Saracen Chronicles

Also by Juan Goytisolo and published by Quartet Books:

Forbidden Territory
Realms of Strife

Saracen Chronicles

A Selection of Literary Essays

Juan Goytisolo

Translated by Helen Lane

QUARTET BOOKS

First published in Great Britain by Quartet Books Limited 1992
A member of the Namara Group
27/29 Goodge Street
London W1P 1FD

Contents

Mudejarism Today

In the approach of one culture to another or, better put, of the member or isolated individual of one of them to the vast, exotic, apparently refractory general *corpus* of the other, a series of personal, fortuitous factors intervenes which, inevitably, mediatizes or colours the perception of this other culture. The phenomena of accommodation, permeation, rejection or decantation vary from one person to another as functions of their life situations, their spheres of interest, and – why not say it? – their particular illusions. Thus, from the purely scholarly or scientific approach to the Islamic world by the majority of professional Arabists to the passionate, involved, contradictory one of that handful of writers and adventurers called Turmeda or Burton, Lawrence or Isabelle Eberhardt, fascinated by Islam and its magnetizing effect on them, the radii of our possibilities unfold, in truth, like the ribs of a fan. Without pausing here to point out the shortcomings and advantages of extreme attitudes towards the problem, I shall simply note that the lines of separation between them are frequently shifting and ambiguous: whereas the vitalist focus of one who assumes his situation with all its complexes and, along with it, the centuries-old Islamic scenario anchored in the European subconscious, in both its positive and its negative aspects, proceeds without misgivings to sack and appropriate Arabic cultural elements and models in the service of an art founded on promiscuity and hybridization, the 'pure' scholars, that is to say, those who mount *ab initio* to the lofty plateau of a presumed objectivity, frequently handle Islamic particularity by confining it to the channels of a method or an ideology that have nothing whatsoever to do with its premises. This aseptic, deconditioned, 'scientific' approach to the problem does not eliminate, however, the feelings of sympathy, the solidarity and at times the aversion of the Arabist or Islamologist with regard to the thematic object of his study. As we know today, by excluding from their explanations and probings their own subjectivity and co-ordinates – the emotional components of their lives – certain of these 'scientists' infect the whole of their schemata with a hidden irrationality: what is swept out of the door immediately filters back in through the window and permeates their discourse – as was the case yesterday with Simonet and today with Sánchez Albornoz – with a delirious mythification. Now that I have touched on this point, I shall merely add that the differences that distinguish those whom I shall call Mudéjares *from Arabists properly speaking* lie first and foremost in their different conception of their commitment to the human and cultural world which they approach – from the serene and distant attitude of a García Gómez, whose orientation towards the Arabic legacy is almost that of a Latinist towards Latin, to the posture of militant fraternity of Martínez Montávez with the Arab peoples and his exemplary defence of the processes of decolonization and the cause of the Palestinians: a passion not only intellectual and political in the second case but also, to cite a handful of eloquent words of Artaud's, 'physical, physiological, anatomical, functional, circulatory, respiratory', etc, of one who accepts his contradictions and ambivalence and thanks to them forges that bastard work, fecundated by the clash of two opposed cultures, which we call Mudéjar.[1] I am not setting up a scale of values here between the two but, rather, demarcating fields and dispelling errors. My knowledge of Arabic culture is certainly quite inferior to that of a García Gómez or a Martínez Montávez, and because of my inability to read a classic text, I have not been able to, nor will I be able to perform as they have an admirable labour as an Arabist; none the less, my somatic, vital approach to what is Islamic has enabled me to create a way of writing that in one way or another is connected to the one that arose more than seven centuries ago in the domains of Castile: neither the anonymous author of *El cantar del Mío Cid* nor the Archpriest of Hita were, in all likelihood, two erudite Arabists, but, rather, simple Mozarabic[2] storytellers or bards, to whom the values and customs of Al Andalus were familiar, and whose work was contrived in the marketplace or the street, in the innermost recesses of life in creation and in movement. The same distinction between Arabists and Mudéjares shows up, as we have pointed out, in the area of their objectives: whereas the former endeavour in so far as it is possible to avoid the European or specifically Hispanic myths that deform or blur the correct perception of what is Arabic, the latter may use them for mythopoetic ends since every rich, profound and complex text is composed not only of rational factors but also penetrates to the depths and secret corners of the individual and collective subconscious where myth is hidden. To tax the artist – whether his name be Goya, Rimbaud or Joyce – with such an attitude and call his creation irrational, mythifying or oneiric, as do certain professors of literature who are not exactly paradigms of rationality themselves, would be equivalent to condemning and blocking the hidden sources from which art and literature draw their sap, their vitality and their lusty vigour.

But I shall now leave aside a subject which, in view of its vastness and multiple implications, would merit treatment in another context at greater length. My intention today is to emphasize the roots of my personal interest in Arabs, an interest whose seminal, genesiac value has in some way, as all of you know, changed my life and my writing. The curiosity which at the beginning of the 1970s brought the subject of Arabs to my attention was above all else human, not cultural or bookish: having settled in France at the height of the Algerian War, I lived in Paris amid the daily horror of racial persecution, humiliations, Arab-bashing *ratonnades*, and murders committed with impunity by the police. To my natural solidarity with the victims – whose aspirations I shared – there was added little by little an unforeseen factor: the physical beauty of the Arab immigrants – which was no doubt a determining factor in my approach to their vital and cultural domain. As I wrote of the figure of the English Orientalist Sir Richard Burton, in so many ways akin to my own:

> The alchemy through which passion is transmuted by a body – a physical and cultural model of the body – into a voracious form of knowledge, capable of converting the lover into a linguist, a researcher, a scholar, a poet; of making him leap from the individual to the collective and opening his eyes to the tragedies and injustices of history, or impelling him to militate in the ranks of anti-colonialism and penetrate the language, literature and thought that the beloved body evokes [. . .] is a *baraka* or grace that accompanies anyone who, with incorruptible rigour and sincerity, remains faithful to what is most secret and precious in himself.

There is no point in my explaining that, on speaking of that singular species of writers viscerally attracted to Islam, I was speaking of myself, of my own literary and moral journey. Without that liminal, fecundating force exerted by the North African immigrants – a seduction that called

up in my mental space the exuberant, motley 'Moorish theatrical spectacle' of the Hispanic subconscious – my narrative works after *Señas de
identidad* would simply not exist. From the gradual vital Mudejarism of
the last twenty years – my familiarity with the models of Arab conduct,
customs and sociability; my apprenticeship of the dialects spoken in
the Maghreb – there has thus flowed a body of novelistic works,
Don Julián, Juan sin tierra, Makbara and, to a lesser degree, *Paisajes
después de la batalla*, whose characteristic features, structure and style
are linked, consciously or unconsciously, to the basic texts of Castilian,
the common denominator of which is founded on *mudejarismo*.

To point out, as a number of critics have already done, that my
novel *Makbara* is closely linked with the *Libro de buen amor* is
primarily due to the current, much more precise reading of Juan
Ruiz inaugurated by Américo Castro in his brilliant and far-sighted
essay on the Islamic-Occidental crossbreeding of the poems. My faithful
and vital relations with the popular world of the Maghreb have had
their counterpart, on the creative plane, in a living dialogue between
my recent texts and certain works of classic Arabic literature and of
medieval Castilian literature that are hybrids of the latter. The fantastic
motifs, the oneiric passages, the wavering between reality and dream,
the leaps in space and time of the text in *Don Julián, Juan sin tierra* and
Makbara; the open structure of the latter two works and the apparent
lack, in *Juan sin tierra*, of a clear narrative line; the insertion of
digressive and heterogeneous subtexts, the repeated use of arabesques,
so subtly grasped by Sylvia Truxa; the fundamental value conferred on
the linguistic sign and its potential variations; the euphuistic preciosity
and frequent recourse to polysemy, etc, derive *in part* from Arabic
literature or from the primitive Castilian letters influenced by it.
A novel such as *Makbara*, written to be read aloud, according to
the medieval Andalusian and Castilian tradition still observed today
among the storytellers of the public square of Xemáa-el-Fna, is thus
an essentially Mudéjar text: conceived first as an essay that was to
be entitled 'Reading of the Archpriest in Xemáa-el-Fna', it was subtly
transformed, as I wrote it, into a vast oral poem in which prosody plays,
as in its model, a decisive role.

I believe that the examples cited suffice to confirm the current
continued effects of the imprint left by Mudéjar literature which, since
the twelfth century, often in a subterranean way, has never ceased to
play an active part in our literature. The presence of Islamic elements in
authors as unlike as Cervantes and Galdós, the mysterious alternating

currents between the Andalusian mysticism of an Ibn Arabí or an Ibn Abbad 'el Rundi' and that of St John of the Cross or St Teresa, to mention only a few cases, are still in need of thorough research. In view of these facts, it is to be hoped that in the future, taking advantage of the momentum of Arabic studies – both of the classical era and the modern – in Spain at present, there will develop a more profound, open, pluridisciplinary analysis of this culturally hybrid area, living astride Occidentalism and Islamism, that undoubtedly constitutes one of the most original and most surprising zones or fields in Hispanic letters.

Notes

1 The term Mudéjares was originally applied to Moors living in Christian territory in the Iberian Peninsula, especially during the eighth to the eleventh centuries, who had not been forced to renounce their own religion.

  Mudejarism (in Spanish *mudejarismo*) is a term introduced into the field of literary criticism by Américo Castro to describe Hispano-Arabic intercultural cross-fertilization. Originally the term referred to architecture, principally from the thirteenth to the sixteenth centuries, combining elements of Arabic, Romanesque and Gothic styles [*translator's note*].

2 Mozárabes were Christians living in territories occupied or controlled by Moors before the Reconquest [*translator's note*].

Medievalism and Modernity:
the Archpriest of Hita and Ourselves

For a number of years now, the idiolect of certain professors of literature, reviewers and critics has drawn on a whole arsenal of military terminology that invariably makes me bristle: terms such as avant garde, rearguard, or the ineffable *chef de file* that our fellows so readily mouth strike me as not only grotesque but redundant and absurd. To use the term 'avant garde' – as yet others speak of 'experimentation' or 'ludic intention' – when they examine the tessitura of certain authors of the twentieth century with regard to the life work that these writers are undertaking and their determination to occupy and assimilate new expressive territories is to paste an inadequate label, full of time-bound, reductive connotations, on a meditation and a long journey shared by periods of literature that are far-distant from each other and seemingly quite dissimilar. If we define modernity in terms of openness, rebellion against established rules, a mixture of styles aimed at a superior aesthetic unity, or the author's reflection on writing itself and on the configuration of a text, then an approach – no matter how limited and superficial – to a series of works representative of other eras will very soon reveal to us that they too should be included in this category or subsumed under this heading. What is clearly formulated and explicit today existed tacitly yesterday, with no great public flurry or fanfare, in compositions as disparate as the *Libro de buen amor*, the *Corbacho*, or the *Retrato de la lozana andaluza*. To group together a number of traits and attribute to them a distinctive character that can be identified with a given historical moment is to disregard the fact that these very same traits also manifest themselves in times and contexts very different from the one that is supposedly being defined. It is also to perpetrate the sort of nonsense so often encountered among professionals who speak of 'the inherent realism of Spanish literature' and proffer other such fake pearls of wisdom. There admittedly exist eras and periods which are subject to ideological or aesthetic norms that level what is new to a lowest common denominator, reduce it to a stereotype, asphyxiate it. By contrast, there also admittedly exist eras and periods in which circumstances favour a freer, more open conception of the text, and as a consequence originality, individuality, innovation stand out in high relief. From this point of view – as the Romantics discovered in their day – a dip into our rich and delightful medieval literature affords us agreeable surprises. The unhurried personal pace of certain authors, their spontaneity as they create, their saving lack of attachment to or exclusive respect for one and only one precise model, extend to us a bridge that spans several centuries and brings us into unexpected intimacy with them. It was this contemporaneity – not to mention other convergences and affinities that I found I shared with the work of Juan Ruiz, Martínez de Toledo, or Delicado – whose strong structure or sturdy build of a *monstrum horrendum, informe, ingens* so horrified Menéndez y Pelayo and obviously excluded them from Renaissance canons – that most attracted me to them. It was this aspect I kept emphasizing when I analysed certain medieval texts with my students at New York University, who ordinarily find the subject dull because the approach to it is tedious and uninspiring. Mine was simply to show what strikingly modern angry men certain authors were – authors who never perorated on the subject of experimentation or their role as an avant garde, and whose work not only shaped my experience as a reader but also had a decanting, seminal effect on my writing.

The long and regrettable mutual disregard which literary investigators of the present century and of the Middle Ages have had for each other's area of study is the real explanation of the numerous prejudices and stupidities concerning both subjects that I keep seeing in print. Excessive specialization acts as a pair of blinkers, restricting their field of vision: while on the one hand there are those who amply demonstrate that they are incapable of discerning the dynamic values of the authors and works they approach, as though they were deliberately trying to make them more remote and inaccessible, there are others who joyously hail Mediterranean writers whom a little more curiosity and broader reading would have kept them from so ingenuously 'discovering'. An exaggeration on my part? Let us say, rather, a sad, discouraging reality, the handiwork of those who appear to be bent on sweeping away – from the vantage point of their academic chairs, their publications, their journals – the dangerous, deadly addiction to literature.

I will mention in passing a recent example. In my novel *Paisajes después de la batalla*, there appears a passage in which the amanuensis or compiler sets down the words:

> *escribir escribirme: tú yo mi texto el libro*
> *yo: el escritor*
> *yo: lo escrito.*[1]

Having been put on the spot and obliged to comment on these lines, a swashbuckling critic began sounding off about the influence of Lacan, Derrida, or one or other of the current cultish Parisian schools. The over-eager commentator was not aware, obviously, that the *Libro* of the Archpriest expresses itself in the first person and at times becomes the subject of the narration:

> *De todos estrumentes*
> *yo, libro, só pariente:*
> *bien o mal, qual puntares,*
> *tal diré, ciertamente;*
> *qual tú dezir quesieres,*
> *y faz punto, y tente;*
> *si puntarme sopieres*
> *siempre me abrás en miente.*[2]

Had he come across these verses without knowing who their author was, I have no doubt that this same person would have gravely pronounced that they were the fruit of a minor disciple of structuralism, suffering from a bad case of indigestion brought on by his reading of *Tel Quel*!

If in the delightful interchanges among women in the *Corbacho*, Martínez de Toledo invents a type of narrative discourse very close to the inner monologue; if Delicado masterfully dramatizes the materiality of writing, weaving a complex and amusing net of relations between the author and his characters, we find ourselves forced to a disturbing conclusion. The 'avant-garde excesses', 'formal games', and 'foreign experiments' so virtuously denounced by a certain sector of criticism and academic scholarship, in the name of the sacrosanct, immutable principles of the vaguely defined 'natural style', and of a no less nebulous and problematic 'artistic realism', are not the fruit of a capricious current vogue or of a perverse personal mania. They go back, in fact, to the very first centuries of our literature. But I shall leave this point for the moment, since the vastness of the subject and its broad implications call for treatment in another context.

What I am interested in speaking about at some length here are the many reasons which in the last few years have led me to confront the work of Juan Ruiz in a way at once literary and existential, to the point that I found myself impregnated by his fecund *mudejarismo*. If my reading of the Archpriest in Xemáa-el-Fna helped me to place the book within a suitable framework, that of the world of wandering storytellers, jesters and jongleurs traversed by Juan Ruiz's Don Carnaval, and most likely by the author himself in his travels and adventures, the intuition that was to lead me to the awareness of his incredible contemporaneity stemmed less from my familiarity with the marketplace or agora of Marrakesh than from my personal experience of metropolises such as New York or Paris. My long stay in them revealed to me the provocative reality of their complex pluriracial nature, their dynamic intermingling of cultures and ethnic groups. For an inveterate stroller in the city such as I am, as thoroughly persuaded as Walter Benjamin that 'wandering in a city, like wandering in a forest, requires a complete education', my medinas of Paris and New York have disclosed to me not so much the classic varnish of cosmopolitanism as the multiplicity and the cohabitation of different styles, their reciprocal contagion, the energizing value of osmosis. Suddenly the unilateral, homogeneous, compact vision of things dissolves, loses its interest.

Today's hero, the urban animal, sees for himself that there are no closed, uniform cultures, curled up into a warm ball of supposed self-sufficiency, but, rather, diverse cultures, pitted one against the other, mixed together, fused in a vast and fascinating crucible. He sees that literature – following in the footsteps of Picasso and his omnivorous curiosity concerning Asiatic and African art – can no longer be exclusively national, or even European, but instead must be turned upside down and inside out, scrambled, bastardized, fertilized by the contributions of any number of different civilizations and geographical regions.

The Babelization of great capitals and their cultural relativism are to me the unmistakable sign of modernity. And it was precisely this sign that pointed me towards rereading, with other eyes, Juan Ruiz's unclassifiable creation: a text carefully marked out with beacons to guide us, one that still seduces us, excites us, entices us, one that shows not the slightest hint of baldness or of wrinkles.

In my essay on Mudejarism included in the present collection (see pp. 97–99), I wrote the following:

> If after more than six centuries the exemplary nature of the Archpriest's work remains as intact as ever, this is owed, I believe, to its atypical and, at first glance, shapeless structure, a hybrid of distinct and opposed genres, an inspired hodgepodge of dialects and vocabularies; to its motley, mongrelized, anomalous nature; to the marvellous interweaving of experience befitting a cleric with the tastes and affections of a Goliard, steeped both in the neo-Latin tradition (that of the *joca monachorum* and of religious-profane farces) and in Arabic culture (erotic stories, troubadours' songs); that is to say, a whole made up of particularities that give it a unique and indispensable place in the history of our literature [. . .] I know of no other work in [it] – whether from the point of view of vocabulary, structure, prosody or syntax – as surprising, as multivalent, as polymorphous as the Archpriest's. The textual reality he puts before us is neither two-dimensional nor uniform: it has sudden breaks, unevennesses, fractures, centrifugal tensions, transmutations of voices: in a word, polyphony. The Castilian of Juan Ruiz does not arouse our excitement, as does that of the epic *Mío Cid* or the poems of Berceo, by reason of its extraordinary historical value in the development and evolution of our language. It is an autonomous literary entity, whose interest lies far above and beyond the merely linguistic or documentary. The ferment of language throughout the fourteenth century lent itself to a creative strategy based on openness and receptivity. The Archpriest introduced into the work language both vulgar and learned, gypsy cant, ruffian slang, dialect, parody, bits of liturgy, Latin, Arabic. This orientation allowed him to escape those verbal hierarchies entrenched in every closed and rigid tradition, to break with the inflexible semanticism of the fixed phrase, to forge with complete freedom a language at once uninhibited and fluent, promiscuous, sly, mocking and jocund, like the one created by the attentive ear of the listener in the gentle winter sunlight of the market place of Xemáa-el-Fna.

The quotation I have just cited is a voluminous one, yet it highlights the causes of the undeniable contemporaneity of the *Libro* and its relationship to works such as *Makbara* or Julián Ríos's *Larva*. Those of us who carry on the lineage may take pride in having such an illustrious and remote ancestor. As I am not at all embarrassed to confess, laying claim to the modernity of Juan Ruiz is a way of laying claim, *a contrariis*, to a heritage, a tradition to which our endeavours belong.

The extreme social and political mobility of the century in which the Archpriest lived, the phagocytosis of a vigorous Castilian language that had neither grammars nor academies, the cohabitation and mutual emulation of three cultures within a common horizon, favoured these phenomena of permeability, interpenetration, influence and decantation that today are enriching and effecting a qualitative change in the life and the artistic expression of great cities. If Cervantes was the creator of the European novel, sweeping his entire field of manoeuvre clean and clearing the way for the work of authors such as Fielding, Sterne, Diderot, Dickens or Flaubert, the atypical *Libro* of the Archpriest, by virtue of its peculiar texture, is linked to the post-Joycean literary adventure and its different conception of character, plot and language in the novel. In the new constellation of our predecessors, his star twinkles merrily alongside that of his crony Rabelais.

All through the little book of '*buen amor*' that *Makbara* is, as much as or even more than the masters of the twentieth century it was Juan Ruiz who taught me how to handle breaks in time, apparent digressions, the autonomous disposition of the parts within the overall framework, the metamorphoses of the characters – alternately young and old – as the rhetorical needs of the text required. Unlike what happens in other more severe and more constricted eras, the delightful contradictions and improbabilities that abound in the *Libro de buen amor* continually contravene the trick laws of realistic illusion. These infractions are forgiven, as in Shakespeare, by reason of their immediate effects on the listening audience or the reader. The freedom that the Archpriest glories in can also be found, *toutes proportions gardées*, by any marauder who ventures into the ever-changing spaces or shifting sands of *Makbara*: a constant permutation of identities, sex, age, grammatical person. Here for him too are the changes of tone or register of the *halaiquí* or public teller of tales, the abrupt breaks and oscillations of the story, the use of foreign words and phrases, the festive integration of different 'speakers' and spiels.

The oral expression of the literary work – which long held sway even after the invention of the printing press, but later on was neglected by the majority of prose writers – again links, across the centuries, the most significant modern literature and that of our medieval creators:

novelists such as Joyce, Céline or Arno Schmidt wrote their works for an ideal public called upon not only to read them but also to train its ear to hear them. Breathing new life into the moribund or dead words of the dictionary, re-experiencing the phonic reality of Juan Ruiz or Fernando de Rojas corresponds to the co-ordinates of contemporaneity as interpreted and felt by those writers and artists who are most aware and far-seeing.

There is a literary ear, just as there is a musical ear. Before Gutenberg, the diffusion of narrative or poetic texts was usually achieved by oral means, and great works of our literature were written to be recited: my ear as an attentive listener in Xemáa-el-Fna has enabled me to re-create the polyphonic text of the Archpriest in an atmosphere not too different from that in which it was engendered. Like other novels of mine and those of certain other writers, *Makbara*, I say in all modesty, establishes a link with this tradition. One of the best readings of it would be a reading aloud. This would allow the different registers to be modulated, the political speeches or commercials broadcast by loudspeakers to be parodied, the sports-caster's excited emphasis to become infectious, the complex stereophony of the marketplace-forum of Marrakesh to come to life once again.

The new boundary marking off textual modernity would perhaps have to be drawn between those novels written in a flat, unmodulated prose and those few in which the reader, in order to apprehend them, is obliged to capture the rhythm proposed by the writing, to find the right 'beat' for each sentence, to forget their humdrum distribution in 'normal' speech. I believe it would be an interesting and revealing experience to invite some of our most celebrated narrators to a public reading of their works and thereby demonstrate, as Julián Ríos proved in the case of one of them, that the texture of their phrasing reproduces the model of prosody and syntax of Don Torquato Fernández Miranda's formal speeches.

To come straight to the point: Modernity/Medievality are not, and cannot be, two far-distant or antithetical terms. If my practice as a reader and a writer is worth anything, I would say, rather, that only the knowledge of, the apprenticeship to yesterday enables one to perceive correctly the distinctive features, the really meaningful and modern elements amid the hubbub and confusion of that shopful of *prêt-à-porter* merchandise that goes by the well-known, but far from precise, name of contemporary Spanish literature.

Notes

1 to write writing myself: you I my text the book
  I: the writer
  I: what is written
2 [free version: HL]·
  Of all instruments
  I, a book, am the parent:
  for good or ill, whatever you point out,
  that will I say – to all apparent;
  whatever you would opine
  whatever point you wish to make;
  if you will always mark my words
  you will always have me in mind.

The Spain of Fernando de Rojas

The recent publication of the extensive work by Stephen Gilman, *The Spain of Fernando de Rojas*,[1] is undoubtedly one of the most remarkable events in modern Hispanic studies. His 'intellectual and social landscape of *La Celestina*' is a valuable, perhaps decisive contribution to our knowledge of an author of a work that has fascinated, fascinates today, and in all likelihood will continue to fascinate successive generations of his readers, a work which, as Gilman himself fittingly pointed out in another context, is 'a triumph of literary discovery, as surprising and, in its own way, as important as any geographical or technological discovery' – a veritable 'literary expedition into the unknown'. For we know little, indeed almost nothing, about its creator: a remote, obscure, enigmatic figure, like that vague, almost chimerical Lautréamont who so intrigued and seduced the surrealists. Despite the universal recognition of a creation comparable in importance only to the other two masterpieces of our literature – the *Libro de buen amor* and the *Quixote* – the glory of the work has not been reflected back on its author. Hence it behoves us to emphasize yet again the unprecedented fact that Rojas has heretofore not enjoyed the official recognition that has been granted to dozens, not to say hundreds, of writers of an immeasurably inferior order: his name has not been invoked at the inauguration of statues, monuments, official centres, avenues; the planners of cultural events have avoided, with suspect unanimity, the task of turning their attention to him; and, contrary to all the documentary evidence, certain of them still stubbornly insist on denying that he is the father of his strange and disquieting offspring.

Admittedly, the biographical data we have concerning him are few and far between. We know the approximate date of his birth and the precise date of his death, and the few documents that have come down to us give us a few indications as to his civil status and family background as well. But these data, however useful they may be to mark off the framework within which his life developed, reveal to us no concrete facts concerning that life, and Gilman has been right to turn the usual procedure of biographical critics upside down. Thus, instead of explaining Rojas's work in terms of the context of its author's life experiences, he has tried to imagine Rojas's life by taking as his point of departure what the text of *La Celestina* itself suggests to us – as though the context formed part of the text, and not vice versa.

Even though Gilman lays claim to the perspective of the visionary, his reconstruction of Rojas's life is not a mere product of his imagination. To repeat: documentary evidence exists and Gilman has minutely and tirelessly scrutinized the archives of the era. In a word, he has endeavoured to use them as seasoning for the biographical schema that *La Celestina* hints at, establishing an extremely complex network of relations between the text and a series of events that took place before and after its creation (e.g. the trial of Alvaro de Montalbán, the tracing of the family tree of the Francos, etc), as though to suggest that not only does the context form part of the text, but that certain features of the writing of the text are authentic elements of the context.[2]

Since Serrano y Sanz's publication in 1902 of the proceedings of the trial of Fernando de Rojas's father-in-law, denounced to the Holy Office for having said, in reference to eternal life: 'Let me be well off here below, since I don't know if there is anything beyond,' we have known that Rojas formed part of that vast community of New Christians whose unsettled situation we see reflected in a great number of works of literature written in this period. It is beyond the limits that we have set ourselves to trace here the lineaments of what it meant at the end of the fifteenth century or the early years of the sixteenth – the era in which *La Celestina* was composed and published – to belong to a family line of converts to Christianity. The anguished clamour that reaches our ears from the depths of the archives of the Inquisition comes not only, as Gilman has clearly seen, from a strong sense of difference, but also from the intolerable atmosphere of suspicion that surrounded the lives of the descendants of Jews:

Suspicious of each other, suspected by everybody else, the *conversos* lived in a world in which no human relationship could be counted on, in which a single unpremeditated sentence could bring unutterable humiliation and unbearable torture. It was a world in which one had constantly to observe oneself from an alien point of view, that of the watchers from without. It was a world of simulation and camouflage interrupted by outbursts of irrepressible authenticity, of commonplace repetition broken by sudden 'originality', of neutral masks removed to reveal grimacing faces and harsh voices of dissent.

A simple *lapsus linguae* by Alvaro de Montalbán in the jovial relaxation of a country picnic had been enough to bury him for a long time in the dungeons of the Holy Office. Years later, another relative of Fernando de Rojas's – Isabel López, his wife's first cousin – had denounced herself to the Inquisitors for having expressed herself in much the same terms when all by herself: apparently, she was afraid that a neighbour could have overheard her, and terrified by the ubiquitous presence of informers, had preferred to turn herself in to the authorities, as proof of her good faith, before her neighbour might betray her.[3] But if these two incidents so close to the family circle of the author of *La Celestina* shed harsh light on the daily burden borne by the convert, the interminable list of possible enemies drawn up by one Pedro Serrano – a peasant and a contemporary of Rojas's, and like him, a New Christian – for the purpose of identifying his possible accusers, that invisible hydra with countless heads that supported and sustained the judges of the Holy Office, surpasses in horror all the recent testimony concerning denunciation in modern monolithic societies. Caught in the infernal machine of that omnipotent organization, Serrano rakes up and minutely examines the most trivial incidents in his life, dramatically illustrating the celebrated Sartrean dictum that *l'enfer, c'est les autres*. Serrano's delirious, feverish defence – the product, one might say, of the imagination, at once logical and absurd, of a Kafka – allows us a truly exceptional, blinding glimpse of the inner torment of the convert, his permanent feeling of persecution.

Rojas had lived since early childhood immersed in this hostile milieu, and in order to explain the context in which his amazing literary creation was produced, Gilman reproduces a list of the autos-da-fé of the Inquisition of Toledo in the year in which the young man who had just received his bachelor's degree completed his final draft of *La Celestina*: dozens and dozens of persons handed over to the secular arm, among whom there surely must have been friends or neighbours of his family. His painful experience at this time was not limited, however, to the knowledge of the abuses suffered by his community. In 1484, one year after the establishment of the Inquisition in Toledo, several members of his family had had to subject themselves to a humiliating ceremony of public penance, becoming the object of the contempt and the derision of the rejoicing multitude of their fellow townspeople. The social stigma that such condemnation brought did not end with the death of those so punished nor that of their kinfolk: when in 1606 – half a century after the demise of the author of the tragicomedy entitled *La Celestina* – a distant cousin of his family's had the unfortunate idea of seeking a legal document testifying to the purity of his lineage, the prosecutor immediately brought to light his kinship with the Rojases of the Puebla de Montalbán, still stigmatized by public opinion as people of 'impure blood'. This document is of particular importance inasmuch as it adds a new and decisive element to the grievous ordeal that, from the cradle, fate visited upon the author of *La Celestina*. With the aim of voiding the claim to a minor title of nobility by Hernán Suárez Franco, the prosecutor includes in the latter's family tree the 'Bachelor of Arts Rojas who composed 'Old Celestina', and adds that this Rojas was 'the son of Hernando de Rojas, condemned as a Judaizer in the year 1488'. That is to say, as Gilman puts it on setting forth the documentary proof of the genealogy of the Francos, that 'when Rojas was perhaps twelve years old his father was arrested, imprisoned, tried, found guilty, and in all likelihood (in that initial period of Inquisitional rigour) executed by fire in an auto-da-fé. The horror of the fact needs little imaginative decoration. The "Medieval and Renaissance elements", which according to extreme historicists created *La Celestina*, have no father whose carnal vulnerability is the precondition of one's own.'

As Américo Castro, María Rosa Lida and Gilman himself, among others, have recently shown, Rojas's marginal and controversial situation with regard to Spanish society of the period was the real determining factor in the development of his tragicomedy. The 'horrifying story' that society told him was to be transformed into the admirable 'horror story' that, in the final analysis, *La Celestina* represents. Eccentric, peripheral – in the meaning that Deleuze assigns to this term – Rojas escapes, with unique centrifugal force, the despotism of a centripetal administrative machine.[4] Impossible to carry his mockery of common opinion, his parody of sacred values, any further. Nearly five centuries after its publication, this tragicomedy continues to be the most virulent and subversive work of literature ever written in Spanish. The unprecedented precautions with which the bemedalled zombies of supposed critical officialdom surround the study of it – neutralizing it, watering it down as though it were too strongly flavoured a dish – are abundant proof that its corrosive power is still as great as ever.

Rojas rends to bits, turns topsy-turvy, destroys received ideas and conventions with a boldness unique among us. If we hold to the modern doctrine of verisimilitude, in its twofold sense of conformity to the laws of the genre and to the ideology of the period, *La Celestina* is, *par excellence*, a work of total inverisimilitude, the work situated at the antipodes of the 'aesthetic of identity': whereas the theatre of a Lope de Vega, for instance, embodies an artistic system founded not on transgression but on the observation of certain very precise rules – or, if you prefer, on the complete identification of the events and values represented onstage with those which the audience knows and accepts a priori – *La Celestina* offers us a situation whose rules are unknown to the reader or spectator at the beginning of the performance or the reading. The acts of the characters of the tragicomedy are 'unbelievable' in so far as they do not conform to the maxims accepted by the public of the period, and Rojas must fight at each step of the way against the dramatic canons and prejudices of the reader or spectator in order to force him to accept his crude, negative and distressing vision of the world.

When Rojas finished writing *La Celestina* in 1501, he was about twenty-five years old. From this time on, until his death on 3 April 1541, we know nothing, or next to nothing, of him except for facts that turn up incidentally – by virtue of the trial of his father-in-law Alvaro de Montalbán, when the Inquisitor denies the latter's request to appoint him as his defence attorney and forces him to choose instead an attorney 'above suspicion'.[5] Rojas's will – in which he includes the list of books that constitute his personal library – offers us no more than the image of a respectable bourgeois, concerned about the preservation of his worldly goods and unburdened by excessive cultural anxieties. In order to fill this vacuum of four decades, Gilman does not have at his disposal the voluminous family and commercial correspondence of a Rimbaud, who, following his abrupt and total silence as a poet, traces his biographical itinerary for us – the travels in Africa and the Arabian Peninsula in pursuit of a fortune that continually escapes his grasp. Gilman patiently reconstructs, with the aid of archives, the everyday atmosphere of the villa of Talavera in which the author of the tragicomedy exercised his profession as an attorney, far from the world's hustle and bustle. This description constitutes, in a manner of speaking, the mould that shapes the material of his life – a cast whose details are necessarily imprecise despite the sustained effort of imagination in which Gilman takes justified pride and which it would not be fitting to attribute only to the paucity or the entire lack of documents. Rimbaud's letters from Aden or Harar – full of tiresome, meticulous references to the cost of the merchandise that was the object of his wretched and ruinous commercial dealings – likewise shed very little light on the adolescent genius who composed 'Le bateau ivre', *Une saison en enfer*, or the 'Sonnet des voyelles'. In both authors the break with the period of creative effervescence is total, and neither the well-to-do petit-bourgeois of Talavera nor the paralytic who lay in his death-throes – like, in his own words, an abandoned dog – in the Hôpital de la Conception in Marseille, could have told us anything new regarding the genesis of a literary work which in each of the two cases is fascinating and unique. The enigma of the silence of both Rimbaud and of Rojas is perhaps explained if we conclude that, having said what they had to say, the two of them quite simply outlived themselves: Rimbaud in a pathetic effort to escape from himself, 'fleeing our world and its celebrated progress', as Cernuda said of him; Rojas, as Gilman shows us, calmed by a literary creation that was his indispensable personal reply to the merciless hostility of life. Once the tragicomedy was written and published, it was no longer a matter of anxious concern to him to wear the close-fitting mask of apparent conformism – without the careless slips of the tongue and outbursts of true feeling that were to doom so many of his relatives and friends – to the end of his days. The debt had been cancelled, and after having thrown his horror story back into the face of society, he was able to agree to accept his condition for the remaining years of his life, as Gilman puts it. In all truth, the learned attorney who carefully administered his estate in the provincial quiet of Talavera had made his peace with himself, and if the creative violence of his youthful rejoinder to the world may have seemed excessive to many, we must now grant, in the light of documentation that has come to light in recent years, that the personal situation that provoked it was also *excessive*.

For Spaniards of the Hebrew 'caste' who experienced the dramatic events of the reign of Isabella and Ferdinand – the establishment of the Holy Office, the edicts of expulsion of 1492 – the change of direction taken by the monarchy, and in its wake the entire society of their country, meant a cataclysm without precedent whose enduring consequences were to pursue them implacably for generations. Once the centuries-old coexistence of the three 'castes' – Christian, Jewish and Moorish – had been destroyed, and confronted now with the dilemma of choosing between conversion or exile, they found themselves the helpless witnesses, as in a nightmare, of the collapse of the values that sustained their lives – real victims condemned to death on the instalment plan, potential victims of a system expressly created to keep a close watch on them, repress them, torture them. Under these conditions of panic and pressure, it is easy to imagine that the sincerity of numerous conversions was more than dubious. Alvaro de Montalbán's slip of the tongue – like dozens of other cases revealed by the documents of the period – gives us reason to suppose that there were many converts who, having lost the faith of their ancestors, had none the less not embraced the new religion in their heart of hearts and were encamped, so to speak, in a no-man's-land between the two, adopting a position of cautious agnosticism, and at times overt atheism.

That Fernando de Rojas belonged to this group of marginal figures – genuine 'inner immigrants' – is scarcely subject to doubt if we are to judge by what his work and the documentation concerning him that we possess reveal to us. As Gilman rightly points out in the prologue of a recent edition of the tragicomedy,[6] instead of the vaulted and enclosed medieval world, where man was protected if he kept to his creaturely role, the world of La Celestina is a world exposed to constant danger. The universe, Rojas explains to us from the very first pages of the work, is nothing but a generalized chaos, in the face of which human intentions and acts of will are laughable and futile: the wheel of Fortune goes blindly round and round, crushing in its movement our dreams, plans and desires; good and evil, prosperity and adversity, glory and suffering – everything loses in time the accelerated force of its beginning; there is thus no Creator nor harmony nor order; all is tumult, frenzy, disorder, clamour, war, strife.

Although the description of this world in the prologue of the tragicomedy is simply an expanded translation of Petrarch's De remediis, a careful reading of it reveals that, in his use of this model, Rojas goes much farther than his source. Whereas Petrarch proposes a stoic acceptance of the ravages and calamities of Fortune, the author of La Celestina suggests no virtuous acceptance whatsoever. The description of the natural world as a battlefield serves him as a mere pretext to trace a parallel portrait of human society, and something about the violence of the description warns us that we are here confronted with no commonplace bookish influence or any ordinary literary device. This viper or guilt-ridden serpent that in the act of conception slowly squeezes to death the head of the male and whose son fractures his mother's pelvis as he is born – causing her to exclaim, 'What more terrible strife than to engender in one's body one who devours its entrails' – is this not the Castile that devours its sons, the Castile 'that makes men and then squanders them'?[7] Is not the reference to the fact that the life of men 'from the earliest age until their hair grows white is a battle' and to 'all things having been created as a violent contest' an expression of the cruel, terrible experience that the society of his country has visited upon him and his family? 'For what will we say among men to the one subject to all the foregoing? Who will explain their wars, their enmities, their covetousness, their hastiness and restlessness and discontent? That change of costume, that demolition and erection of new buildings, and many other diverse attachments and caprices that are forthcoming from our weak humanity?' The clichés of an old medieval tradition, doubtless; but the personal situation of the author has injected them with a vital new sap.

An unblinkered reading of the tragicomedy shows us that the Christian elements that figure in it are few in number, and in most cases, obviously fraudulent in intent. The characters of *La Celestina* lead us to understand, both by their conduct and by their words, that they do not believe in the beyond or in the existence of a hidden Providence: 'Enjoy your youth, the good daytime, the good nighttime, good eating and drinking. When you have the chance, don't miss it. Let what has been lost be lost. Don't weep over the estate that your master inherited, for that you will take from this world, which we have only for this one life of ours,' Celestina counsels; 'Let us take much pleasure. As long as we have enough to eat today, let us not think about tomorrow [. . .] We won't live for ever, for few see old age and of those who see it not one died of hunger,' Elicia says. This attitude is far from being only that of the bawd, servants and harlots. The behaviour of the two lovers, their blind self-regard, also takes no account of the reality of a well-ordered Creation or a God who deals out rewards and punishments with total justice. When Calisto describes to Sempronio the intensity of the fire of love that consumes him, and his servant reminds him that his words violate the teachings of the Christian religion, he answers him thus:

CALISTO: What is that to me?
SEMPRONIO: Aren't you a Christian?

CALISTO: Who, me? I'm a Melibean and I adore Melibea and believe in Melibea and love Melibea.

When she announces to her father her 'agreeable end', her 'forced and joyous departure', Melibea in turn shows no remorse or fear in the face of an act – suicide – which, according to official Catholic dogma, will exclude her from the future kingdom of the blessed: 'My end has come, my rest and your passion, my solace and your pain, my accompanied hour and your time of loneliness.' More revealing still: in the helpless, moving soliloquy that crowns the work, Pleberio too fails to include among the reasons for his grief any reference to his daughter's eternal condemnation. His disconsolate meditation on Melibea's tragic end turns, on the contrary, into a no less desolate meditation on a strange, alien and dizzying world, a world in which 'death is a blessing because of the insane and impotent energy of being alive'. As Gilman astutely points out, ancestry, honour, social position are but masks concealing a vast emptiness: the denial of the self by authors and characters – he says – is accompanied by a denial of all meaning.

The protagonists of the tragicomedy live their lives literally obsessed by the certainty that the world consists of nothing but 'sound and fury' – a cold, impersonal and inhuman world, feeding, so to speak, on its own delirious frenzy: 'The world is thus, let it pass, let its wheel revolve, let its water buckets go round and round, some full, others empty. It is fortune's law that nothing long remains in being: its order is change,' Celestina says;

Every day we see new things and hear them and pass by them and leave them behind. Time diminishes them, makes them subject to chance. Why be so amazed if people were to say: the earth shook or some other such thing that you did not immediately forget? Such as: the river is iced over, the blind man can see, your father is dead, a bolt of lightning struck, Granada has been taken, the King is entering the city today, the Turk has been vanquished, there will be an eclipse tomorrow, the bridge has been swept away, that fellow is now a bishop, Pedro was robbed, Inés hanged herself, Cristóbal got drunk.[8] What will you tell me, save that after three days have gone by or on seeing such a thing for a second time, there is no one who is astonished by it? Everything is like that, everything happens that way, everything is forgotten, everything is left behind.

If the influence of Heraclitus and of Petrarch is evident in these and other passages of the work, Rojas has performed the miracle of interiorizing and embodying his doctrine in the lived experience and personal situations of his characters: the world in which the protagonists of La Celestina live is, in fact, a precarious and transitory world, subject to an inexorable process of destruction.

All the loose ends and scattered elements that the reader finds throughout the tragicomedy are found once again – carefully assembled, perfectly disposed, artfully woven together – in the concluding pages of the work. In them, Pleberio bitterly inveighs against love, fortune and the world. The more desperately he seeks counsel, lamenting his lot, the less reason for consolation he finds. Love is wicked, the enemy of all reason, and acts without order or harmony. Fortune pours forth its ever-changing waves, ruining out of pure caprice whomever it pleases. As for the world, he says in vituperation,

> I thought in my tenderest years that you and your deeds were ruled by some kind of order; today, seeing the pros and cons of the luck you bring, you seem to me a labyrinth of errors, a frightful desert, a den of wild beasts, a game of men who go about in circles, a lake full of slime, a region full of thorns, a towering mountain, a stony field, a meadow full of serpents, a flowery field without fruit, a fountain of cares, a river of tears, a sea of miseries, work without profit, a sweet poison, a vain hope, a false happiness, true pain.

Deprived of the company of a daughter who ought to have been the protection and refuge of his old age, Pleberio discovers at the same time his irremediable loneliness and the bitter certainty of a life that has had no sense. 'How lonely I am!' he exclaims pathetically. That the old man is the spokesman for Rojas himself seems more than likely if we consider that the final soliloquy is something of a summing up, for the reader or the spectator, of the moral of the tragicomedy. As Rojas depicts him, Pleberio, no longer afraid, and knowing that he now has nothing to lose, traces a gloomy picture of a world that has become unhinged and absurd, a universe in which man is born alone, lives alone and dies alone, the plaything of the uncontrollable violence of his own passions and impulses. 'I complain of the world because it created me in and of itself,' he cries out, and in his lament his cry of pain is accompanied by a recrimination addressed to a vacuum – or to the deaf, dumb and worthless god who condemns him to unbearable loneliness *in hac lacrymarum valle.* As Gilman observes: 'the implication of a Godless natural universe is about as explicit here as at the time it could be'. Although Rojas (*et pour cause!*) takes numerous precautions and protests his fidelity to the Catholic religion, along with professions of aversion against Judaism, his reasons are transparent enough to enable no one to bring him to book on the grounds that he has been taken in by them. A contemporary of his, and like him a *converso*, justified his own hypocrisy by saying: 'I kept my mouth shut, because life is a most pleasant good.' As the French translator of the writings of the scientist Jorge Juan comments in reference to the fact – at first thought surprising – that Juan took the opinion of those who maintained that the earth revolves to be false, the author does not speak in such cases with his own voice, 'but as a man who writes in Spain, in a country where the Inquisition exists'.[9]

In the world of *La Celestina* – Gilman points out, commenting on the dramatic confrontation of Pleberio and his daughter at the moment in which she informs him from the top of the tower of her decision to kill herself – the endless dialogue of the characters is counterbalanced by their intimate awareness of their profound isolation:

> During all the years of Melibea's life Pleberio had been deceived by domesticity – the dialogue of daily coexistence – into believing that he was accompanied. And only now across vertical space and an unsubstantial bridge of words, does he realize the distance between her mind and his. Only now, only when his daughter finally does tell him everything that she has kept hidden, does he understand the radical nature of his loneliness. As usual in *La Celestina*, the physical situation and the human become one. The tower and Melibea's confession express Rojas's sudden subtle understanding that awareness equals incommunicability [. . .] His [i.e. Pleberio's] is an irremediable loneliness, built into the human condition.

The observation is a penetrating one and merits our dwelling on it for a moment. Américo Castro, María Rosa Lida and other commentators on the work had previously emphasized the fact that *La Celestina* was a drama without heroes or villains, 'a battle of equally destructive egoisms'. The paragraph by Gilman cited above takes a further step: in an absurd universe, marked by war, chaos and strife, man lives by himself and accepts no law other than the sovereign force of his passions. If the universe has no meaning – if God is in reality an immense emptiness and Providence a mere blind, unbridled agitation – man lives in a state of total solitude, in which he has no need of his neighbour or any reason to offer him any explanation for his actions. This thought, dating as far back as Plautus – *homo hominis lupus* – in fact pervades the behaviour of all the characters of the tragicomedy, with the exception of Pleberio and his wife (and the final ordeal to which destiny subjects them is for that reason even more bitterly absurd). Egoism is the one rule: amorous self-regard in the case of Calisto and Melibea; self-interest and greed in the case of Celestina, Sempronio and Pármeno; rancorous selfishness, interwoven with envy, in the two harlots. But if the image of the noble class traced by Areúsa and Celestina cannot be more devastating:

> The noble gentlemen of today love themselves more than their families and kinsmen. And they are not wrong. The latter should do the same. Charitable deeds, proofs of generosity, noble acts are a thing of the past. Each one of them, a petty captive, basely seeks his own interest among his kith and kin. But the latter should by all means observe the same law as they do, since they have lesser powers,

the portrait of servants and commoners that Rojas paints is far from flattering. When it comes to money matters, there is no such thing as friendship. Aware of this truth, Sempronio strikes a deal with Celestina in order to exploit his master's passion: 'He had need of you and of me. Since he needs all of us, let us take advantage of him together [. . .] Let us all profit, let us all share the benefits, let us all enjoy ourselves,' and after a brief initial resistance, Pármeno falls in with their plan: 'Destroy, shatter, break, give what is his to go-betweens, and my rightful share will come to me, for as they say: "A roiled river is the fisherman's gain."'

Selfishness, loneliness, lack of communication, war, strife: the denial of one's fellows ignores social rules of respect and friendship and knows no limit. The gold chain with which Calisto rewards Celestina's good offices will bring about the death of the procuress through the work of the servants, and their death in turn at the hands of the law. That is to say, the selfishness of the characters in the tragicomedy leads to the total denial, of others first of all, and in the end of themselves. Their loneliness asserts itself by way of a far-reaching negation, as Melibea will discover in the solitary watchtower, deprived, through Calisto's death, of the pleasure whereby she had been able to communicate with him. All the rest – the social comedy of piety, filial love, supposed family ties – counts for very little alongside the terrible discovery: the physical reality of her separation from others, the awareness of her inevitable isolation.

Fernando de Rojas's atheism and his lack of faith in a possible social ideal confers on the heroes of the work a tragic dimension that makes them brothers in spirit with some of the most representative characters of the literature of our own time. But his rationalistic conception of the world – in the meaning that the Age of Enlightenment gave to that term – is compensated for, as we shall see, by a rebellion of the sign 'body', whose most perfect expression likewise goes back to the last years of that century – and Gilman points to it in a paragraph on Pleberio's helpless accusation that we shall permit ourselves to cite at length:

> What is the fate of man in such a situation? It is precisely the answer to this question that Pleberio's unseen audience has just listened to in the previous twenty acts of *La Celestina*. Man is engaged in a feverishly logical Dance of Life composed of two fundamental movements. On the one hand (as explained in the Prologue and copied directly from Petrarch), there is continuing, relentless conflict [. . .] On the other hand, there is an equally relentless erotic urge [. . .] reducing us all to animal fury.

This is where the coincidence with Sade commands our attention. Like Rojas, he too has an account to settle with society: flung into the dungeons of the *ancien régime* through the intrigues of his powerful mother-in-law, the prisoner of the Bastille likewise wants to throw back in society's face his 'horror story'. Accused of committing acts of physical violence against the persons of several prostitutes, instead of defending himself against the accusation, he transforms himself into the accuser, not only of his judges, but of society, of God, of the world and nature, that is to say, of everything that stands in the way of, limits or denies the sovereign force of his passions. It is a commonplace that in periods of little or no faith, when hallowed moral and social values clearly reveal – at least to the eyes of the thinking minority – their oppressiveness and injustice, the so-called 'animality' of the human being – his sexual exuberance – becomes the one element preserving the individual from being turned into a mere thing and restores his awareness of existing for and by himself. Whether it be the industrial religion of today's bureaucratic societies – a religion that reduces man to the status of an object in a world of objects – of the enlightened despotism of absolute monarchy, or of a society structured on the basis of this 'immanent Inquisition' of which Unamuno once spoke, we are witnesses to a rebellion of the sign 'body' against the dominant ideologies and their all-embracing rational constructions. In the face of an absurd, asphyxiating, tyrannical social pyramid that crushes men in its inexorable infernal machines, Rojas, like Sade three centuries later, will lay claim to the primacy of the erotic drive and also to its blind, inexorable fury.

Maurice Blanchot writes:

Sade reasons more or less along these lines: the individual represents a given quantity of energy; most of the time he scatters his strength for the benefit of those simulacra called one's fellow, God, the ideal; through this dispersion he commits the error of exhausting his possibilities, in an act of sheer waste, and what is even worse, of basing his conduct on his weakness, since if he lavishes his energies on others it is because he feels the necessity of leaning on them for support. A fatal weakness: he enfeebles himself by futilely squandering his strength and uselessly expends his strength because he believes himself to be weak. But the man who is aware knows that he is alone and accepts being so, denying everything in himself – the heritage of seventeen centuries of cowardice – that binds him to his fellow, destroying, for instance, feelings of piety, of gratitude, of love; and on destroying them, he recovers all the forces he would have had to devote to these debilitating impulses, and what is even more important, he extracts from this work of destruction the beginning of a genuine energy.[10]

Chaos, lack of communication, loneliness likewise lead in *La Celestina* to the sovereign affirmation of an egoism that has no room for the debilitating impulses of piety, gratitude or affection, nor does it sacrifice itself to what Sade calls 'simulacra': God, ideals, one's fellow. To recognize a link of solidarity with others means placing limits on the sublimity of one's own ego. Hence the 'glory' of lovers admits of no impediment that will counteract or lessen its fever. Those who have commented on the tragicomedy have often, quite rightfully, emphasized the violence of the erotic relationships between its characters: in the seventh section, Celestina forces Areúsa to accede to Pármeno's desires, even though the girl suffers racking pain in her womb, and the procuress is consumed with joyous *voyeurisme* on witnessing the inevitable cruelty of copulation; after placing herself in the 'shameless hands' of Calisto, Melibea bewails the 'severe treatment' she received from him, in one of the most daring and meaningful passages in the entire work: 'Leave my undergarments alone, and if you want to see if the garment on top is of silk or of wool, why do you finger my chemise? [. . .] don't rip and tear or treat me roughly as is your habit. What does it profit you to damage my attire?' To which Calisto replies: 'Milady, he who wishes to eat a bird must first remove the feathers.'

The loneliness, lack of communication and isolation inherent in the characters of the tragicomedy presuppose the disappearance of all restraint. Once they are obliged to have recourse to Celestina's services, the two lovers do not hesitate to humble themselves before her and greet her with a servility that borders on the grotesque: 'Wise woman and great teacher,' Melibea says. 'My heart leaps for joy on seeing this estimable presence, this noble ripeness of years,' Calisto says, going one better on Melibea. To attain the satisfaction of arousing Melibea's passionate 'fury', he will happily sacrifice honour, wealth, renown and even the life of his close kin. Overwhelmed by the enslaving power of passion, Melibea, after cursing the portals that hinder her access to 'glory', shouts in Lucrecia's face: 'I take joy in thinking of him, I reach the height of pleasure in seeing him, I exult in hearing him [. . .] Let my parents take pleasure in him if they wish to please me [. . .] I regret nothing save the time I wasted in not enjoying him, in not knowing him, *now that I know how to know myself.*'[11] A knowledge thus linked to the discovery of her own fever. As Georges Bataille – probably Sade's best analyst – says, only through this frenzy (of the act of love) 'do I reveal to my fellows who I am *intimately*; [erotic] consumption is the way whereby *separated* beings communicate'.[12]

Calisto's introverted character, his retiring nature, that odd, solitary, nocturnal life of his that has so intrigued those who have seriously studied the work, run counter to the general rule of an era in which reality appears to bow before the dreams of grandeur of the Old Christian caste and its 'imperative dimension' – thereby leading us to suspect that by portraying him the author was somehow portraying himself. A critic has recently observed, most insightfully, that Calisto not only loves solitude but also darkness, as though night were the only refuge in the face of the wordless threat of a city in the midst of which he lives like a foreigner.[13] Cloistered in his residence, fleeing the light, he puts the day between parentheses, so to speak, and awaits the coming of darkness to steal away to Melibea's garden – in search of the coveted body that kindles and feeds his 'fury'. The frenzy of carnal love is, in his eyes, the one certainty in the world, in 'this *intimate* world which is opposed to the *real* world as excess is opposed to restraint, madness to reason, intoxication to clearmindedness';[14] and, as Bataille says, 'the world of the subject is night – that ever-shifting, infinitely ambiguous night which, during the sleep of reason, *engenders monsters*'.[15] Calisto's 'crude and powerful' love, Rojas indicates to us from the very first pages of the work, 'is not ruled by reason, turns a deaf ear to advice, lacks counsel'. Night is its sole mentor and its counsel scorns the abject niggardliness of the real, the mean and petty fears of 'good sense'. Only fury counts. The lord and master of its own dream, it alone can develop – as occurs in the works of the 'Divine Marquis' – thanks to the profound awareness of its isolation. Sadean morality, Maurice Blanchot explains, is founded on the basic fact of total solitude. Sade said as much and repeated it in a thousand different ways: nature has caused us to be born alone; there is no sort of relationship between one human and another. Consequently, the one rule of conduct is that I am to prefer everything that is to my favour without taking into consideration in any way whatsoever the ills that my preference may bring to my neighbour. The greatest pain of others is always of lesser importance than my pleasure. It matters not at all if I must pay the price of the most minimal enjoyment with an unheard-of accumulation of evils, *since pleasure gratifies me, is within me, whereas the effect of crime does not touch me, is alien to me*.[16]

The radical egoism of Sade's heroes also moulds the conduct of almost all the characters of *La Celestina* and drives them to the denial and the death of others and of themselves. The solitude of humans, abandoned in a world that lacks meaning, is as oppressive in Rojas as in Sade. In accordance with the logic of his condition, Calisto places pleasure (his own) before the death (the experience of another) of Sempronio and Pármeno. 'Why should the gaining of the glory that I hope for matter more to me than what those who died lost by dying?' he thinks; and scorning the weakness of remorse, he adds in terms that the author of the *120 Days of Sodom* might well have put into the mouth of any of his libertines: 'Remember, Calisto, the great pleasure you have enjoyed in the past. Remember your lady and all the things you have enjoyed. And your life is in no way owed to their service; *you will not have to die the deaths of others, for no pain will equal the pleasure received.*'[17]

Looked at from this perspective, we may conceive of the tragicomedy as a remarkable precedent for Sade's universe. A Sadean *avant la lettre*, Calisto abandons himself completely to the fury of his violent passion, wasting his physical energies and squandering his fortune through the breach opened within himself – the bodily frenzy that pays no attention to rational utility and the sacrosanct laws of economy. In the face of the ordered continuity of a world ruled by the notions of God, the common good or progress, the chaotic fever of the body and its blind convulsions. *La vérité de l'érotisme est trahison*: the truth of eroticism is betrayal, Bataille says. Confirming his words, Calisto brushes aside the death of his servants, just as Melibea pays no heed to the truth owed to her parents. Both of them – like Celestina, Sempronio and Pármeno – draw their energy and vitality from their imperious egoism, and, significantly, Calisto will die when, forgetting this principle, he submits to one of those 'debilitating impulses' that friendship represents and hastens to defend Sosia and Tristán, believing that their lives are at stake. A fatal error that, as with Sade's hapless Justine, will occasion all sorts of disasters. Whereas, by virtue of the same cold logic that governs Sade's universe, Melibea's self-willed death is, paradoxically, the affirmation of a sovereign plenitude that cancels out the moral weakness of the pain felt by Pleberio and Alisa, Calisto does not die through an act of self-assertion, in accordance with the egoistic norm of pursuing one's own pleasure, but instead, by reason of his weakness, as he endeavours to come to the aid of his two subalterns who, as a crowning touch of irony, are in reality in no danger whatsoever.

We thus find in *La Celestina* all the elements of a general state of discontinuity, lack of communication and abandonment that Sade's delirious imagination was later to push to the ultimate limits. Taking advantage of the absolute freedom of the blank page – the all-consuming vertigo of writing – the French author, in the inhuman isolation of the Bastille, was to wreak an exemplary vengeance on the society that was oppressing him: that of stripping bare and giving voice to everything repressed and unspeakable, transforming, as Roland Barthes puts it, the impossibilities of the referent into possibilities of discourse.[18] If the logic of Fernando de Rojas does not go that far, I am not one of those willing to throw that in his face. Without falling into the excesses of Sade and his icy monstrosity, the author of the tragicomedy has offered us the vision of a world infinitely closer to our own: a world that after almost five centuries still obsesses us by its amazing reality and one in which we still recognize ourselves.

One last footnote to Gilman's book: his analysis of self-distancing and marginality in the work of converts touches on an essential point that as far as I know no one before him has so much as commented on – I am referring to the fact that an author such as Rojas was forced to dissent in a language that inherently extolled a great deal of what he wished to reject, to war against values that were not 'theirs' but 'ours'. 'The almost unlimited stylistic complexity of La Celestina [. . .] the superimposed layers or meaning underneath its verbal signs can only be understood [. . .] in terms of this dilemma,' as Gilman points out.

A dilemma, I would say, that was not restricted to converts, but to all dissenters and rebels who venture into the language in which they write as though it were enemy territory – occupied by the defenders of the omnipresent official ideology: a territory strewn with traps and snares through which it is necessary to advance with infinite precautions and probings before sowing it in turn with mines and time bombs meant to explode at some later date in the hands of unwary readers. By expressing myself in this way I wish to emphasize that I am not setting forth a mere theory: my personal experience in fact coincides, centuries later, with that of the author of the tragicomedy. Obliged to mistrust his own language, and indeed, to think against it, the disaffected writer strives, today as yesterday, to instil within his ambit an element of subversion – ideological, narrative, semantic – which corrupts it and wears it away. The work that adds to the general tree of letters is thus a double-edged weapon – 'a false gift in the tail of a scorpion, a deceptive offering with in cauda venenum', I have written elsewhere.[19] When Gilman writes at the end of the paragraph that we are citing: 'Ambiguity is here not an abstraction for critics or a strategy for poets but a way of existence,' he is offering, perhaps unwittingly, the key of an entire sector, perhaps the most significant and dynamic one, of today's literature – that of the Genets, Burroughses or George Jacksons, pariahs of a system against whose inhumanity and outrages they have rebelled and in whose language they have unwillingly incorporated texts outstanding for their unprecedented virulence amid the dozens upon dozens produced by 'accepted' authors.[20] Writing is then a subtle act of treason, and the work of the marginal writer a 'horror story' whose germs – as we see clearly from the power of *La Celestina* today – pursue their clandestine labour of sapping and undermining in the mind of readers and – even after five centuries – move, upset, disturb and, with honeyed words, contaminate them.

Notes

1 Princeton University Press, 1972.

2 Cf. Tzvetan Todorov, 'L'analyse du récit a Urbino', *Communications*, no. 9 (1968).

3 'I, Ysabel López, wife of Francisco López, state that not paying attention to what I was saying nor believing that I was in error, said the following words, 'In this world never mind that I'm sinning because in the next I won't be paying for it,' and I state that I said this because it's a commonplace that everybody repeats.' Cited by Gilman, op. cit., p. 92.

4 Gilles Deleuze, 'Pensée nomade', in *Nietzsche aujourd'hui*, Paris, Collection 10/18.

5 See Angela Selke, 'Un ateo español', *Archivum*, VII (1957).

6 *La Celestina*, Madrid; Alianza Editorial, 1969. [All translations from Rojas's text are mine: H. L.]

7 'Castile is better at winning the new than at preserving what it has won, for many times what it did it itself undoes it,' the convert Hernán Pérez de Guzmán wrote. See Américo Castro, *La realidad histórica de España*, Mexico City: Porrúa, 1966.

8 The commentators on the tragicomedy have rightly emphasized the audacity, a real sacrilege in those days, of placing on one and the same level the taking of Granada by the Catholic Monarchs and vulgar, everyday happenings such as 'they robbed Pedro' or 'Cristóbal got drunk'.

9 Cf. Paulino Garagorri, *Revista de Occidente* (Diciembre 1965).

10 Maurice Blanchot, *Lautréamont et Sade*, Paris: Editions de Minuit, 1949.

11 Emphasis mine. [J. G.]

12 Georges Bataille, *La part maudite*, Paris: Editions de Minuit, 1967. [Brackets mine: J. G.]

13 'In the face of this desire of Calisto's, we must ask ourselves, in the end, what the city and the society from which he wishes to flee and with which he has so few relationships is like.' Julio Rodríguez Puértolas, *De la Edad Media a la edad conflictiva*, Madrid: Gredos, 1972.

14 Ibid. On Sade, see also Bataille, *L'érotisme*, Paris; Collection 10/18, 1964, pp. 165–219.

15 Ibid., pp. 220–1.

16 Emphasis mine. [J. G.]

17 Emphasis mine. [J. G.]

18 Roland Barthes, 'L'arbre du crime', *Tel Quel*, no. 28 (Hiver, 1967).
19 *Juan sin tierra*, Barcelona: Seix Barral, 1975, final chapter. Edition in English, *Juan the Landless*, translated by Helen R. Lane, New York: Viking, 1977.
20 In his introduction to *Soledad Brothers. The Prison Letters of George Jackson*, Genet himself has raised the problem in a masterful way.

Notes on *La Lozana andaluza*

I

An exemplary destiny, that of *La Lozana*: the marginalized work of a marginal Spaniard, unknown to its contemporaries because of its anonymous publication in Italy, ignored by generation after generation until Gayangos's discovery of the only copy of it, it has remained in a state of hibernation for four and a half centuries, without ever being able, until today, to break through its petrified chrysalis. A negative exemplarity that confirms the sad reality that still confronts us: that of a history of literature perverted and falsified by the a priori arguments and antipathies that determine the scale of values of the country in accordance with the particular perspective of its cultural programmers. The deeply rooted Hispanic custom of judging literary works according to criteria that have nothing to do with literature explains the amazing fact that a novel of the quality and the importance of Delicado's has vegetated in a sort of limbo, the victim of the repressive mentality of the majority of our authorities. An aggressively erotic work in a century in which the purity of written expression was gradually transformed in Castile into an immutable trait of its 'character', the virulence of its social criticism, the liveliness and freshness of its language, its most original technical innovations, the introduction, in the manner of Velázquez, of the author himself within the ambit of the characters portrayed, none the less constitute, for every alert reader whose vision is unblinkered, an inexhaustible source of feelings of admiration and surprise.

Once again, we must necessarily allude to the judgements of the renowned scholar Marcelino Menéndez y Pelayo, for the reason that, owing to our proverbial critical indolence, his encyclopaedic knowledge continues, even today, to be the wellspring from which the authors of literary textbooks drink, manuals in which new, and ever unfortunate, generations of Spaniards are formed, or deformed. For the indefatigable polygraph from the peaks of Santander, blinded as usual by his ideological prejudices and his caricatural Spanish detestation of the written expression of sex, *La Lozana* is a book of 'frivolous outward show and shameful content', of 'no aesthetic value whatsoever,' that 'barely belongs to [the realm of] literature'. After informing his readers that he refuses to analyse its content 'because this is not a task for any decent critic', he adds:

La Lozana, as regards the majority of its chapters, is a filthy and ugly book [. . .] an extreme case of photographic naturalism, with all the consequences inherent in this mode of elementary and vulgar representation, in which reality is shown without any sort of artistic selection and indeed without any overall plan of composition or organic interconnection. When one discovers that there are one hundred and twenty-five characters who figure in this fable, whether or not it deserves such a name, one may form some idea of the disorder and confusion that reigns in it. It is not a comedy, nor is it a novel, but an altarpiece, or rather, a cinematograph of obscene little figures, who pass by making faces and pirouettes as they engage in incoherent dialogues.

He winds up his fulminating anathema with these significant words:

Perhaps we have dwelt on this book at greater length than it merits, inasmuch as there is no one to whom the reading of it can be recommended. It is one of those which, as don Manuel Milá remarked, 'ought never to emerge from the most hidden recess of the scientific necropolis'. The three reprintings made of it in modern times were altogether unnecessary, and the Vienna copy sufficed to satisfy the curiosity of philologists, who would already have known how to find it, and whose very profession steels them against the good or bad contents of the works whose vocubulary and grammar they examine.

We shall disregard for the moment the curious reserving of works belonging to the common patrimony to an exclusive nucleus of philologists 'steeled' by their erudition – as if the fact of having earned, let us say, a doctorate in philosophy and letters were sufficient proof of morality, as was true yesterday, in Franco's day, of the passport that allowed its fortunate possessor to frequent the sex shops in Biarritz or Perpignan specializing in 'hard-core porn' – so as to dwell at greater length on the castrating effect that for years and years has been exerted on books such as *La Lozana* or the *Cancionero de burlas* by this repressive mentality: preventing not only their circulation in Spain but also making an object of horror of them, conforming to the animosities and aversions of the critic-prosecuting attorney. Then, incapable of equalling his perverted but real curiosity and his rare and laudable diligence, the authors of the bird's-eye histories and overall summaries of literature have ordinarily limited themselves to repeating the authoritative negative opinions of the eminent critic from Santander:[1] taking as their source the solemn decree of its 'utter worthlessness' in Menéndez y Pelayo's *Origines de la novela*, the majority of run-of-the-mill manuals devote a few brief lines at most to *La Lozana*, more or less excusing themselves for doing so and insisting that it is a question, as one of them states, of 'a scarcely recommendable work owing to its cynical prurience and the moral disorder that are its outstanding characteristic'.

At the risk of being included yet again on the list of 'obscene' writers, I shall allow myself to examine briefly a few of the compositional features of this masterwork.[2]

II

Despite the absence of documents concerning the author, the abundant autobiographical data scattered throughout the 'portrait' of *La Lozana* lead us to believe that he belonged to a family of Andalusian converts who may have left the country as a consequence of the infamous decree of expulsion promulgated by the Catholic Monarchs and who, like so many others with the same background – Juan Luis Vives, Juan de la Encina, Bartolomé Torres Naharro, etc – had abandoned the Peninsula more or less voluntarily in search of new and more amenable horizons. The problems of 'pure blood' did not overly disturb the Italians, and this perhaps explains why, instead of following his countrymen to Rome after its sacking by the Emperor's troops and the evacuation of the city, Delicado chose to go off to Venice, where, as he says in the final digression of the book, he found no other Spaniard. More than half a century later, Arias Montano, likewise a New Christian and Philip II's ambassador to the Republic of Venice, confidentially reports in his letters that he feels most comfortable in that city 'because there are no Spaniards here'.

But it is above all in the general atmosphere and typology of the heroes of *La Lozana* that we find arguments in favour of Delicado's Judaic background, and it is significant that even today a number of serious students of the work choose to take no notice of them. Like his contemporary and fellow countryman Fernando de Rojas, Delicado continues to evoke a Spain inhabited by people of three castes and religions when their coexistence was already a thing of the past and the edifice firmly established by several centuries of tolerance had come tumbling down on top of the vanquished castes. The *Retrato de la Lozana andaluza* is full of allusions and references to Moorish and Jewish customs, and as in *La Celestina*, we find a bitter scorn for blood lines and a no less sarcastic claim to honour on the part of ruffians and harlots.

When Aldonza – a name derived from the Arabic *alaroza*, meaning fiancée, as the author himself explains – strolls through the streets of Rome for the first time, the sight of veiled prostitutes brings back to her the memory of the Moorish girls she knew in her childhood, and when she explains to her aunt her culinary merits and skills, she sets forth a veritable catalogue of Judeo-Moorish cuisine:

> I learned to make noodles, turnovers, couscous with chickpeas, whole-grain rice, dry rice, rice with oil, round, tightly packed little meat balls [. . .], waffles, crullers, honeyed fritters, ring-shaped pastry made from a dough of walnuts, almonds and honey, fried cakes of hempseed and sesame seed, nougat, marzipan, puff pastry, semola toasted with oil, almonds and milk porridge, sorghum and turnips without pork and with cumin seed. (II)

These and many other elements take on meaning if we keep in mind the way in which the author suggests to us, step by step, the origins of la Lozana. Her parents, he says, were fond of her 'because she was clever' (I), and Diomedes, he adds later on, felt love grow in his heart, 'noting in her the cleverness that her country and her parentage have given her' (IV). Thanks to Américo Castro, Hernández Ortiz, Rodríguez Puértolas and other researchers, we know today the precise import of the terms *inquietud* [anxiety] and *agudeza* [cleverness, sharp wits] on the one hand, and *quietud* [calm], *gravedad* [composure] and *sosiego* [mental tranquillity] on the other, in the hard-fought inter-caste struggle of the period. Whereas the latter set of words served to qualify the conduct and the attitudes of Old Christians ('He was coveted by many as a son-in-law because he had *quietud* written on his brow,' Lope de Vega writes), *inquietud* and *agudeza* were synonyms for Judaism (in Gonzalo Correa's collection of maxims and proverbs we read: 'neither a stupid Jew nor a lazy hare'; according to Huarte de San Juan, '*agudeza* comes to Jews by birth', and in the *Entremés del remediador* Lope writes: 'You're a Jew?'/ 'No, sir.'/ 'You would appear to be one from your *agudeza*.' We shall add that in the secret report on the composition of Charles V's privy council, cited in its entirety by Castro, those of New Christian origin are branded as *agudos* – sharp, quick-witted – and this adjective frequently appears in the trials and official records of the Holy Office in which Jewish converts are mentioned.)

Upon her arrival in Rome, Aldonza meets several Spanish women of Hebrew origin, and although her family background is not explicitly mentioned, the relationship between her precipitate departure from Spain and her travels in the Eastern Mediterranean, under Turkish rule at the time, makes the women suspect immediately that she is one of their number (VII, IX). Later on, the Neapolitan woman appears to be aware of her origins, for she says to her: 'Here to my house come Moors and Jews who, if they know you, will all help you' (XI). The words 'if they know you' refer, of course, to la Lozana's family background, that is, to the fact that she is *ex illis*.

The references to Jewry and to Jews in Rome run on for pages all through the 'portrait', and it is interesting to note that Rampín speaks with pride of 'our Spaniards', whose culture and fund of knowledge surpass that of the others, he says, 'because there are among them rich and well-educated men, and they are extremely erudite'. And it is to those Spaniards that la Lozana, in a dialogue with Rampín, is probably alluding, thus shedding light on a phrase that would otherwise seem quite obscure.

> LOZANA: I swear, it's something worth seeing and knowing – they say that in those days there weren't two Spaniards in Rome and *now there are any number of them*! But there'll come a time when there won't be a one, and they'll say, 'Poor Rome', the way they say 'Poor Spain'. (XII)

With the resigned pessimism that experience has brought her, la Lozana prophesies that worse times will come for the Roman Sephardim inasmuch as Rome may one day follow the badly misguided footsteps of Spain. But, Aldonza adds, without the Spanish Hebrews, the *alma mater* of Catholics will decline, as today Spain has declined.

The Jewish element in *La Lozana* is stressed even more insistently through the well-nigh obsessive mention on the part of characters and author alike of the problems that the use of bacon and pork products bring to Jews and New Christians. As we have seen, Aldonza cooked without pork, in the Moorish fashion, and in one of his frequent direct interventions, the author, on relating the travels of his heroine in her youth through various territories of the Peninsula, mentions that, as she passed through Jaén, she stopped at the house of a stepdaughter, 'and it was there that she first ate boiled semolina with pork bones' (V). Porkophilia and porkophobia, which in the literature of the Golden Age lays down the dividing line between converts and Old Christians,[3] already poisoned the relations of the characters that appear in the pages of the 'portrait':

NEIGHBOUR WOMAN: Hey, Spanish woman, why don't you tie up that pig? But don't worry. Maybe it's already dead.
WASHERWOMAN: Come on, bend down in the grass and give it a reverent kiss [. . .] Because, mind you, if you look at it or touch it, maybe it isn't a pig to you. Do you think I'm afraid of your blustering cop friend? I'll make the two of you eat it raw. (XII)

Speaking of la Lozana, Silvio's companion notes that 'if they don't please her, she'll say worse things about them [the prostitutes] than about pig meat' (XXIV). As for Rampín, a mere mouthful of ham that Falillo maliciously offers him makes him vomit all over the table linen, the dishes and the cups, and those present joyfully exclaim: 'He's sick to his stomach from the smell of pork' (XXXIV).

As in *La Celestina* – a work that Delicado profoundly admired and had published during his stay in Venice, after *La Lozana* – we find any number of jokes about lineage and purity of blood, whose forthrightness – a sacrilege in the context of the Peninsula – can be explained only by the author's being in exile and the air of freedom that he was breathing:

LOZANA: Do you know what consoles me? What Rampín, my servant said: that they may have it all over me when it comes to money and worldly possessions, but not in lineage or in blood.

SAGÜESO: I'd swear you were right; but to know for certain, you'd have to bleed the two of you, to see which one of you has the best blood. (LII)

Aldonza, like la Celestina, has a lofty idea of her professional honour and exclaims: 'For my honour, I want those women whose faces I paint to go about without shame, and be looked at' (XLVIII); and when the man from Trujillo possesses her gratis, she feels that her dignity has been wounded, saying: 'He duped la Lozana, as though I were Saint Nefija, who let everybody ride her for free for charity's sake' (LI). Sagüeso, for his part, likewise speaks with pride of his métier as a panderer, and in another passage of the work la Lozana addresses the old whore Divicia in these terms: 'Enjoy yourself, harlot, because today is the best part; don't be like the one who said, after having been in a brothel for forty years: "If I get out of here with my honour intact, I'll never go back to the bawdyhouse, because I'm fed up with it"' (LIII).

If we keep in mind these and many other taunts and gibes scattered throughout the 'portrait', we can correctly interpret the passage in which Silvio, conversing with the author, compares Spain with Rome and launches into a sarcastic criticism of Roman freedoms, as three centuries later Larra will do, in a celebrated article on political freedoms in England and the United States:

SILVIO: For that is why Rome is free, because each one does exactly as he pleases now, whether bad or good, and just look at how, if a man wants to go about dressed in gold or silk, or naked or unshod, or eating or laughing or singing, his word is still good in court, and there is no one who says to you that you're acting either well or badly, and yet this freedom conceals a great many evils. (XXIV)

The 'evils' that this freedom concealed were not, however, enough of a dissuasion to cause the author and the characters of the work to renounce them and take refuge in the grandiose spiritual benefits of the regime that the Holy Office had established in Spain. As Luis Ozos y Río says in his admirable prologue to the London edition of the *Cancionero de burlas*, in answer to those who were scandalized at the reference to the Spain of Ferdinand and Isabella as a 'lawless kingdom' by the anonymous author of the *Aposento en Juvera*: 'This was not much of a *rule of law*, at least for those who were burned at the stake.' From his solitary Venetian refuge – if I may be excused the anachronism – Delicado would, in all probability, have agreed with him.

III

In the introductory epistle with which the 'portrait' of his fellow countrywoman begins, Delicado states that he will speak only of what he saw and heard 'so as to call to mind many things that are taking place in our day, which are not a commendation of those we are now living nor a mirror for those to come'. Paving the way for the great masters of nineteenth-century realism and its followers today, after asserting that he neither took his story from other books nor plagiarized the eloquence of others, he declares repeatedly that he has taken everything he has written directly from reality:

> And because this portrait is so natural that there is no one who has known Madame Lozana, in Rome or outside of Rome, who will not clearly see that it has been drawn from her acts and her waggling behind and her words and likewise because I have diligently applied myself to not writing anything that I did not first extract from the work of my model, looking within her or at her.

In the memorandum, *appendicula* and final letters he again insists that his is 'not a work, but a portrait', 'the most natural portrait of which the author was capable', and makes his excuses to the future reader for 'writing once what I saw done and heard said so many times', in words that sound familiar to our ears today, thanks to our reading of authors such as Balzac or Galdós.

This documentary aspect of *La Lozana* is doubtless important, even though, as we shall see later, it by no means exhausts the value and interest of a work which, like *La Celestina*, the *Lazarillo* or the *Quixote* allows for – not to say demands – a plurality of interpretations. The portrait of the corruption of the Roman clergy in the time of Alexander VI and his successors Julius II and Leo X, with its allusions to those abbots who, in order to find favour with a courtesan, go off to the chancery for money to fleece some poor wretch (XXXV), is clearly exact and in Delicado's novel we believe we catch echoes – before the fact – of that admirable and fierce *Council of Love* by Oscar

Panizza – a drama set in the pontificate of Alexander Borgia – which so deservedly aroused the enthusiasm of André Breton. The picture of prostitution likewise helps us to understand the transformation of the Eternal City of the Catholics into the New Babylon that drove Luther to rebellion: in memorandum XXI, for example, the courier touches upon the origin of the prostitutes who have taken refuge in the soft life of Roman cosmopolitanism, and after mentioning in passing his *modus vivendi* and art of placing his worldly goods, well or badly as the case may be, foreseeing worse times to come, answers Aldonza's question as to 'which women are the most kind-hearted' with a joyful outburst of patriotism: 'Oh, Spanish women are the best and the most perfect!' There is also a bittersweet aftertaste to the long, lively monologue in which la Lozana denounces the ingratitude of society towards elderly prostitutes who have served it.

> [...] with their fortunes and honour, and gambled their lives so as to honour the court and fight and battle, for iron doors did not suffice for them and they used their distaffs as bucklers and their ears as helmets, fighting day and night, in bed and in childbed, whatever the cost to them. And now what just deserts are they given? Except that some have been left with broken arms, others, with their persons and worldly goods wasted away, others, pointed out as shameless and suffering physical pain, others, having recently given birth and been abandoned, others who were once respected ladies and are now servants ...

and then brings up next, in today's language of the welfare state or social security, the subject of justice and the necessity of a bonus, in the form of a tavern, for those who have reached the age of retirement after long and courageous service for the common good and the happiness of the republic: 'as in days of old was the custom among the Romans and still is today among the Venetians, whereby all those who had served or fought for the Roman Senate, if they reached old age or had bodily members maimed in battle or in defence of the people, were given the aforementioned tavern as a reward for their merit'. She then further stresses the analogy, being confident that this bonus

> will be given to female combatants [...], and especially to those who have served and are serving with a will in this kindly city; those who, as I have said, placed their persons and their fatigue

in the triumphal car that passed so as to maintain the earth and keep it supplied with the necessary provisions and honoured by their persons. (XLIV)

In this and other passages of the work, we find in Aldonza an unselfish concern for the common good that clearly distinguishes her from the heroes and heroines that Delicado took as a model and a source of inspiration, that is to say, the characters of *La Celestina*. Whereas the actors of the tragicomedy place their own egotism before any consideration of others, since in a world full of sound and fury the one valid rule consists of furthering anything and everything that redounds to the pleasure or profit of the individual, la Lozana seeks her enjoyment and interest without losing sight of the existence of her neighbour: her conduct reveals an ethical meaning that corresponds to what we might call a natural morality, founded at one and the same time on the pursuit of pleasure and the intent to avoid harming another. A whore and a hustler, yes, but always generous and in the service of society:

> I can go anywhere with my face uncovered, for I never acted basely, or acted as a procuress or go-between for a despicable person, for gentlemen and known harlots. With my honour I did my best to interpose words, and soothe ill tempers, and reconcile parties, and make peace and remove rancours [. . .] And this will be said of me, if someone wants to put me in a story some day. (XXXIX)

Let us point out in passing that this sort of natural morality of Aldonza's appears to be that of the author as well, as he leads us to understand in his personal judgement of the protagonist included in the *appendicula* of the work, when he states that she 'took great care not to do things that were an offence to God' and, 'without prejudice, tried to eat and drink without giving offence to any party'. The Divinity, and religious questions in general, are treated in the 'portrait' in a purely pragmatic way, as mere components of the social order, and we never find in *La Lozana* the muted violence of Pleberio's rebuke addressed to the Creator nor the atheism that underlies the world of *La Celestina*. Aldonza's attitude towards religion – be it that of Jews or of Christians – is one of evident indifference. Like a great many of the converts of the time, Aldonza has abandoned the religious practices of her forbears without embracing thereby those of the caste that won out and conforms in her own particular way to a sort of vague epicurian rationalism, shaded with altruistic and humanitarian concerns. As Márquez Villanueva remarks in the article mentioned previously, 'the immediate effect of the lack of beliefs on the part of la Lozana is to free her from the least flaw of inconsistency or hypocrisy as regards an ethic that is not purely natural, thus raising her above the sheer absurdity represented by Rome prior to its sacking in 1527 by the troops of the Empire'.

IV

Unlike the heroes and heroines of *La Celestina* or the protagonist of the *Lazarillo*, Aldonza is not a dynamic character: the events and episodes in which the author involves her throughout the 'portrait' have no influence on her and she experiences no moral or psychological development in the course of the novel. La Lozana's character is static, rather, endowed with an unalterable, prior 'essence'. Delicado has made her, once and for all, an ingenious, picaresque figure, and thereby deprived himself of the possibility of 'building' her, as the anonymous author of the *Lazarillo*, for example, builds little by little the figure of Lázaro:

> And as she possessed great insight and diabolical cleverness and a great deal of practical knowledge, on seeing a man she knew precisely what he was capable of and what he possessed, and what he could give her, and what she could get out of him. And she also observed how those women who were in the city at that time went about things, and noted what seemed to her might be of profit to her, in order always to be free and subject to no one. (V)

From the beginning of the 'portrait', the reader knows, then, what to expect of la Lozana, and her later conduct will serve no purpose save to illustrate this earlier characterization of her. This lack of change is compensated, however, by the exceptional components of Aldonza's personality, and here, a comparison with López de Ubeda's heroine immediately reveals the genuine originality of the figure of Aldonza. Whereas the crafty Justina defends her virginity with tricks and stratagems worthy of a cunning wild animal, the Judeo-Andalusian prides herself on her active and ever-vigilant sensuality. There is nothing more unlike her than the prototype of the woman who is the passive object of the man's pleasure, at one and the same time faint-hearted and resigned to the sexual aggression of the male. In the amorous grammar of la Lozana, the active voice is always predominant. Her character is situated at the antipodes of the honest-maiden-misled-by-men, since, as she explains without the least shame or false modesty, 'ever since I was a little girl I ate what was mine, and on first seeing a man I was roused from my lethargy, and I was eager to go off with one, though I was not yet old enough' (VII). The first time she sleeps with Rampín, she says under her breath: 'May this big cock stick around, seeing as how I've had an appetite from the moment I was born,' and exclaims in amazement: 'Oh, what delicious honey! [. . .] whatever troubles I've had you've taken them away' (XIV).

She is none the less not an exception in the gallery of feminine characters who appear in the pages of the portrait. Delicado's women dialectically wield in turn their own sensuality and their necessities in this regard – Rampín's aunt, for instance, who responds to her husband's boasting in front of la Lozana with these sarcastic words: 'You've been here for two months now without his telling me why, and now he's trying to make himself out to be cock of the walk' (XIV). As Aldonza herself says, discovering the secret desire of many belonging to her sex: 'I wanted the fear of shame to be lost in my day, so that everyone would ask for and do whatever he or she pleased [. . .] for if I didn't feel ashamed, any man that passed by would want to make love with me, and if there were no fear, everyone would come in and ask for what was forbidden' (LXII) since, as she observes in another passage of the work, the woman's sex organ 'ought not to be empty, according to natural philosophy'. It is interesting to note that Rampín's attraction to la Lozana is the effect of a general erotic preference of hers for servants and pimps. Similar in this respect to the whores of today and of all time, Aldonza is on the lookout for a rich gentleman who will keep her and a pimp who will satisfy her:

PILGRIM WOMAN: Tell me, Madame Lozana, what does it mean that young menservants are stronger and better than their masters, however well-off and respected the latter may be?

LOZANA: Because we women are fools. It's certain that in order to sleep at night and sweat freely we don't wear a thin chemise, which then falls apart. The man, if he is fully dressed, is content to look, but he does not satisfy his will, and so young servants are better in this case than their masters. And a thin chemise is fine for festive occasions, and a thick one for ordinary wear; for a woman without a man is like a fire without wood. And a virile man who can set her on fire and who eats pork so that he may play around with her in due course. And her master to pay the rent for the house and give her petticoats. (LXIII)

Money here plays an indissoluble part in sensuality: by buying the services of a pimp or a servant, Aldonza possesses him at the same time that she is possessed and enslaves him by turning him into her master. As a servant-lover-procurer who allows himself to be loved as though he were an object and at the same time protects her and gives her gifts, Rampín is the very incarnation of her erotic ideal. In her relations, she plays the active role: she is the one who seduces him in a scene that is a marvel of humour and verbal liveliness, and the young servant's merits are shown to be exceptional from every point of view, since la Lozana decides, ipso facto, that in the future he will honour her and serve her: 'Look, you poor thing, now that "I know how cauldrons are beaten", I want no one but you to sleep with me at night, and by day I'll eat everything, and by so doing I'll get fat, and you try to card my wool for me if you want me to weave leather sashes' (XXII).

On her arrival in Rome, Aldonza has accepted the lodging that Trigo the Jew has offered her in exchange for working as a prostitute and Rampín's services will be of inestimable value in acquiring her own brothel: 'I have this man who is seeing to my getting my house, and he sets me aflame, and comes inside me with a will, and the only thing people know is that he is my servant, and he never tries to create jealousy between us and he is like a swift stag' (LXI).

The dialogues on erotic themes occupy a good half of the book and if some of them are merely vulgar – in the same linguistic vein as *La Carajicomedia* or *El pleito del manto* – others constitute a veritable model of cleverness and wit. They occupy a unique place in Castilian literature: they did not exist before Delicado (if we except certain passages from *La Celestina*), and we do not find them again later, at least not until our own day. Some of them bear comparison with Aretino's *Ragionamenti* or Machiavelli's erotic comedies. Phallic references and allusions abound, and Delicado very skilfully alternates euphemism – sometimes in the form of metaphor (spear, Paschal candle, reed pipe), sometimes of metonomy (whey, honey), of abstract expressions (virtue), ellipsis or pronouns and adverbs (here, there, that) – and ordinary and direct mention as well: in both cases the repertory of words, tropes and images is remarkably rich and fresh, its vitality revealed to us, after several centuries, thanks to its influence on Carlos Fuentes's recent ambitious novel.[4]

And yet another novelty: ordinarily, when works of this genre depict conduct that the author cannot recommend as a model, punishment lies in wait for the protagonists on the last page; morality is thus preserved and (endangered), equilibrium restored. In *La Lozana*, – as later in *Estebanillo* – punishment does not exist and the traditional reader – accustomed to rose-coloured or black endings, depending on the positive or negative example provided by the protagonists – is in for a disappointment. La Lozana will not perish in the sacking of Rome, as her sins would require if seen from the viewpoint of Catholic morality: before the great cataclysm – because of a premonitory dream – Aldonza withdraws to the island of Lípari in the company of her beloved Rampín, with the obvious satisfaction of a woman who has fulfilled her duty and has the right to a long and enjoyable retirement: 'I shall have repose, and I shall see a new world, and not hope that it leaves me, but that I leave it. Thus the past will have come to an end, and we shall now see the present, as the end of Rampín and of la Lozana' (LXVI).

We are a thousand leagues away from the existential pessimism of Pleberio and the chaotic world of *La Celestina*: Delicado's social and human vision is infinitely more pleasing and it is not venturing too far to suppose that his more or less voluntary exile made a decisive contribution to it. Trapped in the meshes of the gigantic mechanism of repression, vigilance and torture set up *ex professo* against converts, Rojas's absolute nihilism was his exasperated reply to the distressing life experience visited upon him by fate. From his pleasant Italian retreat, Delicado saw things in a different way: the destructive corporeal frenzy that destroys the solitary heroes of the tragicomedy one after the other is countered in the 'portrait' by a harmonious balance of the signs 'body'/'non-body', similar to the one we find in the masterpiece of the Archpriest of Hita. The exile in which the author of *La Lozana* lived and died thus permitted, for the last time, the free, unhindered expression of the ardent corporeal desire repressed by triumphant orthodoxy until far into the present century: the image of a Spain that might have been, and has not been, and whose subterranean existence surfaces at times, in puddles and pools of greenish, stagnant water, on the burning-hot, sterile riverbed of our arid and barren literature.

V

The literary expression of the body, perfectly achieved in the *Libro de buen amor* and *La Celestina*, still appears, in enviable health, in Delicado's novel, though it shows up on our horizon once more, following a long eclipse of several centuries, only in the poetry of Cernuda. As if it did not suffice to confer on it an exceptional significance in the field of our literature, *La Lozana andaluza* may also rightfully claim an important role in the development of the narrative techniques that were to culminate in Cervantes's discovery of the modern novel (I prefer the term 'discovery' to that of 'creation' since even an author of genius such as Cervantes simply realized the possibilities inherent in novelistic discourse, in the same way that the scientific researcher discovers certain natural phenomena which, prior to his findings, were still in a latent state). If we may consider the Archpriest of Talavera as the discoverer of the immediate discourse whereby there emerges the 'I', that is to say, the inner nature of the narrative agent, and Rojas as the first creator of dynamic, totally individualized characters, we ought to recognize in Delicado one of the great predecessors of realistic dialogue, which plays such an important role in the novel of the last two centuries (independently of the fact that, for extra-literary reasons, his contribution was unable to exert an influence on our literature until recently). Whereas in the Boccaccian type of story the author follows the narrative procedure that classical precepts call *diegesis* – that is to say, summing up the conduct and acts of the characters, usually after these acts have taken place – Delicado, like Rojas, has recourse to *mimesis*, that is to say, he allows the characters to express themselves on their own through dialogue and obtains the *progressio* of action by this means, as in the theatre. Thus, rather than depicting Rome for us, we 'see' it as it is being described to us by the characters in their conversations and we have the impression that the author is strolling along at their side with a tape recorder, as often happens in a contemporary novel such as *El Jarama*. The scrupulous reproduction of popular speech in the vast crucible of the Roman metropolis has no equivalent in our literature and despite his prejudices against Delicado, Menéndez Pelayo awards him a modest diploma earned by his originality. In order to establish a comparison, we would also need to refer to the exemplary novel by Sánchez Ferlosio; as in this latter, the protagonists of *La Lozana* use at every turn, in order to substitute for the absence of *diegesis* or commentary, adverbs and pronouns indicative of place – this, that, here, there, etc – which, as Benveniste has pointed out, are realities of 'discourse':

> LOZANA: What is *that one* preaching? Let's go *over there*.
> RAMPIN: He's preaching about how Rome is to be lost in the year '27, but he's saying it as a joke. *This* is the Campo dei Fiori, it's in the middle of the city *here*. *These* are charlatans, tooth-pullers and hernia healers, who fleece peasants and newcomers to the city, who are called greenhorns *here*.
> LOZANA: What's *that*, that crowd *over there* around *that one*?
> RAMPIN: They're young servants looking for masters.[5]
> LOZANA: And they come *here*? (XV)[6]

> – Be careful, my girl, there's a step.
> – I see it. Thanks.
> – Where do we leave the motorbikes?
> – *There* outside for the time being; they'll tell us where to put them.
> – I've never been to *this* place.
> – I have, quite a few times.
> – Hello.
> – Oh, hi there.
> – Fernando, help me please, my skirt is caught.
> – It's already quite a bit cooler *here*.
>
> (*El Jarama*, pp. 21–8)[7]

Only one dissimilarity: although the time of narrative distance is resistant to any attempt at mediation – and for this reason, unlike a musical score or a reel of film, the process of reading a text lacks a specified speed of performance –[8] a comparison of the two works shows us immediately that, whereas Ferlosio's characters move at an apparently 'normal' rhythm, Delicado's wander through the streets of Rome with a camera that moves very quickly, as in the old days of silent films:

> RAMPIN: In *this* street we'll find any number of courtesans crowded together like bees in a hive.

LOZANA: Which ones are they?
RAMPIN: We'll see them at the jalousies. It's called el Urso *here*.
Farther on you'll see lots more of them.
LOZANA: Who is *that*? The Bishop of Cordova? (XII)[9]

La Lozana is, thus, an important milestone on the road leading to the modern novel in so far as the discoveries of the Archpriest of Talavera and *La Celestina* are assimilated in it, while at the same time it departs from the dramatic schema of the latter. From Cervantes on, novelists have been in the habit of combining, as is well known, *diegesis* and *mimesis*, alternating analysis or description of events and the direct expression of the characters in dialogue. In *La Celestina*, on the other hand, Rojas allows the protagonists to speak for themselves while he remains in the wings pulling the strings of the plot, never appearing in person. In *La Lozana*, Delicado conjoins the two narrative systems in his own way, although, rather than resorting to the use of the grammatical third person in the manner of modern novelists, he inserts himself personally in the work, either to intercalate a note of *diegesis* of his own or that of an abstract third person who, as Benveniste has seen, is the absence of a person –

AUTHOR: Next door there lived a blacksmith, who arose at midnight and did not allow them to sleep. And he got up to see whether it was daylight yet and, returning to bed, woke her up, and she said:
– Where were you? I didn't hear you get up. (XIV)

– or else an individual commentary that makes us aware of his presence, like those cysts or enclaves of 'discourse' scattered all through the novels of the nineteenth century and those of the 'omniscient' novelists of today:

AUTHOR: I was trying to find out how to write a pair of snores, whereupon he woke up. And then, because he wanted to make love to her, she woke up, and said:
– Good lord! Is it daylight? (XIV)

Or then again, to intervene as one character more, who mingles and converses with the protagonists of the portrait:

AUTHOR: Show us your chemises or fine pastry, milady, especially if they have been made by the hand of this fair lady.

LOZANA: Upon my soul, your worship has lovely eyes! And this other gentleman appears to know me, and I know not where I have seen him; yes, yes, I swear, I know him.

– Ah, señora Silvana, I swear on the lives of your children that I know him. He is in the service of a Milanese gentleman of my acquaintance. So tell your master that he'll be a godfather when I get pregnant.

AUTHOR: All the more so if you already are, milady.

LOZANA: Ah, sir, don't say such a thing, for I am more chaste than I need be!

AUTHOR: Come, milady, increase and multiply, so that you may bear something of this world. (XXIV)

VI

In a famous and much-discussed essay, published more than half a century ago, Ortega y Gasset, assuming the point of view of the traditional reader, declared that 'the novel demands that it be seen as the novel that it is, that neither the curtain nor the boards of the stage be visible', and stubbornly clinging to his notion of the genre as a 'serious' one, with clearly defined contours, he added: 'The novel cannot be toyed with: it imposes an inexorable decalogue of commands and prohibitions.' In the wider perspective that is ours today, it is evident that, by expressing himself in these terms, Ortega was excluding from the field of the novel a series of works, from Sterne to Raymond Roussel, which are perhaps the densest and most significant works in this genre: along with a majority of literary works of fiction that, as the philosopher pointed out, conceal their signs and the author's process of setting forth his views (the fact that, like Cervantes's Maese Pedro, he is always behind his paper characters, pulling the strings – under a veneer of 'realism', verisimilitude and 'naturalness'), there exist others – far less numerous, it is true, yet qualitatively essential – that purposely destroy the reader's illusion of reality by way of the direct, and at times perfectly arbitrary intervention of a novelist who lays bare his technique, his tricks, his basic method of procedure (and let us recall the fact yet again, at the risk of appearing irksome: naturalness and authenticity do not exist in the field of the novel – an author, such as Galdós, regarded as 'naturalistic' is as artificial as a deliberate anti-naturalist such as the

Unamuno of *Niebla*; the difference lies in the fact that whereas Galdós tries to conceal his intervention in the story, Unamuno does not hide his and even boasts of bringing it out into the open).

In one of the most outstanding works of today's novelistic avant garde – I am referring to *De donde son los cantantes*, by Severo Sarduy – the author interrupts the action at every step of the way. He continually works his way backwards or leaps forwards, he intercalates a series of whimsical digressions that have no relation to the basic narrative, in such a way that the dénouement of the latter is postponed to an ever more distant time and his presence throughout the novel serves as a mere connecting link between the various episodes and at the end, he intervenes to discuss the work with the characters, regrets his inability to deal with the subject at hand and nonchalantly makes ironic remarks about his own 'failure':

> If I were you, Flor dear, if I had realized who The One who is coming this way was, instead of staying there in your steam bath, weighing yourself, drinking vinegar and washing your eyes out with salt, I would have bolted the door to the dressing room. If you go on this way, you're going to stay chaste and pure for as long a time as a *merengue* danced in the doorway of a church lasts.
>
> Auxilio and Socorro (who are playing canasta in the hallway, already dressed for the Amazon number):
>
> – Well! The one thing that was missing: God the writer, the one who sees everything and knows everything before anybody else, the one who gives advice and sticks his nose in everywhere except where he ought to!

This sort of intervention by the author usually has, as is only to be expected, a very bad press among traditionalist and conservative critics of whatever persuasion, concerned only with catching the Message, the 'content', the ideology; with calling a spade a spade and putting aside games, fioriture, gibberish (an attitude equivalent, on the literary plane, to the very bourgeois *time is money*: no wasting time and squandering words, no useless expenditures; eroticism, no, procreative act yes; wastefulness no, thrift yes; writing as a game, Baroque effects, rhetorical figures, *vade retro*: pure information, denotative language, expropriation of productive, physiological, verbal surplus value).

Such critics and readers always accuse writers who adopt a playful attitude towards the work of literature and approach language like an organism – a live body and, consequently, sensual – of all sorts of crimes: obscurity, elitism, presumptuousness, obedience to outlandish foreign crazes, the ridiculous desire to *épater le bourgeois* – and in the magnificent essay on Lezama that figures in *Escrito sobre un cuerpo* Sarduy himself pokes fun at them with great wit and cleverness. But these perverse, decadent, frivolous intrusions by the author, which, according to the guardians of ideology threatened by the formidable power of subversion of literature, correspond to a morbid obsession for always being 'in' on current fashions, are a good bit more profound and essential than they think, since the use of them goes back not only to Roussel or even Sterne, but to much more distant periods and much less widely known authors.

In *La Lozana andaluza*, we were saying, Delicado intervenes in the plot as one character more and mingles and converses with the other principal figures in the work, but his artistic boldness does not stop there. More notable still: the author frequently appears in the act of writing, like Velázquez in the midst of the process of painting, thus reminding us of his function as a chronicler and the material reality of the literary phenomenon (the height of shamelessness for the bourgeois, whose constant concern – in literature as in politics – is to conceal his signs of generation):

> 'as I was in the act of writing the preceding chapter, on getting the cramp in my foot I left this notebook on the table, and Rampín came in and said: "What testament is this?"' (XVII)

> AUTHOR: Come on, brother, you've always been good at bringing me what was best. Here, bring me a bit of paper and ink, for I want to note down here something that just now came back to me. (XLII)

For *La Lozana* is not only, as most critics deem it to be, *une tranche de vie* or a social chronicle: it is also writing that reflects itself, a work whose subject is the genesis of its own creation:

> AUTHOR: I don't want to leave, for it seems to be the wrong moment; but I said to la Lozana that it's been some time since she showed me those signs of affection that I see she's sending your way now, and I don't want to go because they'll say afterwards that I do nothing but look and note down what goes on, so as to write later on, and that I use models. (XVIII)

The characters are aware of their status as heroes and heroines of the book that the author is writing, as Don Quixote knows that he is the protagonist of the first part of Cid Hamete Benengeli's chronicle or of Avellaneda's spurious *Quixote*. Silvano speaks of the author with la Lozana, referring to him as 'that gentleman who is making a portrait of intimate things about you', and she in turn asks him: 'Señor Silvano, what does it mean that the author of my portrait does not call himself a Cordovan, since his father was one, and he was born in that diocese?' (XLVII).

These instances – and we could cite still more not only from Delicado's work but from the Archpriest of Hita as well – are sufficient evidence for us to conclude that if this structural game of juxtaposing, so as later on to shuffle the various literary planes, corresponds to a nefarious desire for fame on the part of the author or to a decadent, capricious and foreign fashion, such desires and fashions are – to the misfortune and consternation of our naîve ideologists – as old as literature itself.

Though Francisco Delicado was, he tells us, of 'slight build', the 'portrait' that he has bequeathed us need in no way feel itself to be smaller in stature than the loftiest literary creations of its author's century. The growing interest that it has aroused in recent years, amid the general public as amid specialists, as in the case of Blanco White and other heterodox figures condemned *ad vitam aeternam* to ostracism by our official programmers, is proof that Señor Menéndez y Pelayo and his peers have, happily, not carried the day.

Notes

1 I shall permit myself to cite a recent example of this typical critical method inasmuch as it concerns me personally: the examples of inexactitude and stupidity that a certain *Panorama* (or *Cinerama*, as Cernuda sarcastically called it) of contemporary Spanish literature attributes to my novels – to all appearances without having read them – that have been collected in the *Diccionario de literatura* by Sáinz de Robles, in an amazing case of nonreading carried to an exponential power, the content of which – full of epithets and value judgements intended to make up for a mental vacuum worthy of an air pump – I heartily recommend to those who wish to verify on their own the 'critical' practice of our reviewers: in a world of well-behaved, well-educated children, I am the black sheep of the class.

2 Among the bibliographical items concerning *La Lozana*, let us mention in particular: Bruno M. Damiani, Introduction to the Clásicos Castalia edition, Madrid, 1969; José Hernández Ortiz, 'La génesis artística de *La*

Lozana andaluza', Madrid; Ricoardo Aguilera, 1974; Segundo Serrano Poncela, 'Aldonza, la andaluza Lozana en Roma', Mexico City, *Cuadernos Americanos*, 1952. As I was putting these notes – the basis of my courses at New York University in 1972 – in final form, there arrived in my hands Francisco Márquez Villanueva's most interesting article, 'El mundo converso de *La Lozana andaluza*', Seville, *Archivo Hispalense*, 1973, a number of points of which coincide with those I make in this essay. My apologies for this to him and to my reader.

3 As is well known, Quevedo, in an allusion to the New Christian origins of his rival Góngora threatens to 'rub his verses with lard', thereby giving new currency to Lope's scornful remarks concerning Arias Montano. On the significance of Cervantes's famous 'sorrows and afflictions', see Américo Castro, *Cervantes y los casticismos españoles*, Madrid: Alfaguara, 1966, and his *Hacia Cervantes*, Madrid: Taurus, 1967.

4 *Terra nostra*, Mexico City: Joaquín Mortiz, 1975; Barcelona: Seix Barral, 1976. (American edition, *Terra nostra*, translated by Margaret Sayers Peden, New York; Farrar, Straus and Giroux, 1976.) See my essay in this volume, pp. 154–185.

5 The allusion to the social framework in which the picaresque novel was to develop later illustrates the complex relations that exist between literature and reality. The narrator in search of a subject is preceded, as we see, by the subject in search of a narrator.

6 Italics mine. [J. G.]

7 Italics mine. [J. G.]

8 Gérard Genette, *Figures*, III, Paris: Editions du Seuil, 1973.

9 Italics mine. [J. G.]

Quevedo: the Excremental Obsession

To Severo Sarduy

The anus is always terror, and I do not grant the fact that one loses
an excrement without being torn apart and losing one's soul in the
process as well.

Antonin Artaud

I

At the end of the Civil War, the maidservant who took charge of me
and my brothers and cared for us with a mother's love and concern,
used to tell us the story of a certain Quevedo who, having lowered his
breeches in order to defecate in a public place, with his back turned
to those passing by, was surprised in this position by a distinguished
Italian gentleman. '*Ah, qué vedo!*' he supposedly exclaimed with horror
on contemplating the miscreant, caught *in flagrante*, not with his hands
in the cash box but with his arse in the air. To which the Spaniard is
said to have replied, with ill-concealed pride: 'Imagine that! They even
recognize me by my behind!'

Eulalia laughed till the tears rolled down her cheeks every time she
told us this anecdote. She who had undoubtedly never read a single line
by the author of the *Buscón* and knew nothing whatsoever about his
literary creation, spoke of him in familiar terms, invariably associating
his comic, bizarre figure with the act of defecating or urinating, with
turds and farts. Whereas critics and serious scholars of the works of
Quevedo are in the habit of dismissing with a grimace of disgust
the writer's scatological obsession or hurriedly dealing with it in a
few concise and condescending, if not frankly condemnatory, phrases,
the example of Eulalia shows that, on the contrary, his abundant

coprophiliac allusions and the legend that surrounds them are well known and appreciated by the mass public, and even by those who, as victims of the rigid social stratification of the country, live entirely on the margin of its culture. This dichotomy, very common in Spanish life, reveals with noonday clarity the divorce that exists between the intellectual asepsis of an elite that keeps itself entirely apart from the problems and traumas of concrete human beings and their frequent bafflement and confusion, which, for lack of an adequate and direct means of expression, manifest themselves in a tangential and oblique way in the form of jokes and wordplay revolving about what is unspeakable, excluded, denied. A neurotic phenomenon that cuts culture off from the fecund realm from which it ought normally to draw its life's sap and in turn cuts the people off from culture because of its anaemia, its rarefied atmosphere, its abstruse, erudite jargon, its absurd mandarinate. The consequences are a matter of common knowledge: a people deprived of a culture that is truly theirs, in which it may find a full-length portrait of itself reflected, and an anti-popular culture, which does away with the flesh-and-blood human being and converts that person, in the name of age-old oppressive Christianity or the present-day religion of progress, into an abstract entity.

II

An examination of the traditional attitude of Spanish culture towards the body, from the Catholic Monarchs to our own day, would merit an entire study by itself. The detestation of corporeal pleasure by the majority of our writers is truly amazing, and a psychoanalytic study of authors such as Menéndez Pidal or Unamuno would no doubt have great surprises in store for us. As we know since Freud, thanks to his debatable but penetrating analysis of culture as neurosis or as a substitute satisfaction for bodily enjoyment, repression still wreaks its effect more forcefully on excrement than on the sexual in the strict sense of the word. With this premise as our point of departure it is possible to understand and interpret the phobias, the complexes, the aversions of a culture that has always proceeded to defend itself and defend us from this physiological reality through silence, concealment, scorn. The simple fact that the subject, fundamental in Quevedo's works, has as yet not been accorded the serious treatment it deserves, indicates what a powerful effect repression and censorship continue to exert today, even among our most avant-garde critics. From this point of view, a careful exploration of the minds of some of our Quevedo specialists would be as instructive as an examination of that of Quevedo himself. Consciously or unconsciously, on the pretext of so-called scientific asepsis, our investigators have tried to whisk the excremental obsession of the author of the *Buscón* out of sight, maintaining that it does not fit in with the broad outlines of their lofty intellectual values. The silence of a great many scholars of *La Celestina* with regard to the Jewish origins of Rojas, along with the rejection of Quevedo's coprophilia, constitute the best example in the field of literary criticism of the persistence and the strength of the taboos with which these specialists have been confronted. Denial, Freud said, is a way of coming to terms with what is repressed: the supposed cultural and moral superiority that Menéndez Pidal wields like a rapier, for example, when he takes up taboo lexical fields in the work of Góngora or Quevedo scarcely disguises the strictly emotional nature of his reactions – such as that of refusing to transcribe for his readers, because of its 'repellent' nature, Góngora's mocking comparison between the eyes of a lady and two chamber pots.

The taboo that, in the majority of the cultural expressions of *homo erectus*, involves sexual activity and corporeal excreta perhaps obeys, as Leach has observed, the desire to suppress the intermediate categories between the 'I', the 'mine', and the 'not-I', the 'not-mine'. In an interesting commentary on his investigations, the North American Hispanist Larry Grimes rightly points out:

> bodily excretions (urine, faeces, semen) constitute a highly ambiguous category; they are products of the body that become separate from it and are expelled into the outer world. Since they have both the characteristics of A [that is is to say, I, mine] and of B [not-I, not-mine], expressions referring to these substances form part of the mediating category C, and are the object of a powerful taboo. The same is true of erotic activity and the sex organs, which represent a zone of confluence and confusion because of the direct contact of two physical entities.[1]

This necessity of distinguishing between two possible objects of infantile desire, between the I and the not-I, would extend equally to individuals of the same sex and family, thereby including them in the proscribed category and creating the taboos of homosexuality and incest.

The behaviour of society with regard to linguistic taboo fluctuates, depending on the period and the country. At times, the severely moralistic attitude of the people contrasts with the laxity and tolerance of writers and cultivated minorities in general. At other times, the rigid, puritanical position of these latter represents a reaction against the tolerance of the popular sectors towards uncomfortable realities and dictates a euphemistic avoidance of them that extends lexical areas that are taboo to unimaginable limits. As is logical, such fluctuations do not attempt to interfere with the unalterable force of the taboo; it is merely a question of degree within the ambit of the neurosis. Contrary to the usual dictum, Quevedo's coprophilia, rather than being a reflection of a sick mind, is, paradoxically, a symptom of good health: the author of the *Buscón* expresses, in his own way, the general neurosis of humanity, giving free rein to the obsessions and fantasies linked to the recognition of our corporeal reality – and it is precisely those who scorn the body and look on it with contempt who discover the incurable depth of their sickness by refusing to admit that physical reality, concealing with genuine hysteria the 'shameful' act of defecating. Quevedo's scatology allows us to see in their true perspective all those elements of his work that exceed that reality, complement it or contradict it: *velis nolis*, the asepsis of pure intellectuals, by virtue of the well-known dialectic of denial and the return of the repressed, excrementizes and marks with a visceral seal the totality of their creative vision in the field of culture. In the eyes of many Quevedo specialists, the neurosis of their subject thus becomes total neurosis – an abstraction that dehumanizes the species and alienates it even farther from the criminal body that belches, drools, spits, pisses, shits and farts.

III

A gradual humiliation of the value of the body, from the Peninsular society of Al-Andalus to the evil called the Golden Age – from the joyous exaltation of carnal pleasure that permeates the work of Ibn Hazm and the Archpriest of Hita, through the ambiguous and cynical attitude of the Archpriest of Talavera, and arriving finally at the traumatized Quevedian vision of woman in certain breathtaking passages of *La hora de todos*: whereas the picture of Eden in the Koran captivates the mind of the Muslim thanks to the colour and sensuality of its palette, Christianity has failed lamentably in its effort to provide us with a representation of heaven. Only the image of hell, traced by its preachers with a terrifying luxury of details, becomes a consistent graphic portrayal. The abstract and insipid descriptions of the utterly tedious realm of the blessed amply establish the clear separation between a religion that denies the body and the joyfulness of the senses and another that prolongs and perpetuates their bliss in a life beyond our earthly one. Religion and eroticism are not contrary terms for the Muslim; his law does not forbid him the satisfactions of physical pleasure and his paradise is a wondrous condensation of all the fantasies and chimerical imaginings of the man of the desert: gardens of delight with fruits, date palms, pomegranates; gently flowing waters; exquisite wine that does not intoxicate; nuptial beds; girls with great innocent black eyes, whom no man will have previously deflowered and who, even after being possessed, will continue to be virgins; wondrously beautiful ephebes who will always remain in the flower of their youth, etc.[2] Thanks to the vital symbiosis of Juan Ruiz, the *Libro de buen amor* is a typically Mudéjar work, in which the terms body and spirit, instead of being opposites and mutually exclusive, act in a harmonious and complementary way. But the defeat of Islam and the long process of eradicating its values from Hispanic society clear the path for the violent anti-feminism and the repression of the body that were to shape our culture from the last years of the fifteenth century down to our own day. The dividing line is formed, as goes without saying, in the reign of Isabel la Católica: during it, not only are the Jews expelled and the Inquisition created so as to keep watch on the converted; the importation of books (in other words, the free circulation of ideas) is prohibited and bigamists and sodomites are sent to the stake (that is to say, one's sovereign disposition of one's own body is condemned). Little by little the cultural life of the country drifts towards the daily schizophrenia of living between two contradictory and incompatible planes – vulgar love and courtly love, lofty poetry and collections of bawdy popular songs and poems.[3] Quevedo's inspired works show better than any other *oeuvre* the seriousness of the insoluble conflict – the adorable image of the desired woman destroyed by the evocation of what she expels: blood, faeces or urine. 'Think of her having her monthly periods' – he writes in *La hora de todos* – 'and she will disgust you, and when she is without them, remember that she has had them, and will have them again, and what captivates you will make you feel horror, and feel shame at being carried away by things that even in an ordinary statue made of wood have a less repulsive fundament.'

This process of abstraction and debasement is not exclusive to literature. The age-old fury of Catholicism against the cleanliness of the body – in so far as it accentuates its status as an erotic object

– manifests itself at an early date in the form of a general attack on public bath houses and the development of an entire corpus of doctrines that excuse physical filth in the name of clean moral habits. 'Although public baths existed now and again in Spain as a Romano-Visigothic tradition before the arrival of the Muslims,' Américo Castro writes, 'their presence among the Christians of the reconquered territories was a reflection of Muslim customs'. When the Infante Sancho, son of Alfonso VI, died in 1086 in the battle of Zalaca, the king asked his counsellors why the martial spirit of his knights had weakened; they replied that it was because they often went to bath houses and were much given to vices. The king then had all the baths of the kingdom demolished. (*Crónica general*, p. 555). Doubtless not all the baths were torn down, and the account is probably a legend. The idea that attending public baths, a common practice among the Moors, was a cause of weakness and vice none the less lingered on.[4] Nietzsche, for his part, mentions in the *Anti-Christ* that the entry of the Castilian monarchs into Cordova was accompanied by the destruction of all the bathing establishments in the city. Little by little public baths fell into disuse among Christians, 'and from the year 1526 attempts were made to suppress those of the Moriscos [. . .] In 1576 a solemn ceremony was held and all the artificial baths in Granada were torn down,' Castro adds. 'People forgot the custom of washing frequently, in Spain as in the rest of Europe, until well into the nineteenth century.'

The feminine characters of the Archpriest of Talavera still mention in their delightful dialogues their visits to public bath houses. A century later, in one of Timoneda's *Patrañas*, the narrator includes in the idealized description of an unsually beautiful girl, on whom he furtively feasts his eyes, the following phrase: 'Her maidservant was removing fleas from Finea [. . .]' The act of ridding the beloved of fleas was thus not out of place in a sublimated portrait of the loved one. Bodily uncleanliness included all social classes and awaited, so to speak, the arrival of a genius to describe it. Quevedo then represented the vengeful apotheosis of the physiological and visceral – the dawning consciousness of the denied body with its filth, excreta, saliva.

IV

Systematic repression of the body acts through its being radically dispossessed of verbal expression. The all-embracing expansion of an oppressive system of thought denies it, humiliates it, insults it. Until it reaches the limit-situation that unfortunately we are all well acquainted with: the reality of a mute, defenceless, guilty organism, condemned without appeal by language – a rebellious impulse that cannot name itself, that must fight every step of the way against the monopoly of the dictionary, that must think and affirm itself against its own means of expression. Giving the body its voice back again still strikes us as a quixotic, almost rash undertaking – a bold incursion into mined territory, into the heart of the enemy camp: to seize the condemnatory words one by one, to engage in a violent struggle with them, to turn them inside out like a sock, to transform them into a boomerang that launches a surprise attack on the zealous guardians of language.

The universality of desire, the search for a pleasure that has no knowledge of the miserable limits imposed by reality, inevitably clashes with the grandiose 'rational' edifices erected by creeds, religions, ideologies. Civilization, as we know, has been the result of a fierce struggle for existence that has subordinated the satisfaction of the primary impulses of the individual to urgent social objectives. Owing to the age-old opposition between libido and productivity – of which a thinker such as Ibn Hazm was fully aware – humanity little by little loses contact with its corporeal reality – organic, evacuatory and sexual – in the name of a series of inhuman abstract values – apparently rational schemata that in the final analysis lead to monstrous tyrannies. Monolithic ideology and its offspring, the totalitarian state, dispense with the physical reality of human beings, metamorphose the person into a glorious body, dehumanize him or her: a mere cipher or incorporeal entity whose salvation or well-being requires the elimination of anyone who claims to be different, marginal or unassimilable; a simple instrument in the service of the intangibility of the creed or doctrine.

Neither Nazism nor Stalinism invented anything at all. The expulsion of the Jews, the persecution and burning of apostates, heretics or sodomites already imply the triumph of a 'rational' conception that leaves aside persons of flesh and blood for the sake of the purity of principles. The reprobate handed over to the secular arm is not a human being who writes in pain and screams, but a perverted soul, a completely abstract and unreal entity. The Spain that Quevedo knew is the perfect paradigm of a process of coldly developed sublimation, in which those who hold power, the custodians of the doctrine, can discuss, for example, the fate of their Morisco countrymen in terms resembling those that the Nazis will use three and a half centuries later as they put forward, with perverted logic, the inevitable 'final solution':

the documentation published by Boronat shows us the ruling class of the period – government officials, noblemen, high church dignitaries – recommending in turn pure and simple extermination of 'that accursed riff-raff', death for the parents and slavery for the children, 'putting them in abandoned ships without oars, rudders, grappling hooks or sails', exiling them on a desert island, and even castrating them and then sending them to the most desolate areas of Labrador or the Straits of Magellan – all of this seasoned with protestations of fervent Christian charity and invocations to the Divinity.[5] Subjected to the implacable tyranny of this hostile discourse, the body resists as best it can the sublimating process that hides it and makes it abstract, without, however, confronting the dominating ideology – which would be impossible. To evoke excrement, saliva or urine will be a discreet way of reminding us of its presence, of making us feel that 'it is there'. Seen from this perspective, Quevedo's much-debated coprophilia expresses the protest of a body that rejects its 'glorious' status and provocatively assumes its *unclean guilt*.

V

In a well-known episode of the *Life of the Adventurer Don Pablos of Segovia* during the stay of Pablos and Don Diego in Alcalá, those sharing the room at the inn in which they are lodged subject the former to a nasty initiation: they defecate in his bed. The discovery of the excrement and the smell it gives off fill the unfortunate protagonist of the tale with shame and distress. When his master enters the room and notices the smell, Pablos tries to conceal the faeces all round him. Don Diego insists on getting him out of bed and pulls him so hard by one of his fingers that he dislocates it, thereby forcing Pablos to uncover the shit he is lying in, amid the jeers and laughter of the malicious band of students.[6]

The abundance of scatalogical incidents and allusions throughout the book frees me of the tiresome task of enumerating them: the floods of urine, faecal matter, spittle are essential ingredients of the novelistic plot and undoubtedly have a primordial function. Although these elements are fairly common in the literature of the period – and often are employed as a formal theme – the importance they assume in Quevedo's work, not only by reason of their social implications but also because of their psychoanalytic ones, takes on truly exceptional dimensions.

To Maurice Molho – who merits the fairly rare distinction of having taken on the subject without prudery – Quevedo's evident pleasure in showing his characters in the act of shitting, pissing or spitting, and in general perceiving the human being as an essentially excremental body, corresponds to a process of reification and reveals an 'insuperable scorn for man'. Commenting on the episode in which the prankish students cover Pablos with gobs of phlegm, leaving him dripping from head to foot, Molho states that we see 'man degraded to the point where he appears beneath the reifying image of an organism, or rather of a physiological automaton, a shitter and a spitter, capable of secreting at will the excrement and the mucus he is stuffed full of'; and the passage in which the narrator eats with a band of blackguards who get drunk and drink face down from a trough of wine suggests to him the following observation: 'The degradation consists here in making the physiological person descend to the level of the animal that drinks from a trough, wallowing about on the ground, as though the erect posture, the specific attribute of man, were forbidden him.'[7]

There is no need to say that Molho is perfectly correct about the great writer's intention to offer us a portrayal of the human being at a strictly physiological and visceral level – but our own interpretation of this aim proves to be diametrically opposed to his. In the face of a monolithic ideology that disregards the being of flesh and blood and substitutes an abstract entelechy for him, to remind us that man is an animal that gulps down its food, pisses, spits and shits, far from humiliating the human being and transforming him into an object, contributes, as Bataille saw very clearly, to preserving his awareness of existing in and for himself. Whereas the ideology of tyranny denies the body in order to reach heaven or reduces it to the condition of a work tool in the service of productivity, the individual's presumed animality spares him the nightmare of Judeo-Christian abstraction and capitalist and bureaucratic reification. Given the stigma that marks sexual pleasure in the eyes of Catholicism – more than once the heroes of the picaresque novel, taken in by the wiles of a lady of easy virtue, escape the latter's boudoir with all possible haste and fall into a dung heap or a barrel full of excreta – the physiological and excretory functions of the being of flesh and blood become, so to speak, a last pocket of indomitable resistance which, instead of degrading and making an object of the person, affirm and humanize that being. Quevedo's coprophilia then appears to us in a different light: as a reply of the mortified body to the alienating process that sublimates it.

The subversive nature of Quevedo's thought appears even more clearly in his satirical poetry. Quevedo expresses the *inter urinas et faeces nascimur* after his own fashion in one of the crudest and most suggestive verses in our language: '*La vida empieza en lágrimas y caca*': 'Life begins amid tears and shit'. But, leaving aside the numerous references to excrement and breaking wind so liberally scattered throughout his poems, I shall refer only to the sacrilegious boldness with which he pairs the face and the arse, imposing on the pyramid of intellectual and social differences of human beings a radically egalitarian and anarchic vision:

> *Que tiene ojo de culo es evidente,*
> *y manojo de llaves, tu sol rojo,*
> *y que tiene por niña en aquel ojo*
> *atezado mojón duro y caliente.*

> *Tendrá legañas necesariamente*
> *la pestaña erizada como abrojo,*
> *y guiñará, con lo amarillo y flojo,*
> *todas las veces que a pujar se siente.*

> *La voz del ojo, que llamos pedo*
> *(ruisenor de los putos) detenida . . .*

> *La llaneza de tu cara*
> *en nada la disimulo,*
> *pues profesara de culo,*
> *si un ojo no le sobrara.*[8]

The hierarchy of faces, Quevedo tells us, is a mere mask intended to make us forget the uniform, common condition of our *inferior face* that has been whisked out of sight. To compare face and arse, to evoke the extremely close relationship between the two faces – the one shown and the one hidden, the free one and the imprisoned one – is equivalent to attacking at its very roots the arduous process of sublimation, and is a first step on the path that will one day lead us to the indispensable reappropriation of the body. On this point and others that I cannot touch upon here, Quevedo's work – quite apart from those factors which, as we shall now see, make it odious to us – reflects with great clear-sightedness the insoluble conflict between body and reason and is a cry of alarm by the former against the attempt to turn us into angels or machines – a process of abstraction or reification that by contrast lends dignity to our so-called animality and humanizes its humblest excretions.

VI

Quevedo's scatological obsession can be compared only with that of two other great European writers: Rabelais and Jonathan Swift. But whereas the references in Rabelais to physiological functions and their products play an integral part in a unitary conception of life more characteristic of the early Middle Ages than of the Renaissance – and hence his numerous points of contact with the world of the Archpriest of Hita, Chaucer and Boccaccio – [9] in the case of Swift, his neurosis stems from the same traumatic root as that of the Spanish poet and their differences of shading are owed only to the divergent course followed by the two societies in whose midst they lived.

We owe to Norman O. Brown the first serious and systematic study of the excremental vision of the Irishman – a monomania that is especially evident in Part IV of *Gulliver's Travels* and in his last poems: 'The Lady's Dressing Room', 'Strephon and Chloe', and 'Cassinus and Peter'. The underlying material of these is the irreducible opposition between our animality, manifest above all in the act of excreting, and our prideful pretensions to a sublimated, platonic love. 'The peculiar Swiftian twist to the theme that Celia *****,' Brown says, 'is the notion that there is some absolute contradiction between the state of being in love and an awareness of the excremental function of the beloved.'[10] We referred previously to Quevedo's horror at the evocation of the female body 'having its monthly periods'. Swift replaces the profaning image of menstruation with that of evacuation. By confronting the fact, he admits and forces us to admit that the platonic sublimation of the beloved is founded on an implacable repression of anality, with the result that the revelation of the truth necessarily takes on a traumatic character. As for the portrait of the Yahoos that Gulliver meets in the course of his travels, the repeated faecal episodes in which Swift delights – the tribal ritual, for example, of pouring excrement on the head of the deposed chieftain – irresistibly bring to mind other incidents and passages from Quevedo in which coprophilia attains the dimensions of a veritable apotheosis. To cut a long story short, we may say that the relation that the two writers establish between the body and the soul, the physiological and the spiritual, is an exploration of the vast area of cultural sublimations that psychoanalysis was to study later, and in its own way breaks the vicious oppressive circle in which the human being is trapped.

The discrepancies that exist between the two correspond – as Octavio Paz has clearly seen –[11] to the different attitudes towards the body and bodily effort on the part of Spanish Catholicism and English Puritanism. For the one, the human person is a battlefield where war is waged between God and the Devil; for the other, a tool subjected to the rational imperative of work. Catholicism lays the burden of guilt on the body and humiliates it; Puritanism makes an object and an abstraction of it. Hence, in the case of Swift, the scandal of consciences at peace with themselves will be even greater. The intellectual repression of Hispanic Catholicism denies the bodily reality of the sodomite or the heretic to the extreme of annihilating them in the purifying ritual of burning them at the stake, but excuses the orthodox believer's baseness and abjection by attributing them to original sin and the fallen nature of man. English Protestantism – though much less rigid in the sphere of ideology – acts, however, with greater violence against sexual pleasure even when it is 'legitimate', and proceeds for the first time in history neurotically to conceal the act of defecating. The triumph of aesthetics and olfactory asepsis was to bring as its inevitable corollary the filthiness and the stink of the mind: in the refined, pleasing realm of the sanitary water closet, toilet paper and deodorants, we are all indebted, in one way or another, to the liberating excremental fantasies of writers such as Quevedo and Jonathan Swift.

VII

In the prologue to his excellent edition of Quevedo's *Obras completas*,[12] Manuel Blecua, on examining the satirical compositions of our author, says that 'three or four subjects become obsessive, among them importunate damsels, cuckolds and the power of money'. While this is indeed true in purely quantitative terms, it is regrettable that Blecua has disdained to concern himself with other much more personal and significant material, whose repetition throughout Quevedo's work borders on the obsessive – not only the already-mentioned *idée fixe* of excrement, but also a number of manias and stubborn phobias that unveil hidden twists and turns and secret recesses of the complex, tortuous figure of the great writer: fear and loathing of venereal diseases (and hence the allusions to the Antón Martín hospital and the wordplay and puns on the 'French disease'); virulent racism directed primarily against anything smacking of Jewishness, but also against Moors (see his poems 'A una mujer afectada', 'Matraca de paños y sedas', 'A un morisco llamado Moisés' and even Africans ('A un ermitamulato', 'Boda de negros'); an unhealthy aversion, finally, against the 'abominable' *crimine pessimo* ('A un bujarrón', 'Epitafio a un italiano llamado Julio'). These subjects – which also crop up in the writings and the psychopathic attitudes of the author of *Mein Kampf* – may well constitute the secret key of reactionary thought, invariably built on a morass of fears, rejections and hatreds (less contradictory than might appear at first glance): of promiscuity (sexual enjoyment), the unassimilable and alien (different races, cultures) and the traumatic reality of the anus and the latent attraction to the faecal (sodomy).[13]

The intimate phobias of Quevedo – a repulsive and fascinating character who has few equals, a fantastic mixture of the anarchist, the warrior for Christ the King, and the NKVD or CIA agent – seem to be summed up in the numerous poems – more insulting than satirical – that he wrote against his rival and enemy, the poet Don Luis de Góngora. The persecution mania of the poet from Madrid leads him to centre his venomous attacks on those points liable to discredit the Cordovan poet in the eyes of his fellow citizens and include him in the ignominious ghetto of the proscribed: Judaism and homosexuality – horrifying images *par excellence* that the sentinels of faith and decent morals took great pains to exorcize in those accursed times by sending guilty parties to the dungeons and stakes of the Holy Office. Let us look at a few examples:

> *Por qué censuras tú la lengua griega*
> *siendo sólo rabí de la judía,*
> *cosa que tu nariz aun no lo niega?*

> *En lo sucio que has cantado,*
> *y en lo largo de narices,*
> *demás de lo que tú dices*
> *que no eres limpio has mostrado.*

> *Muy dificultoso eres,*
> *no te entenderá un letrado,*
> *pues, aborreciendo puercos,*
> *lo puerco celebras tanto.*

> *Yo te untaré mis obras con tocino,*
> *para que no me las muerdas, Gongorilla.*[14]

If the anti-Judaic references are very nearly continuous, the anti-sodomitic ones are no less frequent:

> De vos dicen por ahí
> Apolo y todo su bando
> que sois poeta nefando
> pues cantáis culos así.
>
> Poeta de bujarrones
> y sirena de los rabos,
> pues son de ojos de culo
> todas tus obras o rasgos,
>
> Bosco de los poetas,
> todo diablos, culos y braguetas,
>
> y dicen lenguas ruines
> que de atrás os conocen florentines,
>
> éste, en quien hoy los pedos son sirenas,
> éste es el culo, en Góngora y en culto,
> que un bujarrón le conociera apenas.[15]

In these passages and others, Quevedo stresses the excremental nature of the 'abominable sin': *'dejad de ventosidades'* ['stop breaking wind'], *'albañal por do el Parnaso'* ['cesspool for Parnassus'], *'almorrana de Apolo'* ['haemorrhoid of Apollo'], *'doctor en mierda y graduado en pujos'* ['doctor in shit and graduate in bowel-straining'], etc, thus condemning the *pecado nefando* less because it is a pleasure freed of procreative ends (as is the case, for example, with onanism or coitus interruptus) than because in the act of copulation (whether heterosexual or homosexual) the phallus and the anus, semen and faeces are coupled – a doubly traumatic image for a conscience that denies the reality of the body and conceals, with disgust, its physiological 'servitudes'.

In his unique and exemplary way of expressing alienation in a totally alienated form, Quevedo transforms the anus into an eye and the mouth into an anus, thereby impressing upon us, if only to stigmatize it, the identity of our inferior and superior countenances, the arse and the face:

> Hombre en quien la limpieza fue tan poca
> (no tocando a su cepa),

que nunca, que yo sepa,
se le cayó la mierda de la boca.
Dícenme tienes por lengua
una tripa entre los labios,
viendo que hablas con ella
ventosedad todo el año.[16]

His anti-sodomitic aversion will be all the stronger the greater the secret power of attraction exercised on him by the anus and faecal matter. It is not necessary to be a specialist in psychoanalysis to know that what is forbidden or censored is necessarily the object of a desire: it would be absurd to prohibit (and to include in the lexical area that is taboo) what no one – even in dreams – has the least desire to turn into a reality.

VIII

If the repressed unconscious that occasions a neurosis is, as certain people think, a collective unconscious, there is a possibility of interpreting Spanish literature, if only as a working hypothesis, in terms of retention, of constipation. Thus the scanty, lumpy fruits – in truth coprolites – of our letters over the space of two centuries (excepting those of half a dozen authors of whom everyone knows) and the supposed qualities of a hard, concise, direct, dry style – usually attributed to the severity and austerity of the Castilian plateau – would in reality be the product of a stingy and secretive attitude towards the material that we expel. The close relationship between writing, sexual impulse and excrement can no longer be disregarded by anyone. Studying Quevedo's coprophilia without blinkers or repugnance – wresting it from the tweezers and medical gauze of an erudition that so frequently sterilizes it – may constitute an excellent point of departure for the understanding and eventual cure of our centuries-old wounds and traumas.

Notes

1 Larry Grimes, 'El tabú lingüístico: eufemismo, disfemismo e injuria en México', a study as yet unpublished.
2 The most detailed descriptions of paradise figure in suras 37, 47, 52, 55, 56 and 76 of the Koran. It would be pointless to add that these fantasies are exclusively masculine.
3 The question of literary genres has nothing to do with this.

4 Américo Castro, *La realidad histórica de España*, Mexico City: Porrúa, 1966, p. 271.

5 Pascual Boronat, *Los moriscos españoles y su expulsión*, Valencia, 1901.

6 Like *La Celestina*, the *Buscón* is a work without heroes or villains – a struggle of selfish interests fought under the law of the strongest. The recent analysis by Carroll B. Johnson, '*El Buscón*: D. Pablos, D. Diego y D. Francisco', *Hispanófila* (1974) sheds new light, in my opinion, on the secret intentions of its creator.

7 M. Molho, *Introducción al pensamiento picaresco*, Salamanca: Anaya, 1970.

8   That it has the eye of an arse is obvious,
      and a bunch of keys, your red sun,
      and that it has as that eye's pupil
      a dark, hot turd.

      It will necessarily be sticky
      With eyelashes as bristly as thistles,
      and will wink, as the yellow flood passes,
      every time it sits down to empty its bowels.

      The voice of the eye, that we call a fart
      (the nightingale of sodomites) held back . . .

      The familiarity of your face
      I hide in no wise,
      for it could easily pass itself off as an arse
      had it not one eye too many.
                                              Translation by H. L.

9 As Mikhail Bahktin says in his admirable essay on Rabelais: 'faeces and urine personify matter, the world, the cosmic elements [. . .] Urine and faecal matter transformed cosmic fear into a mirthful carnival scarecrow.' Cf. *La cultura popular en la Edad Media y en el Renacimiento*, Barcelona: Barral, 1974.

10 Norman O. Brown, *Life Against Death*, Middletown, Conn.: Wesleyan University Press, 1959, p. 186.

11 See my essay 'The Language of the Body', below, pp. 128–48.

12 Francisco de Quevedo, *Obras completas*, I, Barcelona: Planeta, 1963.

13 Reference to Wilhelm Reich and his analysis of fascism seems to me to be indispensable here.

14   Why do you criticize the Greek language
      when you're only a Jewish rabbi,
      something even your schnoz does not deny?

      By the filth you've celebrated in song
      and the length of your nose,
      you've proved more than you say,
      that you're unclean.

      It's real labour to read you,

scholars will not understand you,
since, detesting swine as you do,
you celebrate the swinish so often.

I will rub lard on my works,
so that you don't bite into them, Gongorilla.

Translation by H.L., following
J. G.'s word-for-word version

15   'Tis said of you round here
by Apollo and all his band
that you're an abominable poet
because you sing of arseholes as you do.

Poet of buggers
and siren of backsides
for all your works or features of your face
are arses' eyes.

The Bosch of poets
all devils, arseholes and codpieces,

and wicked tongues say
that Florentines know you from the back,

this, in whom farts today are siren songs,
this is the arse, in Góngora and verse so cultivated,
a bugger would scarcely recognize it.

Translation by H. L., following
J. G.'s word-for-word version

16   Man in whom there was so little that was clean
(not to mention his lineage)
that never, as far as I know,
did shit fall from his mouth.

They tell me that for a tongue you have
a length of gut between your lips,
seeing as how what you say with it
is but a fart the whole year round.

Translation by H. L., following
J. G.'s word-for-word version

The *Viaje de Turquía*

For José Angel Valente

In the year 1557 – when the new monarch, after having set up a veritable *cordon sanitaire* intended to prevent the spread of the germs of Lutheran heresy in his domains in the Iberian Peninsula, methodically proceeds, with the aid of the Holy Office and its informers, to ferret out, capture, try and eventually burn at the stake those presumed to be contaminated – an anonymous writer, like the author of the *Lazarillo*, dedicates 'to the most high and most powerful, most Catholic and most Christian sovereign Don Felipe, King of Spain, England and Naples', not as a learned scholar, he states, but as a faithful interpreter of everything that he has seen, the recollections of his two years of captivity in Constantinople, so as to inform His Majesty of the 'power, life, origin and customs of his contumacious and capital enemy'. But if the fervent apologia of the prologue – the proclaimed eagerness to support the King in his determination to 'defend and further the holy Catholic faith' – scarcely concords with the cautious concealment of the name of the author – a very common recourse at the time against the winds of intolerance sweeping the Peninsula – even the most cursory reading of the dialogues between the protagonists of the *Viaje* – three persons with names as suggestive and symbolic as Pedro de Urdemalas, Mátalascallando and Juan de Voto a Dios[1] – immediately dispels all our doubts. The bold mockery of relics and pilgrimages, the virulent anti-clericalism, the lack of respect for the Sovereign Pontiff, the daring satire on the credulity of the common herd and its superstitions, the denunciation of the corruption and immorality reigning in Rome, are expressions of a religious dissidence that, once the innovative tide of Erasmianism had been forcefully beaten back, no longer offered an author any possibility of expressing an opinion without exposing himself to the rigours of the Inquisition. The trial of Cardinal Carranza, the tight net that trapped the supposed Protestants of Seville – 'Those gentlemen want to burn me at the stake, but they find me pretty green,' Dr Constantino ironically remarked – the tireless activity of the tribunals, the legal subjection of suspects to torture, the more and more frequent autos-da-fé, all understandably inclined dissenters towards caution. A work such as the *Viaje de Turquía* was doomed to remain unpublished: like another basic book of the sixteenth century – I am referring to *La Lozana andaluza*, published anonymously in Venice in 1528 – it was able to reach no more than a handful of readers and its influence on Spanish cultural life was unfortunately non-existent. When Serrano y Sanz brought out his edition of it in 1905 it was practically unknown. Since then, numerous studies, articles and doctoral dissertations have made a valiant attempt to solve the enigma of its authorship, although to date no definite proof in support of any one hypothesis has been forthcoming. The work, later edited for a wider audience by Solalinde in the Calpe Colleción Universal, contained a large number of errata, however, and made even more evident the lack of a careful and readily accessible edition that would put before curious contemporary readers the politico-religious ideas of a critical and nonconformist Spaniard in the days when 'the sun never set on our empire', as well as his personal evocation of that literary cliché *par excellence*, that stubbornly persistent, truly obsessive fantasy engendered for Europe by the proximity, at once threatening and fascinating, of the power, the institutions and the army of the Great Turk. The meticulous edition recently offered us by Fernando García Salinero has filled this gap, and we should all be grateful for the scrupulous care that he has devoted to this undertaking. The *Viaje de Turquía* can at last be read in a trustworthy transcription and the well-documented introduction that accompanies it contributes new and suggestive evidence concerning the long-standing and much-debated problem of its authorship.[2]

The elucidation of the mystery surrounding the figure of its creator is not simply the result of scholarly curiosity. Since Serrano y Sanz edited the manuscript discovered by Gallardo, attributing it to Cristóbal de Villalón, specialists in the study of the *Viaje* have also attempted to settle the controversy between those who hold that it is an autobiographical work and those who are persuaded that it is a purely novelistic invention. For some (Serrano y Sanz, Schevill, García Villoslada and others), the author of the work faithfully transmits in it his own recollections of his captivity, as is proved by his numerous and precise references to the language, history, topography, life and customs of the Ottomans; for others (Bataillon in particular), Urdemalas's dialogue with his companions is 'a travel novel ingeniously commingling solid information garnered from books and memories of a life rich in experiences'. The arguments advanced by the former (the manifest 'sincerity' of the author when he avows that he has been the protagonist or the eyewitness of everything he recounts, his acquaintance, *de visu*, with the places he describes, etc), suffered a rude blow when Bataillon offered documentary proof that even those pasages which insistently proclaimed that the work was autobiographical were in reality a mere transcription, at times word for word, of previous works (Menavino's *Trattato de costume et vita d'Turchi*, Belon's *Observations*, Münster's *Cosmographia*, Paulo Jovio's *Comentario*, Vicente Rocca's *Hystoria*, printed in Valencia in 1555, etc). According to the great French Hispanist, the author might well have taken from these sources his descriptions of the way of life of the Turks, their religion, character, administration, army and institutions, as well as a series of details and anecdotes concerning the Sultan's palace, without his necessarily having suffered the ordeal of captivity or ever having set foot in Ottoman territory. After refuting, with good sense and solid arguments, the thesis of those who supported Villalón's authorship, Bataillon attributed the paternity of the *Viaje* to Dr Andrés Laguna, an Erasmian and the descendant of Jewish converts to Christianity; utilizing the most heterogeneous materials, Laguna proposed to entertain the reader with the pleasing tale of his apocryphal adventures as a pretext for putting before him the reflections of a cultured and independent Spaniard on the religious orthodoxy imposed by the Tridentine Counter-Reformation, and its harmful effects on the moral and social life of the country. This attribution to the Segovian humanist – disputed by Schevill, Dubler, Luis and Juan Gil, among others – is merely a hypothesis. While Bataillon argues persuasively in favour of the predominantly bookish nature of Urdemalas's story, he remains a long way from convincing us when he exhaustively lists plausible but not entirely reliable presumptions and coincidences that lend support to his candidate.

The original and well-constructed theory with which García Salinero concludes his introduction to the *Viaje* strikes us as more probable: it is really the work, he maintains, of Juan de Ulloa Pereyra, Knight Commander of the Order of St John of Jerusalem, whose military career in the galleys of this order and participation in the Algerian and Buginese expeditions explain his extraordinary acquaintance with naval matters and his uncommonly extensive geographical and maritime vocabulary. Taken prisoner by the Turks, he escaped by way of Mount Athos and the Aegean Sea and eventually landed in Messina. On his return to Spain, as we know from Llorente and Menéndez Pelayo, he made contact with the Lutheran group in Valladolid, and when its members were caught in the dragnets of the Inquisition, he was imprisoned, despite his having voluntarily handed himself over to his judges; he was subjected to a trial, eventually abjured, and was taken back into the Church in the celebrated Valladolid auto-da-fé of 1554. The *Viaje* would thus presumably have been written in the period between his return to Spain and his detention, although the circumstances enabling him to keep his manuscript or manuscripts of the book out of the hands of the greatly feared and fiercely zealous officers of the Inquisition have yet to be explained. If García Salinero's philological and stylistic arguments in favour of Ulloa's authorship are not entirely convincing, his hypothesis none the less appears to be more solidly grounded than those previously mentioned. A New Christian such as Laguna could scarcely allow himself the privilege of expressing opinions not merely pervaded by Erasmianism but potentially heretical at a moment when the Holy Office was hunting down and sending numerous descendants of converts to the stake. Moreover, García Salinero rightly notes that the attack on Church authorities by the person who penned the *Viaje* goes far beyond the mocking jests and sarcasms of Erasmus and his followers. The professions of Catholic faith that we find in the *Viaje* in no way invalidate the heterodoxy of the book: the recourse to the ritual formulae of fealty to official doctrine – so common today in the case of intellectuals subject to the iron rule of Soviet orthodoxy – has no more real significance in *La Celestina* or the *Viaje* than in Bakhtin's pages on Rabelais. The dissidence of the creator of the figure of Urdemalas makes its surreptitious appearance all through the book's meaty dialogues, and it is in this context of dissent that we must interpret his praise, no less clear for being indirect, of the religious tolerance of the Turks: it is by no means a mere happenstance that among the European writers who scrutinized Islam with friendly fellow-feeling we find many members or friends of the new Reformed Churches. Guillaume Postel, the author of *De la République des Turcs* (1560) was imprisoned by the Inquisitors of his country; as for Philippe du Fresne-Canaye, the creator of *Le voyage au Levant* (1573), he made no effort at any time to conceal his Huguenot convictions. Later on, when Catholic polemicists resorted to the tactic of equating Lutheranism and the 'barbarity' and 'impiety' of the Muslim religion, it was likewise Protestants such as Bayle and Reland who emphasized the positive and rational aspects of the latter by contrast to the dogmatism, intransigence and superstition of the Papacy. In the eighteenth century, Voltaire's ineradicable enmity towards Catholicism led him, as Hadidi reminds us, gradually to adopt an attitude favourable to the permissiveness and indulgence of the Ottomans, to the point that his adversaries branded him the 'patriarch *in petto* of Constantinople'. Juan de Ulloa Pereyra would thus have been, at least up until his recantation, the unknown precursor of a brilliant line of writers who held that the Christian nations had a great deal to learn from the Turks and their respect for beliefs different from theirs.[3]

Even if, as is the case, García Salinero's attribution of authorship of the *Viaje* to Ulloa is purely hypothetical, he none the less points the reader in the right direction when he places the work within the historico-cultural framework to which it belongs: at once the real protagonist of the events he relates (as the supporters of Villalón maintain) and a moralist disguised as the narrator of adventures (as Bataillon believes Laguna to have been), the author of the *Viaje* can be said to combine the virtues and merits of both, commingling erudition and personal recollection in his exposition in the form of a series of dialogues. In all truth, the structure of the *Viaje* reproduces, without any particularly remarkable novelty, the one that we find in the usual run of Ottoman novels and travel descriptions: in the first part, Urdemalas recounts to his companions his adventures as he wandered about the Mediterranean, his captivity, his escape from Constantinople and his return journey to Spain; in the second, he describes the life and customs of the Turks, with a multitude of details and reflections concerning their capital city, their religion, sexuality, organization, diet and dress. Turkey held a veritable fascination for Europeans of the time: as García Salinero pertinently reminds us, the number of books and pamphlets published about Turkey and about Islam 'amounted between 1500 and 1600 to more than two thousand titles'. The Ottoman Empire, in those days at the apogee of its power, extended from Hungary to Algiers, directly threatened Vienna and Sicily, and commanded the respect and admiration even of its enemies. Europe was living through an experience somewhat similar to that undergone by the Christian kingdoms of our Peninsula during the first centuries of its struggle against the Muslims: these latter were the mirror in which they were reflected and through which they acquired, by contrast, the awareness of their own identity. The Turk of the sixteenth century was to be the Other of the European, just as three centuries before the Saracen was the Other for those – Castilians, Aragonese, Navarrese, or Galicians – who were beginning to feel themselves to be Spaniards. In both cases, the dialectic of affirmation/negation permitted the projection on to this inverted double of all the rancours, anxieties, griefs and longings swept away and rooted out of the very depths of the ego: the Peninsular Christian of the twelfth century was simply a 'non-Moor', the reverse, negative image of the rival that he feared and of whom he dreamed. There is a Turkish 'mental stage production' that includes the comedies and tales of Cervantes, the theatre of Shakespeare, Racine and Voltaire, Mozart's opera, etc, as in our *Romancero* there existed a Saracen 'mental stage production'. The projection on to the Other of everything we detest and find secretly fascinating obeys, naturally, the necessity of inventing for ourselves a comfortable cultural dwelling, a living space in which we can cohabit without too much trauma with what we have inwardly censored. The Turk of the sixteenth century, like the Moor of the thirteenth, exacerbated people's imagination through the attraction of the forbidden: he was envied, yet at the same time hated. Only after the politico-cultural twilight of the Muslims of Al Andalus, and of an Ottoman power that in the end became the symbol of the 'sick man' for Europe did the earlier consideration and respect on the part of Westerners give way to a global attitude of scorn and repulsion that was to last down to our own day. But in 1557, the Turk found himself at the height of his power and his spectre – the scimitar and the harem – haunted the muse of writers, inspiring visions and fantasies.

Travel books, histories and novels on Ottoman themes appealed to the tastes of a public that eagerly devoured exoticism and novelty: the seraglio concentrated in its mysterious and hermetic space the frustrations and secret appetites of readers and lovers of theatrical spectacles. The topography of Constantinople came to be as familiar in those days as that of Paris or New York is today thanks to the movies; at the same time, the forays and the adventures in 'infidel territory' were the equivalent of the plots of latterday novels or films based on the theme of the American Far West. Without leaving Madrid, Lope de Vega was able to situate the action of one of his novels dedicated to Marcia Leonarda in the capital of the Great Turk as easily as he would do so today with the aid of a map or a description in the Michelin guide. The Sultan's palace – the Topkapi Sarayi – had been described in minute detail dozens of times: it was, so to speak, a ready-made setting for a story, and any writer sitting at his desk could enter it, plunder it, use whatever he pleased of it as an all-purpose background for his plots and the fabrications of his imagination. The vast volume of stories and first-person accounts had created a genre, with its own rules and requirements, and even a real live visitor to the Sublime Porte had a hard time escaping the tyranny of the conventional. Whether the author wrote *de visu* or not was of little importance in the final analysis. When, paraphrasing Schevill, García Salinero explains that the author of the *Viaje* is obliged 'to have recourse to books on Turkey and the Levant in general, because he writes from memory and his recollections keep gradually fading away into nothingness', this description of the creative process is of no help to us. The problem does not lie in whether or not the author refers to actual personal experiences – and whether or not he is 'sincere' – but, rather, in the fact that when he sets these experiences down on paper, he invariably passes them through the filter of a previous reference, an earlier cliché: like a fearful child making his way into unknown territory, he immediately retraces his steps and takes refuge in another text. Whether Villalón, Laguna or Ulloa possessed or did not possess medical knowledge sheds no light at all on a work whose principal source is its own rhetorical conventions: Urdemalas does not enter the private precincts of the seraglio by virtue of his supposed qualifications as a physician; the author, rather, has him pass himself off as one in order that, in accordance with the laws of the genre, he may have an entrée into the seraglio that the reader will find believable. It is evident that, whoever the writer may have been, he will multiply the signs attesting to his presence in the story being recounted. The rhetoric of persuasion obliges him to punctuate the text with a series of statements intended to ward off the suspicion that it is a fiction and emphasize its claim to be eyewitness testimony. This is, of course, a trick that goes far back in time; its sole aim is to lull the reader's sense of disbelief. Greco-Latin tales and chronicles are liberally seasoned with assurances and oaths deliberately inserted in order to enhance the credibility of the narrative, and the author of the *Viaje* will also constrast everything that he has seen with his own eyes and heard with his own ears with the 'twenty lies' that every 'blusterer' endeavours to drum into the heads of Christian princes. But the objective impossibility of proving the truth or falsity of his assertions – that insurmountable margin of doubt between narrator and reader – leads Urdemalas craftily to underline the ambiguity of the literary work by harking back to the example of the first classic:

Ulysses you say! You can believe, as firmly as you believe in God, that I will tell my tale to the very end [. . .] because the one who tells the story about Ulysses is Homer, who was blind and never saw what happened, but he was a poet as well; whereas I saw everything I went through and you will hear it from the one who saw it and lived it.

The reference to the author of the *Odyssey* as a 'poet', one who, according to the Greek literary convention, pursues the pleasure of the ear and not the truth, shows that Urdemalas is not unaware of the suspect status of the teller of a tale that is a supposedly first-hand account. If, as Marrou asserts, history 'is not made up of texts alone', but is none the less largely based on them, by virtue of their exactitude, which 'nothing can replace', a hybrid genre, such as that cultivated by true or false travellers to Turkey and the Near East, 'creates' the object that it narrates by relying on an infinite succession of previous references, to the point that it might truly be said that 'in the beginning was the text' and not the real model. The reading of some of the sources of the *Viaje* and a dozen works that come after it leads us in any event to the following conclusion: individual vision or direct experience is of very little significance as compared with the crushing weight of written proof. Fidelity to the truth is measured by the exactitude of the copy: the real Turk is the one who figures in books. Thus, rather than constituting a supplementary corroboration of their existence and imperishability down through the centuries, the repetition of certain occurrences, incidents and anecdotes in works based on the Ottoman theme is, quite to the contrary, the sign of an inexorable process of formalization. The seraglio offers us an inexhaustible mine of examples of thematic formalism and is a confirmation of the principle, applicable to all firmly codified genres, namely, that within such genres, the tie that links one work with the entire body of works that have preceded it is always more solid than the one that links it to 'reality'. Whether a traveller or a stay-at-home, a novelist or an eyewitness, a scholar or the author of an autobiography, the creator of the *Viaje* respects the primacy of what has already been written. Everything having to do with harems and the fantasies associated with them finds its place in a pre-existent framework: the Occidental subconscious.

Scholars and exegetes of the odyssey of Urdemalas have exhaustively studied the manifestations of heterodoxy which, from the official religious point of view, infest the work. The list of them is long and I shall not dwell on it. The author in fact speaks irreverently and insolently of the hypocrisy and opportunism of confessors, the ridiculous ignorance of monks, the traffic in fake relics (Juan de Voto a Dios earns his living exhibiting a reliquary which contains, among other things, locks of hair and drops of the milk of Our Lady, thorns of the crown of Christ, a 'good bit' of the Cross: a collection which lacks, he tells us, 'only a feather from the wings of Saint Gabriel the Archangel'), the obtuseness and dullness of Scholasticism, strewn with citations from St Thomas, supposed theologians, the simony and prostitution reigning in a Rome that, despite having been chastened by a thorough pillaging, appears to have changed very little since the happy days of la Lozana.[4] To Juan's question as to how the Pope can permit all this, Urdemalas merely replies: 'What can he do if he is ill-informed? Doesn't he answer: *si sic est, fiat?*' Bataillon rightly calls attention to the extraordinary description of the head of the Church offered by the ex-captive: 'He has the shape of an onion, and feet like a jug [. . .] what else can he be but a mere man like all the rest? Who was a cardinal first and then was made pope. He has but one particularity: he never goes anywhere on foot; he is carried about, rather, on men's shoulders, seated in a chair.' We have only to imagine a similar portrait of Brezhnev from the pen of a Soviet writer or of Wojtyla the superstar from that of a Pole to measure the self-assured cheekiness of Urdemalas.

Along with the social and moral criticism of the Church and its institutions, the *Viaje* abounds in condemnations and sarcasms concerning Spanish civil and military administration, in which the author judges his country, as Bataillon remarks, 'with the same impartiality as a Vives'. Whenever the opportunity presents itself, he also casts his darts at the Spanish Inquisition, responsible according to him for the anguish and the calamities afflicting the kingdoms of the Peninsula:

> There would be many trials here on this account if all the gossips and informers were to be burned at the stake: because there is not a single official who does not delight in having in each town persons such as you have described; I see guards who tell them what this person or that said when he saw the new royal magistrate as he was strolling in the main square, and what sort of relations he has, and the way he lives.

In the face of the Catholic intransigence towards alien doctrines and opinions, Constantinople offers an example of peaceful coexistence between persons and groups of different origins and creeds. Urdemalas thus mentions the case of

> [. . .] Morisco women who flee each day from Aragon and Valencia with their husbands and their worldly goods out of fear of the Inquisition. And don't say that there are few Jews who flee! There were so many of them that I had news of the whole of the Christian realm, given the number of those who took off in this way because they were Jews or Moors.

Among Europeans who in later centuries were to write about Islam and the Turks, we may distinguish two tendencies. The first of them, exemplified by essayists such as Montesquieu and Boulanger, raise the spectre of Asiatic despotism in order to further a political strategy whose real aim is to combat the emergence of absolute monarchical power in their own country. When Montesquieu says, for instance, that the despot leaves the affairs of government in the hands of the vizier, may he not be describing the reign of Louis XIII and the omnipotence of Richelieu? When he observes that this tyrant concentrates in his person the prerogatives of the prince, the laws and the State, is he not painting the portrait of the Sun King? When he depicts this potentate as a naturally insensitive, idle, pleasure-loving being, manipulated by his favourites and his courtesans, to whom is he referring if not to Louis XIV's great-grandson, his namesake and successor? As Voltaire saw very clearly, Montesquieu fabricated *pro domo sua* 'a despicable spectre': that literary fiction, the Oriental despot – Persian or Ottoman – that his disciple Boulanger was later to sum up in the epithet *Monstrum horrendum, informe, ingens* – a huge, shapeless, horrible monster. Mingling together the fantasies, prejudices and ideas of Homer, Herodotus, Plato and Aristotle concerning the 'barbarians' – Persians, Trojans, Scythians – his denunciation of the autocracy, cruelty, decadence and lasciviousness imputed to the Turk was eventually to have a boomerang effect on an institution, the reigning dynasty of his own country, which had abandoned its previous principles of moderation and kept the aristocracy and the people from participating in public affairs.

The second tendency, represented above all by Lutheran authors and Encyclopedists, was to find its most outstanding spokesman in Voltaire: the author of *Candide* relied time and again on the example of the Turks to fustigate *a contrariis* the dogmatism and intransigence of Christianity.

By turns a bugaboo and a model, the Ottoman was always a pretext for a different discourse, intended exclusively for an Occidental public. Both Montesquieu and Voltaire invented a Turk that suited their purpose: while they pretended to describe and inform the public about Ottoman laws and customs, the urge to prove their point, the rhetorical requirements of the text, the organization of the discourse imposed their own criteria in the end, insidiously undermining the authors' supposed objectivity. Like the 'Moor' of Spanish literature, the Turk who was to obsess Europe for four centuries was, depending on the writer, a spectre or an entelechy, but in either case a mere fantastic fiction.

The author of the *Viaje* wavers, as we shall see, between the two tendencies, nimbly making use of the one that better suits his purpose and as nimbly abandoning it in favour of its contrary if the occasion presents itself. In the lively, meaty dialogues that make up the book, Urdemalas does not hesitate to compare Turkey with the Christian nations and lead us to see that the comparison is often to the advantage of the former. Like the authors in the tradition of Postel and Fresne-Canaye who came after him, Urdemalas celebrates the magnificence and generosity of the Turks, their natural kindness towards animals, their frequent acts of charity – 'they give many more alms than we do' – their industriousness and frugality, their aversion to alcohol and card playing, their tolerance of alien beliefs – 'The justice of the Turk applies to all alike, be they Christians, Jews or Turks. Every important judge has on his desk a cross for Christians to swear by, and a Bible for Jews' – their diligence and uprightness in official matters – 'letters seeking special favour, I assure you, are of no avail there and their strong point is the rapidity with which they settle official business; you need have no fear that they will dally as they do here, where he who has right on his side ends up agreeing to a settlement out of sheer despair'. The description of temporary marriages or concubinage, permitted by law, until such time as one of the contracting parties wearies of the arrangement or has second thoughts gives rise to a delightful dialogue among the characters:

MATA: And you, father, why did you not marry?
PEDRO: Because I came at the very best time [to pursue the Crusade]. Otherwise, believe me, I would have profited from this windfall, for there were lots of women who were chasing after me.
MATA: Damn, if only a papal bull were to come that allowed such a thing, I'd leave the crusade cold this minute!

PEDRO: If one did come, I'd much rather be a preacher than the archbishop of Toledo.

JUAN: There wouldn't be many who'd refuse to take themselves a woman, even two of them, in case one of them dropped out of the picture.

The opposition between the Turk who is idealized in conformity with the needs of the anti-Catholic argument and the Spanish experience shared by his listeners lead the latter to lament the behaviour of their compatriots: 'Oh, blessed be the Lord!' Mátalascallando exclaims. 'It is the infidels who, in their sect, are holy and just, while we are not and content ourselves with the name alone!'

Winding up the list of the merits and virtues of the Turks – full of accounts and stories culled from earlier books – Urdemalas launches into an enthusiastic apologia of this 'contumacious and capital enemy' of Christianity, ritually described to Philip II in the dedication as an 'Ottoman monster, a disgrace to human nature':

Don't cudgel your brain over this and do not listen to those charlatans who come back from there, and because they were badly treated in the galleys say that those who dealt with them in this way are miserable so-and-sos, just as bad soldiers habitually speak ill of their captains, blaming them for everything, for few of these slaves can recount what happens in those parts, since they are not allowed inside houses but are kept shut up in prison. In the countries through which I travelled, constituting a good third of the world, I have seen no people more virtuous and I do not think that such exist even in the Indies, or in the places I did not visit, apart from the fact that they believe in Mohammed, and I am well aware that they are all going to hell, but I am speaking here of the law of nature.

Of greater interest to us are those passages in the account centred on the depiction of the sexual customs of the Turks and the inner distribution of power in the seraglio, since we find in such passages the sort of Greco-Roman phantasmagoria combining in the prodigious and monstrous personage of the despot the notions of boundless pleasure and limitless power. In these fragments, visibly influenced by the authors who inspired the *Viaje* – marked in their turn, let us not forget, by the classic Hellenic representation of the 'Asiatic barbarian' – today's curious reader can trace the genealogy which, by way of the subsequent writings of Baudier, Coppin, Tournefort, eventually leads to Montesquieu's *Persian Letters* and *The Spirit of the Laws*. For several centuries, the idea of the harem – a word derived from the Arabic *haram*, that is to say what is sacred and forbidden by religion, by contrast to what is permitted, or *halal* – was to sum up for Christians the totality of aberrations, pederasty and libertinage that Catholic polemicists traditionally attributed to Islam: a close circle of unbridled pleasure, an exquisite den of iniquity and excess. It is not surprising, then, that a visit to a harem and the description of it become obligatory *topoi* of any text having to do with Turkey: historians, travellers, former captives, storytellers, poets, dramatists all made use of it in their stories, tales, autobiographies, novels, poems, theatrical works. The space of the seraglio created by literature took on the connotations forged by some twenty centuries of imaginings, first Greek and later Christian, centred on Asiatic despotism: it is not simply a reproduction of a forbidden, though concrete, space but a palimpsest formed by the superposition of literary spaces, and transformed by the European imagination into a realm of repressions, terrors, desires, anxieties, appetites, spectres. To enter it, to unveil the mystery that enveloped it, was to be a requisite that, with varying degrees of talent and inventiveness, the writer whose aim was to attract the ordinary run of readers found it necessary to fulfil. For the reader of the time the fascinating world of the *Topkapi Sarayi* was as exciting and remote as the dissolute life and the licence of Paris, Copenhagen or Amsterdam will be, centuries later, for the Spaniard addicted to wild daydreams: cities in which promiscuity reigns and, as a celebrated preacher of Francoism put it, 'the natural role of the sexes is confused'. It should come as no surprise, then, that the eyewitnesses of the secrets of the seraglio are almost as numerous as the aficionados who swear to heaven that they were in Linares on the fateful afternoon when a Miura bull fatally gored Manolete.

García Salinero hits the nail on the head when he writes that the author of the *Viaje* 'turns into a self-proclaimed doctor in order to satisfy literary needs and enters the apartments of sultans thanks to the powers of imagination'. Others had already done so before him and would continue to do so for a long time afterwards: the supposed medical consultation lends a certain credibility to the arduous undertaking of violating this *sanctum sanctorum* of every imaginable sin, and countless writers resorted to this literary device, plagiarizing each other without the slightest scruple. Urdemalas's story of the visit he paid to the daughter of the Sultan and the wife of Rustán Bajá strictly observes the canons and conventions of the genre: accompanied by the husband, he is introduced into the apartment where the sick woman lies in bed.

> He says, I saw nothing, save a hand hanging down; as for the woman, they had thrown a gold cloth over her that covered her entire head. They ordered me to kneel, and I dared not kiss her hand out of fear of jealousy on the part of her husband, who, when I had taken her pulse, began to press me to leave, saying that that sufficed and we had best leave.

A century and a half later, Tournefort gives an account of a similar scene in his *Relation d'un voyage au Levant*: called to the bedside of an illustrious lady, the physician does not even manage to make out her silhouette and must content himself with taking her pulse through a gauze net. Paraphrasing the episode, Alain Grosrichard observes that the author took it from Baudier and Baudier from Courmenin.[5] The anecdote of the hand emerging from amid veils, curtains, shadows was thus to become a cliché of any seraglio story. There is no doubt that we are moving about in – and only in – the exclusive domain of literature.

Favourites, slave girls and eunuchs are roles that are *de rigueur* in this mental spectacle – Edward Said *dixit* – presided over by the absent, yet omnipresent and omnipotent, figure of the despot. Urdemalas will inform his comrades that

> [. . .] the great lords and kings do not marry, because there is no one suitable, and since they do not wish their lineages or their estates to be inherited by primogeniture to disappear, they buy a slave woman who strikes them as good-looking and sleep with her, or if not, one who is offered them as a gift, and if she has offspring, she is regarded as their wife and they live with her; when they build a house for themselves they make another separate one if possible [for her], and if not an apartment in their house, with no window overlooking the street, with many rooms like nuns' cells, where they put all the women they have.

The Sultan, so he says, has sixty-three wives, with four of whom he has had children. The eldest of the wives rules over the others, like an abbess, and all the doors of the gynaeceum are guarded by blacks called 'agas'. The seraglio, he will insist, has the appearance of a monastery, and the wives and favourites of the Sultan, like those of the noble gentlemen who have a bath in their own house, never go out on to the street, 'any more than do the strictly cloistered nuns of the Order of St Claire'. Outside of these unfortunate women and their masters, despite the obstacles and barriers, there is no noble gentleman or ordinary husband who is not a cuckold, 'because of the great freedom that women enjoy, going to the public baths and to weddings and other festive celebrations'. The reader will perhaps conclude from this that the future creator of Don Juan had probably been intoxicated by such readings. On the other hand, the alternations between the façade of austerity and virtue – nuns, abbesses, cloister – and the reality of the profligacy – the furtive relations with Christians and even with black slaves – adds a piquant note to the effusions of the unbridled imagination. Eroticism linked to the absolute power of the despot implies in reality a series of transgressions whose meaning we shall try to unravel.

The imaginary surveyor of the seraglio, Urdemalas offers a lengthy, gloomy description of the triple-walled fortifications surrounding it. The concubines are cut off from the world by three successive doors: the Cerberus guarding the first one announces the arrival of the intruder to the guardian of the second, who then warns the personal guard of the recluse, and he in turn, pounding on the floor with his staff, obliges the women, with the exception of the one who is ill, to withdraw from the sight of the stranger. These doorkeepers, and all the guard of the gynaeceum, are castrated blacks:

> By this you must not conclude that their testicles have been removed as is done here, but, rather, that their member, along with all the rest, has been cut off down to the belly, for it if were otherwise they would not be regarded as worthy of confidence: not all of them are black, for there are also whites among their number. When they have a boy whom they are very fond of, they castrate him in this way, so that he never grows a beard, and when he grows old, he serves to guard the women or the pages, who are also shut up within the redoubt. The greatest presents that the princes of this land can be given are eunuchs,

and it is for this reason that those who capture Christians in that realm single out a few lads to be castrated and many of them die from it.

Despite this description, Urdemalas adds a little farther on that when the Sultan wishes to favour a slave of his retinue – which was made up, as we know, entirely of eunuchs – he gives them as a wife one of his female servants, whom 'he tries out first, as one samples a melon'. This somewhat irregular marriage, at least if judged according to Christian precepts, occasions only an offhanded remark by Mátalascallando on the subject of cuckoldry. The authors who wrote subsequent to the *Viaje*, drawing metaphysical conclusions from such coupling, launched a salvo of insulting remarks and scandalized opinions concerning the perverse practices of the Ottomans. The awareness of this 'perversity' in which the violation of the laws of nature brings about a sexual pleasure that goes beyond every norm and thus knows no bounds, obsessed the Occidental imagination, in its centuries of confrontation with the Orient, until recently, when the abrupt rise in price of Arab crude oil metamorphosed the spectre and materialized the nightmare by transforming it, if you will permit me the pun, 'from the Arabian nights to Arabian light'.

The European representation of the Great Turk, developed through the reading of the classics, deserves to be examined at length. While Christian authors of our Peninsula interpreted the Saracen invasion as being a punishment for 'Spain's original sin', an explanation reviving the schema of Genesis, European writers of the sixteenth century, steeped in humanist culture, reverted to techniques and procedures which, from Homer to Aristotle, had enabled the Greeks to domesticate the exoticism and the outlandishness of the 'barbarians'. This strategy of assimilation, conceived for the domestic consumption of the people to whom these accounts were addressed, was repeated with no notable changes in the Renaissance perception of the worrisome Ottoman enemy.

In a recent work,[6] François Hartog makes a masterful analysis of the mechanisms whereby Herodotus undertakes to transmit to his fellow citizens his knowledge and his views concerning the Persians, the Egyptians and the Scythians. To describe an alien group, understand its nature and its characteristics, and present them in a form accessible to the intended audience of the work implies a series of mental operations allying intelligence and power: the foreign group comes to be a mere object of the supposedly informative discourse of the narrating subject. The latter acts on his readers, manipulates them and subjects them to his own rule, surreptitiously establishing himself as the criterion of a hypothetical universality. To set forth the difference between two human groups implies, in and of itself, the introduction of a 'rhetoric of otherness', of a play of operative norms the object of which is 'the fabrication of the Other'. To speak of Greeks and non-Greeks presupposes the transformation of a pure and simple lack of similarity into a dissimilarity through the arbitrary introduction of the two terms into one and the same system, ruled by bipolarity. In order to project the universe described into that of the narrator and facilitate the comprehension of the former by the latter, Herodotus explains the differences by stating them in the form of contrasts: the climate, the soil, the nature of the 'others' were shown to be different from 'ours'. When he takes up the subject of customs, the contrast is expressed in turn in terms of an inversion. This inversion is implicitly presented as one related to the whole of the human species, 'but as soon as Herodotus begins to enumerate examples of inversions, the reader notes that by the expression "all other men" what he really means is the Greeks [. . .] Inversion in this traveller's account is an exercise in translation: one of the devices that readily permits the passage from the world that is being described to the world in which it is described.' Though a reader as sharp-witted as Vives had branded Herodotus as a *mendaciorum pater* his warning fell on deaf ears: the 'fabrication of the barbarian', in order to meet the needs of the one who contrived the fabrication, gave rise to a similar falsehood with regard to the representation of the Turk. The dissimilarity of cultures and civilizations was first transmuted into a difference, then into a contrast, and finally into an inversion: if the Christian consumes alcohol, the Turk is abstemious; if the former uses a sun calendar the latter uses one based on the moon; if the one reads and writes in the 'proper' direction, the other does so 'backwards'. The epitome and quintessence of a long list of inversions, the Turk will himself be an *invert*, or to use Urdemalas's expessive summing-up, 'the worst bugger that ever was'.

All travellers, real or imaginary, to Constantinople are in agreement on this point: the Turks are sodomites, and in the give-and-take of conversations, Urdemalas never misses a chance to point this out. When he prescribes an enema as a remedy for the ills of the governor of the city, the interpreter, he says, does not dare translate his words for fear that the recommendation will be taken as a nasty joke. When he describes the Sultan's guard and the young boys in his service, he will calmly remark:

> None of the pages, among all those whom I counted, and there are more than two hundred of them, is permitted to go outside or peek out a window, as is true of the women as well, because their masters are jealous, and as I believe I already told you yesterday, all of them, from the youngest to the oldest, are sodomites, and when I found myself in the private chamber of Zinán Pasha, I saw the youngsters initiating each other, and the older ones giving pleasure to the younger ones.

The author of the *Viaje*, like those who deal with the subject after him, discovers that polygamy, rather than appeasing the passions, instead gives rise to new forms of concupiscence, and first of all, the love 'against nature' between one male and another. In his seven months as physician to Zinán Pasha, Urdemalas says, 'no woman ever came near him', and 'he was better served by the pages and valets than he would have been had the women been there'. The ruling customs among the janissaries are neither different nor better: 'In the entire army of eighty thousand men that I saw there was not one [whore] among them. It is true that, since they are sodomites and have plently of pages with them, they take no notice of women.' The rhetoric of Otherness imposes its own demands; the Turk's sexual inversion must be a rule and not an exception, whereas among other men the contrary is true: 'The Turks live in accordance with reason in only one respect, which is this: they do not esteem women and pay no more attention to them than to the roasting spits, spoons, and pots hanging from the kitchen rack [. . .] [Every one of them] sought more eagerly the favours of the kitchen boy than those of all the Turkish women in the world.' While the most beautiful slave girl cost fifty escudos and no one wanted her even so, a page who costs four times as much easily finds a buyer. Not content to scorn women in this fashion, Urdemalas adds, they do not hesitate to mistreat them and arouse their jealousy for no good reason: 'There are so many wicked scoundrels among them that they live both with women and young lads, and out of spite they put the woman and the boy in bed together with them, and spend the entire night with the youngster without touching the woman.'

In point of fact, Urdemalas limits himself to expressing or repeating the commonplaces of the period, according to which, always by way of earlier stories and tales, the word Turk was invariably associated with the slanderous idea of the sodomite: the photographic negative of the Westerner, the Ottoman allowed the latter to purge himself of his own fantasies, to project them on to his bugbear of a rival, to silence his anxieties and his contradictions and to affirm the superiority of his faith to that which supposedly endorsed the abominable vice stigmatized by the moralists. There is no more graphic and exact expression than 'Turk's head', a phrase used as a synonym for scapegoat: the Turk, the Turk's head, took all our sins upon himself and expiated them. All through Cervantes's *oeuvre*, the fascination for Islam and its rejection subtly coincide with the sentiments inspired in him by sodomy.[7] The daughter of the Morisco Ricote realizes in exile that 'among these Turkish barbarians, a young lad or a fine-looking young man is more esteemed than a woman, however beautiful she may be'. In *El trato de Argel*, *La gran sultana*, *Los baños de Argel*, etc, the equation Ottoman-invert is a constant. The seraglio is the receptacle of the aberrations of the Other, of the feared and censured double: our Mr Hyde. 'A hell of debauchery and perversion', 'a barren desert wherein the difference of the sexes vanishes, where the hierarchical relationships between them are reversed', according to Grosrichard's paraphrase, the harem was to occupy a central place in European literature for more than three centuries. The tenor of the quotations included in Grosrichard's *Structure du sérail* is a perfect illustration of the mechanism of copying and reiteration that re-creates the image of the 'barbarian'; the events, opinions and anecdotes collected in the *Viaje* are related, without the slightest modification, by Ricaut, Baudier, Galland, Chardin and others. The yielding to illicit passions and the contempt for women resulting from it was in turn to spur the woman to seek a remedy among persons of her own sex, 'perverting the order of nature by crimes, the nature of which I shall spare the reader', one of the authors cited by Grosrichard writes with a great show of modesty. More serious still, as we know from Urdemalas's account, eunuchs marry and show themselves capable of giving pleasure to women and receiving it, practising with them, in the obsessive words of Ricaut, 'a sort of brutal and unknown sensual pleasure'.[8] Such a parody of Christian marriage, founded on the natural and religious duty to procreate, is frightening and shocking. The fundamental pillar of society as conceived by God totters and collapses: man and woman cease to form an indissolubly united couple in order to ensure the perpetuation of the species and transform themselves into bodies that produce and receive a pleasure without bounds, an insatiable mechanism, marked by excess and violence, which awaits the pen of a Sade to acquire a vainglorious awareness of its Luciferian irreducibility. Thus the *Viaje de Turquía* becomes in reality the *Journey to Desire* : a leap into the abyss that gapes open within our own selves through the fantastic representation of the seraglio and the monster that inhabits it – the terrifying, enigmatic, ungraspable Oriental Eros.

Notes

1 A possible translation of the three names might be Hatcher-of-Plots, Kill-All-Females-without-Saying-a-Word, and Juan-of-the-Vow-to-God [*translator's note*].

2 Fernando García Salinero, ed., *Viaje de Turquía*, Madrid: Cátedra, 1980.

3 Cardaillac has devoted an interesting chapter of his work *Moriscos y cristianos. Un enfrentamiento polémico, 1492–1640* (Paris: Klincsieck, 1977) to the convergences between Protestants and Moriscos with regard to religious tolerance and to the influence of the former on the latter, before and after their expulsion.

4 A reference to Francisco Delicado's novel *Retrato de la lozana andaluza* (1527), on the life of a Spanish prostitute in Rome. See Goytisolo's essay in this volume, pp. 34–55 [*translator's note*].

5 Alain Grosrichard, *Structure du sérail. La fiction du despotisme asiatique dans l'Occident classique*, Paris: Seuil, 1978.

6 François Hartog, *Le Miroir d'Hérodote. Essai sur la représentation de l'autre*, Paris: Gallimard, 1980.

7 Françoise Zmantar, 'Cervantes y sus fantasmas de Argel', *Quimera*, 2, Diciembre, 1980. Idem, Louis Combet, *Cervantes ou les incertitudes du désir*, Presses Universitaires de Lyon, 1980. See also Albert Mas, *Les Turcs dans la littérature espagnole du Siècle d'Or*, Paris: Institut d'Etudes Hispaniques, 1967.

8 Quoted by Alain Grosrichard, op. cit.

Vicissitudes of Mudejarism: Juan Ruiz, Cervantes, Galdos

I

The literary critic who is also a creative writer has the appreciable advantage of being able both to understand and to relativize the much-debated (and sterile) problem of the influences and sources that contribute to the elaboration of a text. Unlike those critics who have not had this experience and are led to favour certain currents, styles or cultural areas in order better to situate within them the author or work which is the object of their analyses and entomological classifications, those who have produced their own literary texts know very well – although they may not always admit it – that the task of pinning down and circumscribing influences is as vain an exercise as trying to put a fence around free air. The writer is affected by everything he experiences and everything he reads, and except in cases where deliberate imitation or parody on his part gives rise to a preferential relationship to a specific text, his work will be the fruit of a sum total of personal incidents, historical vicissitudes and cultural currents of the time. Every important literary text stems from a profusion of models belonging to different genres, periods and traditions, and the more rich and profound it is, the more numerous and diverse its points of contact with Borges's Imaginary Library will be. Cervantes, Sterne, Flaubert and Joyce offer palpable demonstrations of the pathetic insensitivity of the crude practitioner of reductive criticism. The great writer uses anything and everything for his work of creation: his insatiable voracity impels him to pilfer bookstores, museums, cultures, to penetrate them as conquered territory; to appropriate without remorse whatever interests him or suits his purpose; to base his own unique, irreducible specificity on interpenetration, permeability or osmosis. Such artistic pollenization permits, for example, the discovery of the survival of the Arab epic or of Latin poetry in the contemporary Spanish-American narrative, or the study of the enduring legacy of Cervantes in authors as dissimilar as the Russian Andrei Biely and the German Arno Schmidt. The only imitators are the minor follower, the person who lacks culture, or one who, naïvely attempting to reproduce 'reality', instead unknowingly duplicates the canonized copy of that reality. Any truly significant text, however, is situated at an infinite crossroads – a veritable wind rose – of paths, influences, readings, tendencies and so on, commingled or amalgamated in a heterogeneous melting pot. The literary work is always impure, a hybrid fertilized by its contacts and encounters with the universal patrimony. There are thus no univocal influences or exclusive sources or single geneses; only polygenesis, bastardization, mixture, promiscuity.

The professional specialization of our critics, whether limited either to isolated acquaintance with Hispanic literature or to the Romance languages and literatures that are its preferred province, accompanied in many cases by a total ignorance of works from other cultural areas and – what is worse – by a violent prejudice against them, explains the fact that, with a few honourable exceptions (I am thinking, for example, of Blanco White, whose writings I so admire), the study of a series of key texts in our literature has until recently been partial, pedestrian and halting. Spanish literature was examined, and unfortunately continues to be examined, by minds curiously impermeable to the language of facts – as a function of their Latino-Christian co-ordinates, accepting at most (and as a necessary tactical concession) a passing and superficial contagion by Arabic-Islamic elements. Although the vogue for Romanticism and the development of Orientalism in Europe placed our Andalusian and Morisco[1] past in the limelight, this past was seen throughout the nineteenth century as something colourful and exotic, a mere foreign graft on an Occidental, Christian trunk that has ultimately rejected it. But the gradual development of Arabic studies on the one hand, and the courageous historico-cultural focus of Américo Castro on the other, brought to the fore the weakness of the premises on which traditional analysis of our literature was founded. If the publication of *Huellas del Islam* [*Footprints of Islam*] opened up new and enriching perspectives for study of the classics, the coincidence of Castro's viewpoints and Miguel Asín's searching analyses and explorations had the enormous practical value of including within the vast field of Romance scholarship an area that had previously been restricted to the ghetto of Arabic specialists. To point out, as Castro did, that Spanish literature 'has been inspired by Arabic sources from the *Disciplina clericalis*, which in the twelfth century made thirty-three tales of Oriental origin known throughout Christian Spain and Europe, to Baltasar Gracián's *El criticón*, whose germ is found in a tale preserved among Aragonese Moriscos', was to overturn the received idea that the Christian and Islamic worlds had coexisted in closed compartments in the Peninsula for centuries. The term Mudejarism, felicitously applied by Castro to the work of the Archpriest of Hita (Juan Ruiz), likewise illuminates the reading of *Mío Cid* and of Juan Manuel. It helps to unravel the enigma of the presence of Sadalí mysticism in the poetry of St John of the Cross, as discovered by Asín, and favours a better understanding of the ambivalent feelings of authors such as Cervantes toward the inter-caste[2] struggles, as well as towards the temptation, present for centuries, of Islamic models or alternatives. Thanks to the studies of specialists of the stature of Castro and Menéndez Pidal, the old thesis of the ephemeral influence of Islam on our culture is today difficult to maintain. The more and more numerous analyses and essays devoted to the subject, coming from several camps and disciplines, make new data available almost daily concerning the fertile Romance–Arabic cultural crossbreeding which has been a feature of a broad sector of our literature. Thus the fine-honed and well-documented works of Galmès de Fuentes on the Arabic and Castilian epic demonstrate, in the author's words, that 'the *Mío Cid Campeador* can be understood in its full significance only within an Arabized linguistic and social context'.[3] The Mozarabic bard lives immersed in the world of Arabic epics and the structural Mudejarism of the work is in turn reflected at all levels of the text. Similarly, the obvious porosity of the milieux of Muslim and Christian troubadours from the era of Ibn Quzmán to the time of the poetic tournaments of the court of Alfonso explains the fruitful interchange between Romance lyrics in the Peninsula and Andalusian poetry, an admirable cross between classic and popular currents, revealed to us by James Monroe. Without attempting to be exhaustive, I shall also mention the sober and penetrating essays of Luce López Baralt, who, following in the footsteps of Asín, examined the symbolic imagery of St Teresa and St John of the Cross in the light of Israquí spiritualism and convincingly established that St John's 'Llama de amor viva' is the product of a 'genius, born of the triple-caste Spain', a poet who 'sings his Christian sentiments in Muslim metaphors'. Spanish literature continues to amaze us and promises us limitless surprises whenever we are capable of broadening our focus and admitting the reality of its hybrid nature. In large part, these areas of our poetry and fiction have yet to be explored.

Without pausing here to point out the lexical, thematic and stylistic influences – the use, for instance, of rhythmic units characteristic of Arabic rhymed prose – or structural influences (arabesques, dedramatization, abandonment of the psychological development of the characters, etc) of Arabic literature on my own novels, already studied by such authors as Bernard Loupias, Sylvia Truxa and Malika Jadidi Embarec,[4] I shall endeavour to trace a brief, personal sketch of the flamboyant or discreet Mudejarism that pervades the work of three key writers in the history of our literature: I refer to Juan Ruiz, Cervantes and – although it may surprise some – Benito Pérez Galdós.

II

The ideal or privileged reader of all literary works is one whose spatial and temporal co-ordinates coincide, *grosso modo*, with those of the author: in so far as the context forms part of the text, a lack of acquaintance with the one inevitably clouds our perception of the other. When I am confronted with a novel or short story by a writer distant from me in time and/or space, the lack of a context common to the two of us obliges me to reconstruct it if I wish to reap the benefits of an optimal, total, integral reading. Only a compatriot and contemporary of the author can grasp the endless sea of connotations, intentions and references incorporated in his books without having to resort to a minute and invariably aleatory reconstruction. To re-create the cultural and social atmosphere in which the text was produced, to replace the text within its context, to revive the feeling of immediacy, familiarity and receptivity of the public to which the work was originally addressed – all this would be the unavoidable task of any critic determined to penetrate its darkest zones and bare its supposed secrets.

With these considerations as my point of departure, I undertook, four or five years ago, the reading of one of my favourite works within a cultural and human framework especially suited to a dynamic approach – at the antipodes of the sepulchral silence of the university library where, as I recall, I first devoured it. The text – impossible to catalogue under any of the commonly acknowledged literary genres – was the *Libro de buen amor*, the Spanish literary creation I most admire after the *Quixote* and *La Celestina*, and the context for taking it up

again was the agora or main market square of Marrakesh. The series
of notes and outlines that I began making at that time for a prospective
'Reading of the Archpriest of Hita in Xemáa-el-Fna' took, I admit, a
very different direction from the one I had had in mind: escaping my
original plan bit by bit, they took on a life of their own and were slowly
transformed into the context of another book or novella of 'good love'
– my novel or poem *Makbara*. But that is another story.

If after more than six centuries the exemplary nature of the Archpriest's work remains as intact as ever, this is owed, I believe, to
its atypical and, at first glance, shapeless structure, a hybrid of
distinct and opposed genres, an inspired hodgepodge of dialects and
vocabularies; to its motley, mongrelized, anomalous nature; to the
marvellous interweaving of experience befitting a cleric with the tastes
and affections of a Goliard, steeped both in the neo-Latin tradition
(that of the *joca monachorum* and of religious-profane farces) and
in Arabic culture (erotic stories, troubadours' songs); that is to say, a
whole made up of particularities that give it a unique and indispensable
place in the history of our literature. Reading the *Libro de buen amor*
in Xemáa-el-Fna was one of the most profound and intense literary
experiences of my life: to conjoin the sound of the text (the prodigious
language of Juan Ruiz, light, jocular, gibing, licentious, undisciplined)
and the context (the popular comedy, frank and free, of the oral
halca[5] tradition) was to confirm, in an instant, the inescapable truth of
Bakhtin's observations concerning the carnivalesque world of Rabelais:
'The public square constituted the main point of convergence of all
that was not official, enjoying somehow an extraterritorial right in the
world of order and official ideology, and the populace always had the
last word.'

The visitor or daily frequenter of Xemáa-el-Fna enjoys a truly
singular prerogative – that of being able, in the closing years of
this millennium, to plunge into a world which, from the point at
which we are situated, disappeared centuries ago, a world where
medieval man, whether in the Christian or Islamic orbit, disposed
freely of his time, giving himself over to his playful instincts and his
fondness for spectacle, joining the open, fraternal circle that formed
around public storytellers and tirelessly absorbing their tales, founding
on them the rudiments of his own sociability. The minstrel's universe,
so beautifully described in the poems of Ibn Quzmán, every corner of
it visited by Don Carnaval in his peripatetic travels, still exists today,
unchanged. Clowns, bards, athletes, mountebanks, healers, holy men,

owners of trained animals, all attract a multitude of 'country people, shepherds, soldiers, tradesmen, hucksters who have flocked to it from the bus terminals, the taxi stands, the street stops of jitneys poking drowsily along: coalesced into an idle mass, absorbed in contemplating the daily hustle and bustle, taking refuge in the anonymous freedom and permissiveness of these surroundings: in continuous, capricious movement' (*Makbara*). There, as in the days of Ibn Quzmán and Juan Ruiz, the public square, the plural, effusive space of the *halca*, promote 'immediate contact between strangers, forgetfulness of social restraints, fusing of prayer and laughter, temporary suspension of hierarchies, joyful equality of bodies' (ibid.). Popular literature in the fourteenth century, unlike the learned sort, written in Latin, employed the plain vulgar tongue of Castile and was most often spread orally. Recitation favoured a narrative structure in which prosody played as important a part as semantics. The meter used by Juan Ruiz is possibly linked, in its polygenesis, to the rhythmic units of Arabic rhymed prose and poetry.[6] The minstrel's speech, in obedience to the melodic requirements of the text, is directed as much to the ear as to the intellect. The audience – of yesteryear, in the marketplaces and squares frequented by Juan Ruiz, of today in Xemáa-el-Fna – educates its literary ear there, catching the meter and the accentuation offered by the story, and marks off the phrases in accordance with them, forgetting altogether their humdrum 'normal' pattern.

I know of no other work in all our literature – whether from the point of view of vocabulary, structure, prosody or syntax – as surprising, as multivalent, as polymorphous as the Archpriest's. The textual reality he puts before us is neither two-dimensional nor uniform: it has sudden breaks, unevennesses, fractures, centrifugal tensions, transmutations of voices: in a word, polyphony. The Castilian of Juan Ruiz does not arouse our excitement, as does that of the epic *Mío Cid* or the poems of Berceo, by reason of its extraordinary historical value in the development and evolution of our language. It is an autonomous literary entity, whose interest lies far above and beyond the merely linguistic or documentary. The ferment of language throughout the fourteenth century lent itself to a creative strategy based on openness and receptivity. The Archpriest introduced into the work language both vulgar and learned, gypsy cant, ruffian slang, dialect, parody, bits of liturgy, Latin, Arabic. This orientation allowed him to escape those verbal hierarchies entrenched in every closed and rigid tradition, to break with the inflexible semanticism of the fixed phrase, to forge with complete freedom a language at once uninhibited and fluent, promiscuous, sly, mocking and jocund, like the one created by the attentive ear of the listener in the gentle winter sunlight of the marketplace of Xemáa-el-Fna. Although 'pious' hands subsequently mutilated the text, ridding it of its most offensive 'obscenities', the erotic charge it carries confers on it a place apart in the history of our letters: as Maria Rosa Lida so aptly noted, we will not find its equal either before or after. Its sage amalgam of religion and licentiousness, of hymns to the Virgin and racy tales of skirt-lifting, belongs of course within the rich tradition of Arabic poetry. In stressing here its undeniable Mudejarism, I am less interested in traceable references to the works of authors of the stature of Abu Nuwas, Ibn Quzmán, or Ibn Hazm, than in emphasizing the fact that the same erotico-religious tradition is still alive today among the *halaiquís* of the marketplace. Thus I am not speaking of sources but of a living context. To move freely from an 'internal' listening to Juan Ruiz to an 'external' listening to my friend Abdeslam means adjusting my ear to a duo of voices at once pious and comic, biting and evocative, mystic and pagan: 'stories of love-complications, cuckolding, off-colour language, interlarded with verses, obscenities, suras of the Koran, laughter, imprecations, insults'. The Mozarabic cleric, sensual rascal and pleasure-seeker, friend of matchmakers and wandering storytellers, connoisseur of the female sex, appears to have been reincarnated in the arrogant figure of the *fquí*, his demeanour majestic and solemn, his preaching jovial and libertine, behind the pulpit or the *alminbar* of the *halca*. Both have recourse to familiar language and slang, invoke traditions and legends, exalt and yet mock the vertigo of love, adding as an envoi canticles or verses from the Koran.

To go from one to the other permits savouring the verse of the Archpriest, freed of cut-and-dried erudition, reliving the delight and joy of the audience for which it was originally intended, leaping from a risqué saying to a brief prayer in less time than it takes a fly to copulate.[7] I invite the reader to share the experience with me, comparing and contrasting, for instance, the savoury adventure of the nun highly lauded in the *Libro* by Trotaconventos (a conquest that failed, as we know, because the nun ended up saying no), followed by a few verses of consolation in praise to the Virgin, with the incident which befell the industrious and sharp-witted Xha (a very popular character in traditional Arabic narratives), here translated from the version told by Abdeslam, preserved in a tape recording I made of it:

The young Xha happened to be on a journey, and as darkness fell before he got home, he was obliged to spend the night in the *fondak*, in a men's dormitory. Rightfully fearing for his integrity, Xha invented a strategem to save himself: he went to the market and bought a bowl of *bisara* [a very thick bean soup] and returned to the inn. He waited till the candle was blown out, and lowering his breeches, emptied the contents of the bowl into them. When his neighbour, inflamed by Xha's youthfulness, stretched out a sinful hand towards the lad's privates, he dirtied his fingers with a paste of very suspect consistency. In apprehension, he instantly withdrew it, swearing. One by one, other guests of the *fondak* tried their luck and withdrew, similiarly frustrated [. . .] Thus it was that the youth emerged intact from the tight spot in which fate had placed him by leading him into that den of iniquity, for which we should give thanks to the Merciful, the Subtle, the Well-Informed [. . .] As the Holy Book declares, O true believers, 'God also conspired against them, and God is surely the most clever of conspirators.' (Koran, VIII, 29)

III

The fact that the greatest work in all our literature should be presented to us by its author as an original manuscript discovered among some sketchbooks and old papers bought on the Calle de Alcaná in Toledo for the price of half a *real* from a boy who was on his way to sell them to a silk merchant, and that then a Moorish convert who knew *aljamía*[8] translated it for him for two pecks of raisins and three bushels of wheat, and that said work should be entitled '*History of Don Quijote de la Mancha, written by Cid Hamete Benengeli, Arabic Historian*', is not simply a caprice of its transcriber Miguel de Cervantes, nor is it simply a variation of the then-common gimmick of the 'found manuscript'. The choice of the narrative matrix, placing the work, through the powers of imagination, within the confines of a culture that had only recently met its doom in the Peninsula, goes far beyond anecdotal happenstance or mere concession to fashions of the day. In reality, it reflects the existence of a profound vein of inspiration that runs all through Cervantes's mental universe, half hidden from view by a thousand sinuosities and meanders: I refer to the complex, obsessive relationships of the author with the Moorish-Ottoman world and his fascination with Islam.

The insistence on the Muslim theme in Cervantes's narratives and theatre has quite understandably spawned a copious bibliography, and professional Cervantes scholars or aficionados have outdone themselves attempting to shed light, more or less successfully, on various facets and aspects of his fascination for the subject. The Morisco problem, the religio-cultural confrontation of the two Hispanic communities, the vicissitudes of Cervantes's imprisonment in Algeria, the very real threat of Ottoman expansionism, are treated by our author from any number of perspectives, many of them frankly contradictory. Cervantes, as scholars have noted, never sets himself up as a possessor of the Truth with a capital letter; on the contrary, he acts as a disseminator of a multiplicity of lower-case truths, inasmuch as he allows the Other – the Turk, the Morisco – every opportunity to express a viewpoint opposed to the one commonly held by the public for whom his work was intended. To that end, the novelist dons masks, and shielded behind them, demonstrates rules and sets forth exceptions to them, contrasts opinions and beliefs, points to nuances, and rectifies at every step the reader's over-hasty conclusions. As if in a gallery of mirrors, the reader must feel his way along, and retrace his steps as he searches for the exit. A master of the arts of insinuation, ambiguity and irony, Cervantes takes great pleasure in subtly eroding the reader's most deep-seated convictions and impelling him towards a terrain sown with uncertainty and enigmas.

To appreciate fully the originality of the stance he takes, it is necessary to bear in mind, first of all, the violence of the politico-religious confrontation between the Catholic world, headed at the time by Spain, and a hegemonic Ottoman Empire then at the height of its power. The Great Turk both attracted and intimidated Christian nations by way of a cultural and ideological coherency which, above and beyond its armed might, offered its enemies a possible and potentially dangerous alternative. Like the Soviet Union today, the Ottoman Empire was the object of analyses, portraits, novels, fiction, fantasy and denunciation. A comparison of the anti-Turkish and anti-Muslim literature of the sixteenth century with the anti-Communist and anti-Soviet writings of the last sixty years would allow us to establish numerous parallels and similarities. In this huge collection of works, the testimony of captives, fugitives, spies and renegades looms large. In both instances, those who propagate such literature address an audience eager for first-hand information on the virtues and defects, real or supposed, of the adversary. Though treated for the most part in a manner that today we would dismiss as cheap journalism, the Islamic theme also inspired poets, dramatists and novelists: it was at one and the same time a literary fashion and a concession to popular taste. But no great writer except Cervantes lived the problem from within, or was able to endow it with a creative dimension representing at once the height of genius and of ambiguity. His experience as a captive in Algeria and his intimate dealings with the Muslims enabled him to approach the material from a position of privilege, in life as in letters. From this standpoint, his work is unique in the Western world: and as in the case of Dante and the Archpriest, it would be inexplicable, had it not been for the fertilizing influence of Islam.

To the mystery of the creative process in the case of Cervantes must be added the one that envelops many periods and events of his life the moment we leave the well-beaten paths of his official hagiography. The scarcity of trustworthy data regarding his captivity, in any event, obliges those interested in his work to decipher it in order to reassemble, like a puzzle, the allusions made to his imprisonment. The 'phantoms' of Algiers – so intriguingly interpreted by Françoise Zmantar – [9] point once more to the existence of a *void* – a hole, a vortex, a whirlpool – in the central nucleus of the great literary invention, rotating around what has been omitted, in repeated, obsessive circles, an incessant ritual of hide-and-seek, disguises and masks. The Cervantine *summa*, conceived from the *other shore* (that of what has been excluded and rejected by Spain) thereby becomes, among many other things, the attempted portrayal of an existential and cultural alternative that in the end is rejected. The 'easy and pleasureful' life of the renegades in the service of Hassan or El Uchali, the abundant references to indolent Ottoman customs in *El amante liberal* and *Los baños de Argel,* in the *Quixote* and in *La gran sultana* transport us to a world in which Christian captives ponder their possible defection – permit me the anachronistic word – in somewhat the same terms as those pure, hard-core Communists who suddenly desert and become turncoats, less for ideological reasons than because of the attractions of the soft life and licentiousness offered by execrated Occidental societies. Cervantes's work reflects the persistence and the acuteness of the dilemma in terms that can be directly likened to our present experience. Many times, in my frequent periods of residence in North Africa, I have relived in my imagination the shadows and the lacunae of Cervantes's experience in Algiers, attempting to answer the questions it raises. Exile or transplantation to a cultural area judged a priori to be the reverse of our own, offers the opportunity of looking upon the latter with different eyes: I for my part suspect that Cervantes elaborated his complex and admirable vision of Spain during his imprisonment in African lands, for the express purpose of counterbalancing the rival model with which he had to contend. The problem of the captive, at the crossroads of his beliefs, fears, revulsions, desires, was to transmute the disorder and confusion of his life into a new literary order: that creative enterprise – truly a leap into the unknown – capable of redeeming his failures and weaknesses and projecting him, through the powers of invention, to a higher level of reality. If Cervantes is the precursor to whom I feel myself the closest, it is because of his situation as a precursor of all adventures; if his familiarity with Muslim life gives his work a distinctly Mudéjar air, the novelistic invention by means of which he assumes the totality of his experiences and dreams makes of him the outstanding human example of the attitude epitomized by the dictum *humani nihil a me alienum puto.* Three and a half centuries later, we novelists follow in Cervantes's footsteps (we 'cervantize' unknowingly); writing our works, we write from and for Cervantes. Writing about Cervantes, we write about ourselves. Wherever we stand, whether near or far from his devotion to Islam, he will be that point where our worshipful gazes converge.

IV

To propose a historical reading of Spanish reality on the basis of a novelistic epic as vast and ambitious as that of Benito Pérez Galdós proves to be an undertaking as tempting as it is strewn with dangers and pitfalls. The relationship between the literary text and the social and human referent with which it is linked is neither direct nor simple: on the contrary, it is filtered through rhetorical and technical devices and narrative tricks intended to create an illusion of reality in the reader's mind, one clothed in all the raiment and attributes of truth. The literary critic skilled in disassembling the procedures most frequently employed by the author of the *Episodios nacionales* will find cleverness and ingenuity there where the more naïve historian believes that he has come upon a faithful portrait of historical fact and authentic social drama. Analysis of Galdós's techniques of composition is thus indispensable and demands a certain caution. The 'reality' of the novelistic world of our writer is (pardon the truism) a *literary* reality. The linking of his works with the schemata and narrative models of the era reveals that the latter determine beforehand the instrument with which he sorts out or filters historicity.

The foregoing reflections, which I cannot now pause to elaborate further, none the less appear crucial to any examination of Galdós's art and its relationship to the model depicted. My personal experience as reader and critic teaches me, in any event, that unlike such works as the *Libro de buen amor* or the *Quixote*, which bear a close connection to the totality of the literary corpus of their time and are thus linked to the socio-cultural context of their era at all its many levels, those which call for a univocal, 'natural' reading of reality are connected, rather, to a privileged literary canon – nineteenth-century realism – and its historical background (the avowed intention of rivalling the civil registry) paradoxically leans towards bookishness. To examine the universe of Balzac or Galdós, not, as is usually done, from the perspective of the illusion of reality created in the reader, but, rather, from the standpoint of the stratagems whereby this illusion is brought about) is in this respect a most unusual and most instructive exercise.[10] For the reader experienced in the structural analysis of narrative writing, no genre is as parodic and as full of artifice as the one that demands total allegiance to 'realism'. Galdós's art – in his minor works in particular – offers numerous examples of badly concealed plot devices and violations of verisimilitude never 'explained' (as the rules of the game require) by more or less plausible motives. Rather than an on-the-spot photo, it is a portrait inspired by an earlier preliminary sketch, the effect of which is similar to that of a filter.

If, for instance, we were to read *Aita Tettauen* as a historical fresco of O'Donnell's military campaign cast in the form of a novel, we would be forgetting that this curious and suggestive *Episodio nacional*, assigned the date 1905 by the author, is articulated with and made the definite homologue of another narrative text, the *Diario de un testigo de la guerra de Africa*, published forty-five years earlier. The documents collected by Galdós to compose the work and his utilization of certain Arabic sources, aided by the literary and linguistic counsel offered him by Ricardo Ruiz Orsatti, in no way interfere with the fact that the novel owes its internal coherence to its dynamic confrontation with the model provided by Alarcón.[11] Above all else, Galdós measures himself against the latter, and his hero Santiuste gradually takes shape as a character by opposition to and contrast with the protagonist/narrator of Alarcón's *Diario*.

In another context, I once penned a quick sketch of Alarcón's ambivalent attitude towards the African colonial adventure: a mixture of patriotic fervour and fanciful notions of Arabism, nourished in large part by his Orientalist readings. In constructing his hero, Galdós at no time fails to bear in mind the features, character, and temperament of the narrator of the *Diario* in order to make them the exact negative counterparts of Santiuste's. In order to make this polar contrast strikingly obvious, the author of *Misericordia* takes evident delight in introducing his authorial rival into the gallery of his own characters. In this way Galdós's 'reading' of the war in Africa is insidiously transformed, as we shall see, into an anti-reading of Alarcón. If Alarcón is, in the words of Galdós, the eloquent bard of War, Santiuste – the 'miserable poet and bad orator Santiuste' – will be the poet of Peace. The conversation between the two protagonists in the comfortable tent where Alarcón is lodged permits Galdós to set forth, as the *differential sign* of his novel, the unbridgeable gap separating the two:

> – You will render in mournful prose quatrains the carnage of yesterday and today [. . .] You are the only one who can do this, Perico. You are capable of finding language appropriate to the epic expression of Castilian valour, and to the pitiless scorn with which the poor Moors are regarded [. . .] Here, you are the poet of war. Spain contributes artillerymen for the cannons, and poets who convert military deeds into ringing verse so as to fascinate the populace . . .

Let us leave aside the very different degree of artistic elaboration to which both writers subject narrative prose – a domain in which Alarcón easily outdoes his adversary – so as to concentrate our analysis on the variations and breaks made by Galdós vis-á-vis his rival's model. If Alarcón, the author of *El sombrero de tres picos [The Three-Cornered Hat]*, surrenders all too often to martial ardour, daydreams of crusades, and lyrical reminiscences of the *Romancero* in order to idealize the mean and petty undertaking in which he is participating, Galdós's novelistic character will implacably proceed to strip it of its fancy ornaments and the finery in which it is arrayed: 'The Spaniards went to war because they needed to show off a little to Europe, and give some wholesome, restorative nourishment to public sentiment on the domestic scene [. . .] This was clear evidence of the great generosity of this populace, which resigned itself to living on enthusiasm and glory, meagrely supplemented by dry bread.'

The battle episodes, the arduous march to Tetuán, the ferocity and heroism of the armies afford Alarcón numerous opportunities to parade his talent and offer the avid reader of the time those *morceaux de bravoure* which Santiuste so rightly ridicules. The latter's perspective, on the contrary, is that of a mere foot soldier, doomed to serve as cannon fodder, who demythifies the cause in which he is naively participating, reproducing its horrors and miseries with simple, salutary directness. The 'manly courage' of Prim at Castillejos, trampling the wounded and fallen beneath the hoofs of his warhorse 'with lightning shooting from his mouth', dazzling everyone with 'his incredible madness', will leave in its wake a hideous trail of blood, of hapless recruits mortally wounded, of broken and disjointed bodies: 'The ground was strewn with bodies, the air filled with a howl in which the two languages, Arabic and Spanish, commingled their curses and the accents of human ferocity, a language of animals antedating that of human beings.'

The illusions and ecstasies of poets who devote odes to the celebration of battles vanish in the face of a violent and indefensible reality:

> The dead he saw gathered up to be buried in unmarked graves formed in his mind a funereal legion. The Army chaplain bustled to and fro reciting prayers for the dead with military alacrity, and as he passed by there disappeared beneath the earth a multitude of young men who only hours before were full of vigour, felt intensely the joy of living, and believed themselves to be upholding the honour of their fatherland. For it, they fell into the pit, just as the Muslims perished for the honour of theirs, the two honours fusing beneath the earth, reduced to one and the same honour in the putrefaction of flesh.

If the denunciation of war takes its place within a thematic current that later will be brilliantly cultivated by authors such as Ramón Sender and Henri Barbusse, the 'madness' of Galdós's Santiuste exceeds the bounds of the traditional anti-militaristic tract. His ingenuous, youthfully idealistic evocation of El Cid and Fernán González, of Flanders, Cerinola, Pavia, San Quintín or Lepanto has been transmuted, he says, into 'dead leaves that smell rancid and rotten'; war, lived from within, has become as odious to him 'as it was beautiful when I fell in love with it through my readings'. His disillusionment – in sharp contrast to Alarcón's Orientalist fantasies and eructations in favour of crusades – has a regenerative, baptismal, cathartic effect, transforming him into a new man, an enthusiast preaching a humanitarian, fraternal, pacifistic mission. With this conversion (probably inspired by the example of Tolstoy after his military experience in the Crimea, as Gómez de Baquero has pointed out), Santiuste takes his place among that attractive gallery of Galdosian characters, half mystics and half madmen, in perpetual conflict with a grey, sordid and oppressive society, characters who are more or less outlandish and unbelievable despite the author's efforts to make them 'real', and yet filled with penetrating insights, with affectionate and endearing traits, perhaps because they are just a bit larger than life. Like Benina, Almudena or Nazarín, Santiuste disdains the consequences of anomalous behaviour, defends his right to be different in the face of the conformism of the herd, preaches by example the virtues of a glowing, redemptive, revelatory spirituality. Armed with his quixotic truth, transported in the ecstasy of 'Semitic souls', eyewitness of the butchery of Castillejos, sickened at the moans of the wounded and dying and the curses of those unable to assuage their hunger, he will suddenly discover himself to be 'a Moor, with no memory of having been Spanish'. Without a word of farewell to his comrades, he will make for the enemy camp, wearing a headcloth 'whose loose folds could be taken for a turban'; a spiritual brother of Nazarín, 'the Arab of la Mancha', his air of a beggar of 'Moorish appearance' absolutely impeccable as he presents himself at the enemy camp.

Santiuste's moral and physical itinerary, if properly traced, might have made of him one of the most appealing and complex characters in our entire novelistic tradition; unfortunately, the haste or the clumsiness that so often mars Galdós's most promising intuitions once again ruins their possibilities of development and disappoints our hopes, at least on the aesthetic level. But Galdós's intuitions and interests take an entirely different direction, and it is precisely on that account that his acute historical vision of what is Spanish stands out with such admirable clarity. By contrast to the papier-mâché *Romancero* of Alarcón with his Orientalist reveries in the manner of Chateaubriand and Lord Byron, Galdós opposes a reading of our past which, as Stephen Gilman has shown very well in a recent study,[12] prefigures and presages Américo Castro's vision. Underneath the self-serving official myths of our history, he discovers the half-erased reality of a tricultural and triple-caste Spain, reconstituting the palimpsest written in the blood, sweat and tears of centuries. The presence in his novels and the roles played by characters such as Daniel Morton or Almudena then emerge in bold relief, in all their greatness. Three centuries after Cervantes, Galdós's heroes – often compounded of quixotic traits and touches of Sancho Panza – revive the dramas and the misunderstandings of the Age of Conflict, that familiar and bloody civil war which stamps with its imprint so many painful pages of the modern history of Spain. Mohammedan Jews such as Almudena, or Muslimized Semitic Christians like Santiuste and Nazarín himself, are in fact reincarnations of a fertile *mudejarismo* that transcends the boundaries of art. The pacifistic vocation of the 'Christian prophet Yahia' is thus intended to underline the common roots and convergences of the three revealed religions, beyond their rivalries and disagreements, establishing a generic or common cultural area outside the limits of the intransigency and dogmatism. A fugitive from the victorious Christian camp, he will head towards the defeated Muslims to be received, symbolically, by a group of Hebrews: 'Asked again for his name, nationality and civil state, still not recovered from the mental disorder produced by fever and hunger, he spoke in these terms: '*I am Juan the Pacifier* [. . .] If you are lovers of war, kill me, for I teach the condemnation of the evils of war' [. . .]'

The new Santiuste will discover among the Moors and Jews of Tetuán the half-buried world of ancient Spain. Before his desertion he had asked the military chaplain: 'Do you hold Saint James the Apostle to be the true general of Spaniards and the slayer of Moors? Where is the text in which Christ told his disciples, "Mount your horses and cut off for me the heads of the sons of Hagar"?' Once acclimated to the new social and human environment, he feels the urge to manifest his pacifist ideas to 'the three similar races', and not only by way of speeches but by action as well. A mystic in the Islamic style, to the point that he does not renounce the pleasures of carnal love, courting a Moorish woman, Erhimo, and a Jewish one, Yohar, he will preach his somewhat nebulous doctrine of harmony and peace to the believers in the three religions of the Holy Book:

> In reply to my question as to whether he liked our land [Nasiry will recount], he answered that he did, because all men there address one another in the familiar form, a sign of their complete equality before God, and because Islam and Israel practise their faiths without disturbing each other. This peace between the religions surprised and delighted him. Later he said to me: 'I perceive your language as a triumphal music, and I see your face as the face of a friend.'

Carrying all his fervour on his back, like a snail, he decides to travel around the world, devoting himself to the propagation of his exalted message:

> I hate war, and I want all peoples to live in perpetual concord, with complete freedom in their customs and their religions. To provoke God to fight against Allah, or Allah against Jehovah, is something like the cockfights, with the vile wagers of those who lay bets on them. But peace would not be good and fruitful without love, which means the increase of generations and the continuation of the divine work.

The reality he discovers when he changes skin is reminiscent of that other reality contemporary with the risks and dangers confronting the Archpriest of Hita, in which religious tolerance and lax customs were conjoined. Galdós subtly connects one with the other in terms of which (had he had knowledge of them) Juan Ruiz the licentious believer would doubtless have approved:

> Drifting about Tetuán, the adventurer realized that even though Moors and Jews fought over questions of money, they never fought for religious reasons: synagogues and mosques functioned with absolute independence, in mutual respect of each other's venerated rites. He also observed that Hebrew priests, as well as Muslims who serve in the temples of Islam without belonging to religious orders, were either married or else enjoyed the possession of a woman more or less freely. This, perhaps, was the source of tolerance, since in the opinion of Santiuste, obligatory celibacy is like amputation, bringing as a consequence the development of instincts contrary to love: selfishness and cruelty.

To the Alarcón who wholeheartedly backed O'Donnell's raid because he shared his desire for glory and exoticism, Galdós (disillusioned with progress and 'civilizing' missions) opposed a Santiuste similarly steeped in the rhetoric and the mythology of the *Romancero*, who will cross the Strait of Gibraltar to discover the profound socio-cultural affinity of the two peoples that the Strait separates, the analogies between faces, expressions, formulae and customs beneath the mask of antagonism and repulsion born of their ignorance of each other. Far from 'that

Christianized Barbary which we call Spain', the wandering mystic will address the author of the *Diario* in these terms: 'Thus it is that what should be Moroccan history turns out to be the history of Spain [. . .] Perico, Moor of Guadix, you are a Spaniard turned inside out, or an unbaptized Mohammedan [. . .] You write in Castilian, yet you think and feel like a Muslim.' That Santiuste is the vehicle for Galdós's own opinions is beyond doubt. The latter's Semitic sensibility, in its twofold Arabic and Jewish aspects, appears throughout his abundant novelistic production, betokening a richness and a depth which go far beyond mere historical evocation or appetite for local colour. Unfortunately for us, the hasty and crude construction of Santiuste's character, which fails to provide a 'believable' motive for his psychic lapses and breaks, robs him of the greatness and the pathos of the fervent, maladjusted heroes of Flaubert, Clarín and Tolstoy. We might also regret the fact that, after having set forth El Nasiry's *muladí* perspective with regard to his 'hated brothers of the other band', in a careful and laudable attempt to imitate certain Arabic literary sources, he spoiled this singular, intimate, adverse vision of the *nesraní*[13] by appending to it a final retraction as cynical as it was inopportune. But Galdós must be judged, we repeat, by the far-seeing wisdom of his historical vision and his poetic intuitions, and not by the faulty construction of his works or the sketchiness of his portrayal of his characters. Returning to the subject that we are treating, let me cite, by way of conclusion, these words of old Ansúrez at the beginning of *Aita Tettauen*, lines so revealing of subliminal Mudejarism that they link the author with antecedents as remote as the Archpriest of Hita and Cervantes: 'Moor and Spaniard are more brothers than it appears. Take away a bit of religion, and another bit of language, and the relationship and family resemblance are obvious. What is a Moor but a Spanish Mohammedan? And how many Spaniards do we see who are Moors disguised as Christians? [. . .] This war that we are undertaking is something of a civil war.'[14]

I am the Other; that is, beneath the writing nearly erased, the palimpsest shows us an unthinkable image: that of the writing itself. Islam's stubborn resistance of the European invader betokens an unquestionable authenticity, as Alarcón too will finally admit. Each in his own way, the two writers discover beneath the rigidity and inflexibility of dogmas the profound poetic truth with which the young Rimbaud, in his delirium, reviled his compatriots: '*Marchand, tu es nègre; genéral, tu es nègre; empereur, vieille démangeaison, tu es nègre.*'[15] The steamroller of progress, flattening contours and surfaces, exposes the underlying elements with which we can reconstruct, if we so wish, the integral identity that we have lost. Such is, in the final analysis, the teaching that Galdós offers us through the spiritual adventure of Santiuste.

Notes

1 Moriscos were Moors who were forced to accept Christian baptism and continued to live in Spain after the Reconquest [*translator's note*].

2 The term *casta* [caste] was used to refer to the three communities – Christian, Muslim, and Jewish – that lived together in the Peninsula until the expulsion of the two latter [*translator's note*].

3 The title cited by Goytisolo in the Spanish text is *Epica árabe y épica castellana* [*translator's note*].

4 Bernard Loupias, 'Importance et signification du lexique d'origine arabe dans le *Don Julián* de Juan Goytisolo', *Bulletin Hispanique*, LXXX, 1978. Sylvia Truxa, 'El mito árabe en las últimas novelas de Juan Goytisolo', *Iberomania*, Junio, 1980. Malika Jadidi Embarec, 'Lectura marroquí de Makbara', in *Juan Goytisolo*, Barcelona: Montesinos, 1981.

5 Literally, in Arabic, a ring; in this case, a ring or circle of listener-spectators [*translator's note*].

6 Régis Blachère, *Histoire de la littérature arabe*, Paris, 1964. The Spanish reader may also consult a translation by Carmen Ruiz Bravo of an excellent book on the same topic by the contemporary Syrian poet Adonis, *Introducción a la poesía árabe*, Madrid, 1976.

7 On modern, popular Arabic literary expression, see Serafín Fanjul, *El Mawwal egipcio*, Madrid, Instituto Hispano-Arabe de Cultura, Also, *Literatura popular árabe*, Madrid: Editora Nacional, 1977.

8 Among Moors in Spain *aljamía* was the Arabic word for Castilian, and by extension, Castilian written in Arabic characters [*translator's note*].

9 'Cervantes y sus fantasmas de Argel', *Quimera*, no. 2, Diciembre 1980.

10 I devoted one of my seminars given in the Spanish Department of New York University to an analysis of the composition of *Misericordia*.

11 See Robert Ricard, 'Note sur la genèse d'*Aita Tettauen* de Galdós', Bulletin Hispanique, 1936.

12 Stephen Gilman, 'Judíos, moros y cristianos en las historias de don Benito y don Américo', in *Homenaje a Sánchez Barbudo*.

13 A Christian converted to Islam in Muslim Spain [*translator's note*].

14 Gilman astutely analyses Galdós's variations on the theme of the captive in Cervantes by way of the 'prophet' Santiuste. On the latter's return to Spain, he describes the Carlist Wars in terms of *taifas* [factional quarrels comparable to those which broke out between the *taifas* into which the former Moorish caliphate of Cordova was divided in the eleventh century – HL]. Galdós then fuses two such heterogeneous sources (according to Gilman) as the *Libro de buen amor* and the *Quixote* to elaborate the next episode, *Carlos VI en la Rápita*:

The likable and at the same time horrendous Christian who this time plays the part of Agi Morato is called Juan Ruiz Hondón, the 'Caliph', political boss and Archpriest of Ulldecona. And the young girl who forsakes him is the most beautiful slave in his harem of 'housekeepers and nieces' [. . .] If the streets of Ulldecona recall those of Tetuán, if there is slavery in certain backward areas of the Peninsula as well, and if female bigotry and male violence [among Christians] are more repugnant than the purer, more tolerant Muslim fanaticism, everything is at once reality and vastly amusing caricature. But much more interesting and admirable for the readers of Don Américo [Castro] is the fact that Galdós intuited the underlying Arabism in the Archpriest's book of long ago.

The translation of the Gilman quotation is mine – HL.

15 'Tradesman, you're a black; general, you're a black; emperor, you old itch, you're a black.'

The Language of the Body
(Octavio Paz and Severo Sarduy)

I

A comparative study of the panorama of the literatures in Castilian and French over the last twenty years would probably underline a fact which, even though innocuous and obvious at first glance, none the less merits reflection: whereas the meagre amount of critical works written in our language stands in sharp contrast, because of its rarity, with a choice production of poetry and an extraordinary flowering of narrative – to the point of restoring to the Spanish language, as far as the novel is concerned, a primacy that appeared to be lost for ever following the death of Cervantes – the panorama of French literature offers us a diametrically opposed image. In it the splendid development of the essay and of criticism stands out amid the self-satisfied mediocrity of poetry and the long period of self-criticism and experimentation of the novel, whose avowed search for renewal has not as yet produced the results that we might reasonably have expected. If on the one hand we would find in France very few names to compare with the list of such masters of narrative as Borges and Paz, Carpentier and Lezama Lima, García Márquez and Fuentes, Vargas Llosa and Cabrera Infante, we would, on the other hand, find ourselves in much the same predicament if we were to look for the equivalents of a Benveniste, a Blanchot, a Lévi-Strauss or a Barthes in the Spanish-speaking world: the centuries-old penury of critical thought from which our language suffers (a penury whose roots go back to the sudden break in the coexistence of the three medieval religious 'castes' and 'anti-Judaic' intellectual persecution) corresponds to a spectacular apogee of poetic and narrative creation: the singular 'creativity' of the essay and criticism in France, by contrast, corresponds to a very marked anaemia and insecurity in the traditional fields of poetry and the novel. I say 'traditional' because, as we shall see, such a schema deals with only one aspect of the question and in reality things are much more complex, since one of the essential features of the literature of our time lies precisely in the suppression of the toll houses and frontiers established between the classic genres in favour of a deconditioned textual production that includes them all and in turn does away with them: texts that are at once criticism and creation, literature and discourse on literature, and consequently capable of containing within themselves the possibility of a reading that is simultaneously poetic, critical and narrative. With this in mind, we might consider (this is merely a hypothesis) the unprecedented and admirable explosion of narrative written in Spanish in recent years (in Latin America particularly) as the swan song of a genre whose meaning and vitality cannot long continue in its present form – a dazzling fireworks display meant, perhaps, to hide from us the pure and simple reality of its eclipse in the face of a new vision of the literary phenomenon, seen as a totally free choice of interpretations, at different levels, within the textual space. The wondrous present richness of our narrative would be, in this case, not so much a bet on the future as a formal sign of the past: a restless, hurried, feverish recovery of the time lost after the brutal uprooting of the imaginative dimension of the field of the novel after the *Quixote* – exactly the reverse of what has happened in France, where the gradual exhaustion of the traditional 'creative' genres has gone hand in hand with a development of critical thought, the central aim of which is to lay down the foundations of a textual production that is not yet mature, though already entirely freed of the monosemic censorship inherent in the existence of minutely codified genres. The different stage of development or, better put, of decrepitude of the canonized literary forms would thus be related to the evolution of the critical corpus, which has not kept pace with them – thereby indicating perhaps (this, I repeat, is a mere hypothesis) that the apparent good health our novel is enjoying today is a purely transitory and ephemeral phenomenon, as several symptoms already suggest. Today more than ever, the introduction of a critical apparatus into the sphere of our language is an absolute necessity if the Spanish-speaking countries intend to play a role in the creative assimilation and organization of a historical phase which, like the current one, is reminiscent in so many ways of that undergone by the men of the Renaissance: when Spain temporarily embodied the aspiration to a knowledge without frontiers before cloistering itself for ever in the pantheon of self-sufficiency, monolithic thought and orthodox hard-headedness.

These reflections – which the limits of this essay do not permit me to formulate properly here – help us at any rate to situate the cultural background on which the many prose writings by Octavio Paz are inscribed, a body of work as dense, varied and rich as it is exceptional in a world in which, as Cernuda once pointed out, there exists neither 'a critical spirit nor criticism, and in which, therefore, the reputation of a writer does not rest upon an objective appraisal of his work'. For Paz – it is not beside the point to recall the fact in an ambience still influenced by the segmentation of literary genres – is not only one of the great contemporary poets of our language: he is also one of the extremely rare thinkers who, expressing himself in it, has attained a dissemination that far surpasses its boundaries. Since the publication, more than thirty years ago, of his admirable *Laberinto de la soledad* [*The Labyrinth of Solitude*] to his enlightening study of Claude Lévi-Strauss, passing by way of his *El arco y la lira* [*The Bow and the Lyre*] and *Corriente alterna* [*Alternating Current*], Paz's creative meditation has never ceased extending itself to fields as disparate as art and politics, anthropology and psychoanalysis, poetry and science (without thereby yielding to that Hispanic propensity to popularize and vulgarize that so frequently weakens Ortega's writings), restoring to the Spanish language its ability, lost for centuries, to transform itself into the instrument and vehicle of a thought which yields to no system of dogmas: a thought capable of embracing, without thereby losing its own distinctive character, the various ideological currents that arose from the Enlightenment and the Industrial Revolution, from Rousseau and Sade, Hegel and Marx, Saussure and surrealism, and of exploring the extremely complex and contradictory face of the world of today without resorting to any of the schemata that habitually serve to conceal it. An uncommon attitude that brings us back, moreover, to the reality we referred to previously: the impossibility of separating poetic work and critical work into watertight compartments in the future, since the two constitute different aspects of one and the same process and the growing self-reflection of poetry is symmetrical to the gradual 'poeticization' of criticism. A critic-poet or a poet-critic, Octavio Paz offers us the best example of a work that both embraces and goes beyond the canonized literary forms and sets forth a provocative conception of a text as a dynamic plurality of possible readings. A book such as *Conjunciones y disyunciones* [*Conjunctions and Disjunctions*] illustrates very well, in my view, this multiple option on the part of the reader confronted not only with a genuine, almost Tantric banquet of ideas (oh what a cruel contrast with the austere and niggardly menu of the common run of Hispanic thinkers!), but also (and this is a fundamental aspect of the author's conception) of words: a poetic divagation and at the same time a critical approximation to a series of essential facts of our past, our present and, doubtless, our future; a digression on typical Mexican knavery, but also an impressively profound immersion in the being of a dizzying variety of cultures (from Mexico to China, from India to Spain).

One of the peculiar features of Hispanic self-absorption has always been its lack of interest in foreign ways of life and civilizations, an absence of curiosity which, when added to the already-mentioned lack of critical spirit, explains in large part our meagre contribution to the study of other cultures (including those that are close historically and geographically), a fact that Américo Castro so rightfully lamented.[1] In *Conjunciones y disyunciones*, Paz situates himself at the pole directly opposite the provincial Peninsular tradition: taking as his key concept the binomial expression 'body'/'non-body,' he uses his vast culture to describe an extraordinary network of parallelisms and oppositions that extends from Tantric Buddhism, Hinduism and Confucius to the Spanish Baroque twilight and the politico-economic morality of Puritanism. His inexhaustible intellectual curiosity serves as a trampoline for a series of bold reflections on economics and love, excrement and language which prove him to be one of the most lucid minds of our time.

Taking as his point of departure the analyses of Max Weber, Erich Fromm and Norman O. Brown, Paz endeavours to disentangle and order the spider's web of affinities and divergences that exist between the different cultures of the Indo-European world, and even extends the field of investigation to Chinese and pre-Columbian civilizations with the avowed purpose of establishing a play of symmetries much like the one that Valéry dreamed of when he brought up the possibility of tracing a pattern of the changes that take place in literature, so as to demonstrate that the overall scheme of deviations from the norm obeys a strict *ars combinatoria*, or, if one prefers, 'a symmetrical distribution of ways of being original.' The fluctuation of the signs 'body' and 'non-body' throughout the history of civilization would thus be the axis around which religious and social concepts revolve, with their vast and ponderous ideological, dogmatic and ritual edifices – a highly fertile hypothesis that, like Lévi-Strauss's play of primary dichotomies, allows us to weave a series of complex relationships (made up of similarities and oppositions) based precisely on the uninterrupted dialogue of signs that the author crosses and uncrosses on the rectangular space of the page:

> in contrast to the neutral and abstract vocabulary of morality [he is referring to Protestantism], the genital words and phonetic and semantic copulations [of Tantrism]; in contrast to the prayers, the sermons and the economy of rational language, mantras and their tinkling bells. A language that distinguishes between the act and the word, and within this latter, between the signifier and the signified; another that erases the distinction between the word and the act, reduces the sign to a mere signifier, changes the signified, conceives of language as a game identical to that of the universe in which the right side and the left, the masculine and the feminine, fullness and emptiness are one and the same.

Octavio Paz's thought – not only in *Conjunciones y disyunciones* but in later works such as *Los hijos del limo* [*Children of the Mire*] and *El mono gramático* [*The Monkey Grammarian*] – challenges, with an arrogance unknown among us, the doctrinal foundations of the Judeo-Christian tradition with respect to the body, a perpetual victim of the theological or rational abstractions that have served as a basis for merciless exploitation on the part of the bourgeoisie (and prolonged today by Soviet bureaucracy). In order to do so he has followed the trail left by previous thought (that of the Spanish Middle Ages, marked with the imprint of Islam); a thought which does not deny the body, does not abstract it, does not repress it; which, rather, allows it to speak and promotes the reconciliation of man with himself. This historical tendency – thwarted both by Calvinist ethics and by the arguments in favour of pure, chaste immanence of Hispanic Catholicism – has flourished, on the contrary, in other cultural spheres, some of them close to us (Islam) and others remote (Hinduism). Fascination for this latter has led Paz, moreover, to the capital consideration of the body as a writing and writing as a body, this being the texture itself of *El mono gramático*:

> Just as meaning appears beyond writing, as though it were the destination, the end of the road [. . .], so the body first appears to our eye as a perfect totality, and yet it too proves to be intangible:

the body is always somewhere beyond the body. On touching it, it divides itself (like a text) into portions that are momentary sensations: a sensation that is a perception of a thigh, an earlobe, a nipple, a fingernail, a warm patch of groin, the hollow in the throat like the beginning of a twilight. The body that we embrace is a river of metamorphoses, a continual division, a flowing of visions, a quartered body whose pieces scatter, disperse, come back together again with the intensity of a flash of lightning hurtling toward a white black white fixity.[2]

In *El mono gramático*, Octavio Paz has succeeded perfectly in writing, beneath the 'normal' appearance of the essay, the total text (critical, narrative, poetic) that allows for and requires a plurality of readings. In this respect he takes still farther the tendency, visible in certain writings of Barthes, Sollers and other authors, to 'poetize' critical thought, including in it narrative spaces, verbal lianas, an exciting feast of words. His power as an innovator is not limited, then, to placing the ideological edifice of the Western bourgeoisie in question: it also extends to the practical destruction of the doctrine of literary genres in favour of the multiple reading of a text on all its levels. The fruitfulness of such a proposal, and in general, of bringing Hindu thought to the cultural world – so barren and schematic – of the Spanish-speaking peoples goes beyond the limits of the essay and leaps into the traditional territory of the novel, as we are shown in Sarduy's inter-textual dialogue, in the final sequence of his *Cobra*, along with the *Conjunciones y disyunciones* upon which we are commenting at present. Synthesizing his gifts as a poet, narrator and essayist, Octavio Paz takes for granted the possibility of new and exciting paths, demolishes precepts and dogmas, forces readers and critics to shake off that lethargy of theirs that has been proverbial for hundreds of years now.

The limitations of the present work keep us from analysing as we should like an entire group of convergent and opposed symmetries having to do with food and death, anal retention and language, which express the historical-spatial oscillation of the two basic signs, and we shall confine ourselves to touching now on a partial aspect of the binomial that particularly interests Spaniards: I am referring to the brilliant parallel that Paz traces between Hispanic Catholicism and English Protestant morality by way of the examples of Quevedo and Swift and his masterful study of the undeservedly neglected, and badly interpreted, scatology of the former.

In a seminar on the subject of 'Eroticism and Repression in Spanish Literature', meant for graduate students at New York University, I tried as best I could, in terms of what I knew about the context of the inter-caste struggle, to analyse the reduction and the progressive transmutation of the sign 'body' throughout this period, from its full and free expression in the admirable amorous repertory of the Archpriest of Hita to the gloomy, 'luminous funeral rites for sun-excrement' of the great scatological poet. In fact: parallel to the persecution and the stifling of 'Judaic' intellectual curiosity, even a superficial reading of our literature reveals a systematic repression, from the fifteenth century on, of the Hispano-Arabic tradition of sensuality. Coinciding with the military eclipse of the Muslims, the savoury eroticism of medieval texts little by little disappears from the Spanish literary scene, though not before adopting the aggravated and convulsive forms that even today so surprise and shock a great many Golden Age 'specialists'. From that time on we witness an institutionalization of the repression of the sign 'body', which, accompanied by the repression of the intellect, has come to be one of the essential elements of the modern Hispanic personality. To date, no historian or essayist has undertaken the imperative task of calculating the importance of this phenomenon and its formidable impact on the minds and lives of the Spanish people. As Xavier Domingo astutely observes in one of the few essays devoted to the subject,

the Arab has incorporated the sexual act within the structure of his most basic aspirations. The Christian, on the contrary, tends to exclude sex, to deny it. Feeling and sexuality are indissoluble things for the Arab. For the Christian everything that has to do with sex is abominable and may contaminate his soul. Although Christians and Muslims lived on the very same soil, in a nearly identical way, their concepts concerning a matter as essential as love were so categorically opposed that it is not strange that the war between them lasted eight centuries and ended with the annihilation of the vanquished. Everything that the Spaniard bears within him is cruelly repressed, sexuality first of all.[3]

The sign 'body' is revealed without false pretexts in the days of the Mudéjar poet Juan Ruiz, 'when Castile' – Américo Castro writes – 'was beginning to organize its pleasure and was not ashamed of it'. The *Libro de buen amor* is, in the final analysis, a repertory of the sensual pleasures of the age and its author does not fall into the error of Petrarchian sublimation or of scatological mockery to which, later on, a number of our best writers devote themselves in turn. For that very reason his role in Spanish letters is fundamental, and can only be compared with that of the two other masterworks of our literature: *La Celestina* and the *Quixote*. Juan Ruiz represents the one moment in our history in which the 'body'/'non-body' dichotomy is held in harmonious balance, thereby reminding us, as he reminds Paz, that 'we are not only descendants of Quevedo', and thanks to him I too am reconciled – at least during the time that I am reading him – with Spanish-speaking people. All of this, obviously, was a direct result of the Archpriest's deep-rooted familiarity with the Arab world, a familiarity that allowed him to experience a peaceful coexistence between 'eroticism and religion, impossible for Christianity to enjoy simultaneously, being a belief' – as Castro reminds us – 'which does not allow it to abandon itself justifiably to the sweet pleasures of carnal love'. We Spaniards today cannot help reflecting with irrepressible nostalgia on this image of a pluriracial, free and happy Spain, in which the signs 'body' and 'non-body' are expressed in terms of complementarity, an image which, as we know, we will not find later either in reality or in literature: a Spain that is not a thankless and savage country, imposing its rule after a historical fraud going back centuries, but a habitable, welcoming one, free in mind and body, about which some of us never stop dreaming, not even when we are wide awake – a reality thwarted by those who confiscated, once and for all, for themselves and for those of their breed, country and history, space and language.

Octavio Paz's book helps us better to understand the later metamorphosis of the sign 'body' when he establishes a parallel between the different attitudes of Swift and of Quevedo towards this same sign. Whereas the opposition between the notion of work and sexual exuberance sheds light on the relations that existed between Puritan morality and the spirit of capitalism, the attitude of Spanish Catholicism with regard to the body is much more ambiguous, since, for reasons of caste, Old Christians too found it difficult to adjust to the rational imperative of work. Protestantism makes an abstraction of the sign 'body' and subjects it to the sublimations of reason; Spanish Catholicism makes it guilty, tortures it, contorts it, without thereby eliminating it entirely, and its fresh and succulent expression in the work of the Archpriest of Hita was to be succeeded by the exasperated, convulsive expression of Quevedo and the Baroque poets. Swift, Paz points out, 'is an infinitely freer writer than the Spaniard but his daring is almost exclusively intellectual. Confronted with Quevedo's sensual virulence, especially on the scatological level, Swift 'would have been offended', and in reality 'he was faced with prohibitions no less powerful than those to which Quevedo was subjected by neo-Scholasticism, absolute monarchy, and the Inquisition'. To sum up: 'as repression moves farther and farther away from reason the inhibitions of language increase', and rational capitalist economy is not content to monopolize gold and transmute it into a sign, for it also expels dirty words from the language and sublimates and conceals defecation by inventing the flush toilet. On the one hand: cleanliness, rationality, sublimation; on the other: exasperation, violence, scatology. This explains – as Antonio Regalado proves in his study, as yet unpublished, of Calderón's theatre – why numerous moral propositions upheld by Spanish probabilists (the majority of them Jesuits) in the first half of the seventeenth century provoked a scandal because of their 'laxity' concerning subjects such as fornication, adultery, abortion, etc,[4] not only among the panegyrists of the Reform but also in the circle of Pascal and the French Jansenists, since the dialectical tension between the signs 'body'/'non-body' did not function among our neighbours beyond the Pyrenees in the same way as in the Peninsula.

This reality – frequently whisked out of sight by our most estimable essayists – leads us to the following observation: the unconscious model of intrapsychic censorship, of censorship included, as Freud would put it, in the 'mechanics of the soul', cannot act with the same violence on the body and on reason, and when it wars on the latter it does so at the cost of neglecting the former to a certain degree, and vice versa, as though it lacked the power to operate simultaneously on the two planes, or else simply knew that in the long run the human being would not tolerate it. Once again, the possibility of a synoptic table of the relations of opposition, complementarity and alternance of the signs 'body' and 'non-body' in England, France and Spain appears to be a fruitful hypothesis that no reflective mind ought to disregard lightly. In any event, Octavio Paz's observations shed new light on Spanish art and literature of the Golden Age, and in the future they will have to be taken seriously into account in order to analyse and understand the Baroque. 'If the seventeenth century had forgotten that the body is a language,' he says, 'its poets were able to create a language which, perhaps, by reason of its very complication, gives us the sensation of a living body.' Góngora's evasive art, his typical insistence on avoiding specific naming of objects in order to make the idiom of their illusory transparency stand out, is, in truth, the result of a grandiose, titanic struggle to make language take on substance – of an insane persistence in inflicting on us, using tooth and nail, the dense, opaque, almost physical presence of words so elusive that they are impossible to grasp.

I would not want to end these notes without referring, if only briefly, to the current rebellion of the body against the moral philosophy of progress and its all-embracing rational constructions. This attitude, formulated by thinkers of the stature of Georges Bataille, is based on the distinction traced by Marx between alienated and unalienated work[5] in order to condemn, in the name of the body, the slavery of the modern industrial world and recover sexual exuberance as the one human element irreducible to reification. In other words: whereas the rational imperative of work tends to convert the man of today into merely one more object in a world of objects, his so-called animality preserves his awareness of existing by and for himself. As Bataille writes: 'human life is worn out from serving as the head and the power of reason of the universe. To the degree that it becomes this head and this reason, to the degree that it becomes necessary to the universe, it accepts an enslavement' – a cry of devastated violence that irresistibly reminds the Spanish reader of the one that echoes throughout La Celestina. Rojas's tragicomedy may in truth be deciphered as the anguished outcry of the sign 'body' on confronting the dogmatic ideology that oppresses it, an outcry we hear neither before La Celestina nor afterwards in the pages of Spanish literature, perhaps by reason of the well-known, simultaneous opposition of the Old Christian caste to reason and to work. Today, when Spain appears to be adapting itself at last to the schema of a rational and useful world, subject to the laws of economics and to the need for alienated and alienating work, the body will perhaps take on once again the subversive virulence of the cry of outrage. For La Celestina is not only one of the masterworks of literature: it is also the mordant expression of our repressed bodily desire, and therefore a vehemently contemporary voice of protest.

Aside from its implications for a great many civilizations and cultures, Spanish readers will thus find in Octavio Paz's book an indispensable contribution to the knowledge of some of the basic conjunctions and disjunctions of our own unfortunate history.

II

The wall posters of Sian recently made public the following news item: Wang, a twenty-three-year-old worker, caught in culpable intimacy with a young woman his own age, was sentenced to twenty years in prison by the Party officials of the aforementioned province. In a country where marriage is 'discouraged' before the age of twenty-five for women and twenty-eight for men, and where extramarital relations do not exist, at least officially, an act as selfish and asocial as that committed by the two young people could have been motivated only by strictly political considerations. Two special circumstances played a major role in this interpretation and made the crime more serious still: the young woman was the daughter of a highly placed Party bureaucrat and the event had occurred at precisely the time when the two accused young people ought to have been attending a meeting called to denounce and condemn the reactionary thought of Lin Piao and Confucius. This accumulation of suppositions and 'proofs' turned the unusual case into a routine act of provocation and defiance: de facto disagreement with the political line of the Party and objective support of the feudal ideology of the personalities denounced at the meeting. Wang was then accused of the crime of rape and given a twenty-year prison sentence. But, taking advantage of the plausible fall from favour or the failure of the family of the presumed rape victim to follow without question the latest Party directives, Wang's comrades at work denounced the young woman, accusing her of revisionism and the adoption of bourgeois ways of thinking. In other words: Wang and the young woman were victims of a typical counter-revolutionary manoeuvre and would never have abandoned the correct Party line. The wall posters therefore pressed for a review of the trial and the right of Wang and the young woman to defend their real political opinions.

As readers of the wall posters may have been able to appreciate – though lost, as we are, in the hopeless tangle of arguments and processes of reasoning regarding the ideology and political line of the guilty parties – their trial, their condemnation, and their vindication by means of the wall posters deal with everything except the prime factor in the whole affair: the sensual pleasure of the two young people, their lonely fervour when together. One of the characteristics of all monolithic ideologies has always been the phenomenon of the sublimation of bodies, reduced thus by religious or political powers to the mere status of abstract entities (bodies to be glorified) or mere work tools (proletarians in the service of the exploiting bourgeoisie, Stakhanovite heroes).[6] The sodomite or bigamist condemned to be burned at the stake by the Holy Office does not suffer that fate by the act in and of itself; they are not permitted to invoke the one reason that excuses them: the body's rapture, the delight of the senses. Their crime, like that of the heretic or the deviationist, is the arrogant challenge to the established ideological schema, their perverse resistance to it. The obfuscating syllogisms of Scholastics once again reveal their usefulness over many centuries in that their 'gold-work tattooing' permits concealment of a fearful emptiness: the language of a body deprived of language, the reality of an inexpressible enjoyment.

The same tendency to sublimate – whether or not in the service of a monolithic ideology – is also frequently a feature of the reading of the work of literature on the part of those who reduce it and tear it apart by means of a heterogeneous discourse – one distant from it and foreign to it. I am not denying here the possibility of, nor the right to, an ideological reading of a poem, novel or play – provided that it is carried out with at least a minimum of respect for the work examined and provided that such a reader is capable of distinguishing between verbal ordering and literary devices, and between social mechanisms and the reality of life. But there is no doubt that, even if carried out with this sort of respect and intelligence, ideological discourse (of whatever variety) groups together in a new structure (that of the discourse of the critic) anomalous residues and elements extracted with greater or lesser arbitrariness from the old structure (that of the literary discourse analysed) and thus takes on the peculiarities of *bricolage*, exactly as they have been brought to light by Gérard Genette in his brilliant adaptation to the field of criticism of one of Lévi-Strauss's foremost dynamic principles. At all events, any reductive reading (be it structuralist, Marxist, Freudian, etc) easily falls into the sort of syllogistic discourse (whether approving or disapproving) of texts whose only justification may be – as in the aforementioned example of Wang and the young woman – the pleasure, in this case too both solitary and shared, of writing and of the correlative operation: the enjoyment, possessing exactly the same characteristics, that the reader experiences or may experience.

To mention such a pleasure, to take a stand in favour of a form of playful writing then constitutes the worst of crimes: it is to sanction the unspeakable, to give expression to an enjoyment that escapes the repressive laws of apparently rational discourse. By giving voice to it, the guilty party will mobilize against him any and all ideologies. 'In the face of this transgression' – Sarduy says – 'believers and atheists, capitalists and communists, aristocrats and proletarians, readers of Mauriac and of Sartre find themselves suddenly and definitely in agreement.' The more obvious and fundamental the act (the pleasure of copulation, the enjoyment of reading), the greater the insolence of anyone who dares to make use of such simplicity and incontrovertibility. The logocentrism of our culture (or that copied, outside of it, from our exported ideology) leads to the aberrant situation of a world in which bodily enjoyment must hide itself behind the mask of reason (political, social, religious), thereby providing a powerful alibi to henchmen and hired assassins of every stripe (Pinochet's police or a member of the Río de la Plata Triple A, who physically and morally torture those suspected of leftist sympathies, are likewise not in the habit of openly excusing their sadism by invoking their real pleasure: reducing the enemy body to the status of an object; they hypocritically conceal it beneath the veil of anti-communism and the defence of 'social order').[7] To deny the existence of pure physical pleasure (whether 'innocent' or perverse) in the end implies excusing, in the name of an all-powerful ideology, any and every crime and abuse of history – and here Bataille, in his lucid defence of the exemplary nature of Sade's thought, is absolutely right: on allowing the heroes of *Juliette* or *Justine* to speak freely of the drive to destroy physical bodies, Sade identifies it and thereby strips it of any and every alibi (orthodoxy, purity of the faith, reason of state, etc). Just as Machiavelli was only half a Machiavellian (otherwise he would not have written *The Prince*), the Divine Marquis was quite a bit less sadistic than an Ilse Koch or a Lieutenant Calley, in so far as the two latter justified their actions in the name of an ideological discourse or noble patriotic reasons. But I do not wish to compare the delight of writing and the operation of reading (Allah deliver me from such a thing!) with the pleasure of the murderers of Auschwitz or My Lai: my one intention is to call attention to

the consistent, invariably restrictive attitude of Judeo-Christian civilization towards the notion of pleasure – its desire to 'capitalize on
bodies and material goods', its execration of eroticism and ludic
writing, its pertinacity in silencing the body and emptying it of
language.

To write something and not write about something, as Joyce proposed
to do and Severo Sarduy does, drives theoreticians who do not write
novels and who perhaps do not even enjoy reading them 'out of their
minds', as the latter puts it. The scoundrel who commits such a crime
will unleash against him the entire pack of critics self-invested with
the authority of prosecuting attorneys, the tentacular proliferation
of intricate syllogisms intended to prove that, like the unfortunate
Wang, he is shutting himself up in the private property of his own
self and adopting a heretical, unproductive or revisionist ideology.
When Barthes defines *De donde son los cantantes*[8] as a 'hedonistic
text and *by that very fact revolutionary*', his words could not be
more to the point. In a society such as ours (capitalist or bureaucratic, but inevitably imbued with the Judeo-Christian ideology that
makes the body abstract and transforms it into an entelechy), laying
claim to idleness, play and pleasure (as do a whole line of thinkers,
from Fourier and Lafargue to Bataille and Paz, who work their way
around the logocentrism they denounce) is a healthfully subversive and
provocative art.

A fundamental characteristic of Sarduy's novelistic art is his will
to playfulness: the production of a text (a printed space) freed of
any ideological justification – whose reason for being is based solely
on the pleasure of that duo (solo performer and participant) that
becomes one in the act of reading. From *De donde son los cantantes*
to *Maitreya*, his revolutionary hedonism has developed in a crescendo
of sensuality and humour, parody and spontaneity which, though we
find examples in other languages (cf. *Tristram Shandy*), is a rare
bird indeed in our own. Sarduy – following here in the footsteps
of Valéry – does not believe in writing that takes its own narrative
discourse seriously and whose mannerisms and conventions are all
the more easily detectable to the eye of the sharp-sighted critic when
the novelist tries to hide them beneath a laboured appearance of
realism, verisimilitude, 'naturalness'. Like Sterne, he offers us instead
an enjoyable pastime – the only sort of serious reading according
to Valéry – in which the writer, like Cervantes's puppeteer Maese
Pedro, openly pulls the strings of the narrative in a space with

neither a curtain in front nor floorboards underfoot, that is to say, the opposite of a stage set. In one of the frequent digressions that interrupt the narrative line of *De donde son los cantantes*, Sarduy, on proclaiming his own incompetence to deal with the subject of the work – the *excusatio propter infirmitatem* of the classic authors – gives us the key, or at least one of the keys, that help the reader to understand the structure and intentions of the novel: 'lame words for lame realities that obey a lame plan laid down by a lame monkey', he will say mockingly of himself, just as Sterne begs the reader's pardon for having placed the prologue of his novel in Chapter 20 of Volume III of the books, exclaiming: 'All my heroes are off my hands; – 'tis the first time I have had a moment to spare, – and I'll make use of it, and write my preface' or avows that he is incapable of ending the conversation between Tristram's father and his uncle Toby – four chapters devoted to the time it takes them to go down two steps of the staircase – saying, in the words of the narrator, 'Holla! – you chairman – here's sixpence – do step into that bookseller's shop, and call me a *day-tall* critic. I am very willing to give any one of 'em a crown to help me with his tackling, to get my father and my uncle Toby off the stairs, and to put them to bed.'9

In *De donde son los cantantes* – as in *Cobra* – the novelist moves with self-assurance, converses with the characters, utters erroneous judgements and then disavows them, suddenly changes style and shifts the scene, parodies sentences from classical authors, etc, thus reminding us that the realistic – or to be more precise, the referential – background of ordinary novels is here another discourse. Instead of a 'natural' world, we move in a strictly cultural universe. Transgressions, as in Góngora, take on a supra-rhetorical colouring: a pastiche of culture, culture squared. In other words: literature shorn of a 'message', reduced to what Roman Jakobson calls literaturity:

> Auxilio brushes her locks of hair aside. She assumes a Quevedian air:
>   I shall be ashes, but I shall have feeling
>   I shall be dust, but dust in love.10
> SOCORRO: *Tu me casses les cothurnes.*11 Shut up. I'm at the end of my rope too. Dry that tear. Be discreet. Be circumspect. Hold yourself together. Show your pride. (p. 11)

– We're being metaphysical and it's because we haven't eaten. Let's go to the cafeteria! (p. 15)

Sarduy's intention is to dig all sorts of pitfalls for the reader so as to keep him from going to sleep from the steady purr of traditional narrative discourse and force him to notice the holes gaping open underfoot all of a sudden. In order to do this he must constantly fight with its conventions and its usual procedures, displace it when least expected to another playing field. Cobra[12] could be compared, for instance, with a film entitled 'The Andalusian Holiday of a Swedish Tyrant', in which the protagonist was neither a tyrant nor Swedish but a masseur from the Tyrol, whose travels – for educational purposes – did not take him through Andalusia but Scotland, described in the film as though it were Bombay, yet accompanied by a soundtrack with popular songs typical of Naples. The changes of character in Cobra – like those in Sarduy's preceding novel – are simply optical illusions. As Emir Rodríguez Monegal has aptly pointed out:

> There are no such metamorphoses of the 'protagonist' or of his acolytes; there is only a metamorphosis of the text: a text that coils back upon itself (like a cobra) to quote itself, parody itself, criticize itself, bite its own tail, forming a perfectly circular structure in the centre of which the one noticeable thing is the absence of a subject. The masks that the protagonist uses [. . .] are barely that: the representation of a representation of a representation that exists only at the level of discourse.[13]

Underscoring this super-rhetorical level, Sarduy's heroines are always actresses – whether at the Chinese Opera Theatre in Havana, or at the Lyric Theatre of Mannequins in Pigalle – and in reality transvestites, whose disguise does not conceal but, rather, enhances the existence of a body whose rebellious expression is 'criticism become an act', as Octavio Paz said of Cernuda, since it confers on the being of flesh and bone, reduced to silence by the constant repression exerted by ideology, a 'moral coloration'.

Language that is a body or body that is a language, the vindication of both by Sarduy and Paz implies a new attitude towards the baroque. Whereas the morality of homo faber, of the being-for-work condemns waste, excess and sensual pleasure, the notions of 'play, loss, squandering and pleasure', Sarduy says –

link the Baroque to eroticism, in opposition to sexuality [. . .] Our body is an erotic machine that produces 'useless' desire, pleasure without an objective, energy without a function. A machine for pleasure constantly wearing itself out and constantly rebuilding itself [. . .] To be baroque today means to threaten, to pass judgement on and to parody bourgeois economics, based on the miserly – or as it is usually put, the 'rational' administration of goods in the centre and the very foundation of that administration and everything that supports it: language, the space of signs, the symbolic cement of society and the guarantee of its functioning, its communication.

So clear and so cutting a defence of the language – body binomial and the anti-classicism and excessiveness of the Baroque is condemned to meet with the same lack of understanding and hostility that for centuries confined both the poetry of Góngora and the theatre of Calderón to the pantheon of the abnormal, the unimaginable and the extravagant. The attacks against both, in the name of progress and good taste, on the part of neoclassicists such as Luzán, who had been won over by French styles and vogues, and later on by positivists and realists,[14] admittedly obeyed most noble motives: to bring literature once again into closer contact with the preoccupations of social man and make room in it for the puzzling problems and deep concerns of the time. But the radicalism of this programme and the poverty of the solutions proposed succeeded only in giving the *coup de grâce*, as we now know, to the great literature of the seventeenth century without fostering at the same time new modes of expression – thereby contributing in a decisive way to the depression and the exhaustion of our letters for the space of two centuries, until its brilliant resurrection by a series of authors, above all on the other side of the Atlantic, whose works are linked, more or less deliberately, with the literary current that had been buried (and is once again being attacked with flamethrowers by today's neoclassicists, positivists and realists).

We readers who enjoy Sarduy's work doubtless do so for the same indefensible and egotistical reasons that drove poor Wang to perform the act previously mentioned: our own selfish pleasure. If only we can one day free ourselves of the arduous and tiresome task of having to justify it by resorting, as did Wang's supporters and accusers, to the syllogisms, arguments and disquisitions of some sort of frightening neo-Scholasticism!

Notes

1 The imperviousness of the Generation of '98 to the discovery by Picasso of the *musée imaginaire* in the early years of the twentieth century is a good example of what I am saying.

2 Readers of the Arabic poetry of Ibn Guzmán or Ibn Hazm are familiar with this dialectical relationship between the body and writing, which appears frequently in their magnificent verses.

The passage cited is from Helen Lane's English translation of *El mono gramático: The Monkey Grammarian*, New York: Seaver Books, 1981, p. 42. The original Spanish edition was published by Seix Barral, Barcelona, 1974.

3 *Erótica hispánica*, Paris: Ruedo Ibérico, 1972.

4 The propositions of the probabilists condemned by Innocent XI in 1679 include the following: (1) eating and drinking to satiety, merely for the taste, is not a sin, providing that it does not damage the health, for the natural appetite may licitly enjoy its acts; (2) the conjugal act, prompted by sensual pleasure alone, is free of all blame and venial sin; (3) it is licit to procure an abortion before the animation of the child, in order that the pregnant woman may not die or be disgraced; (4) it appears likely that any foetus, during all the time that it is in its mother's womb, lacks a rational soul, and that therefore it begins to have one only at birth, and consequently it must be said that no abortion is an act of murder; (5) copulation with a married woman, as long as the husband consents, is not adultery, and therefore it suffices to say in the confessional that there has been fornication; (6) it is licit to seek directly the proximate occasion to sin for our spiritual or temporal good or that of our neighbour. See Fray Martín de Torrecilla, *Consultas morales y exposición de las proposiciones condenadas por Inocencio XI*, Madrid, 1684.

5 True wealth is the productivity developed by all individuals. Thus it is no longer work time but free time (available time) that gives us the measure of wealth. To use work time as a measure of wealth is to found that wealth on poverty [...] and it is to situate the totality of the time of the individual in work time, thereby reducing him to the level of a mere worker, worth less than his own work.

(Karl Marx, *Grundrisse*, cited by H. Marcuse in *El marxismo soviético*, Madrid: Alianza Editorial, 1971.)

6 For one of the brand-new leaders of our strikingly brilliant Left, homosexuality is, for instance, 'an economic and social problem with ideological roots' (Diego Fábregas, the leader of OICE, a Marxist-Leninist party that no longer exists). See also the 'anthropological' answers on the subject by Manuel Guedán, Eliado García and Fray Tierno Galván in *Los partidos marxistas. Sus dirigentes, sus programas*, edited by Fernando Ruiz and Joaquín Romero, Barcelona: Anagrama, 1977.

7 Publishers and readers make no mistake in this respect: Henri Alleg's *La question*, an extremely valuable testimonial to the odious racist tortures

committed by the French police during the Algerian war, is a big seller today in the sex shops in Pigalle.

8 *De donde son los cantantes*, Mexico City: Joaquín Mortiz, 1967.

9 See the excellent essay by Shklovsky on *Tristram Shandy* in Lee T. Lemon, *Russian Formalist Criticism*, University of Nebraska Press, 1965.

10 Auxilio's version of the two last lines of Quevedo's famous sonnet '*Amor constante más allá de la muerte*' ['Love constant beyond death'] [*translator's note*].

11 'You're a pain in the buskins.' In French in the original; a pun on the expression '*tu me casses les pieds*' – 'you're bugging me' [*translator's note*].

12 Buenos Aires; Sudamericana, 1972.

13 Emir Rodríguez Monegal, 'Las metamorfosis del texto', in *Severo Sarduy*, Madrid: Fundamentos, 1976.

14 'The Baroque is the most shockingly anti-Occidental art stemming from the Occident itself: relegated by the West to the status of *kitsch* (the art of the "ignorant" masses that continued to attend Calderón's dramas) in the eighteenth century and to official and academic censorship in the nineteenth century.' Cf. Roberto González Echevarría, 'Memoria de apariencias y ensayo de *Cobra*', in *Severo Sarduy*, edition cited in note 13 above.

A Cervantine Reading of
Three Trapped Tigers

When Miguel de Unamuno, in his *Life of Don Quixote and Sancho*, comes to the chapter in Part One in which the curate and the barber scrutinize the gentleman's library, he dismisses the episode with these few cursory and sententious lines: 'All of which is literary criticism, that should be of little concern to us. It is about books, not life. We shall ignore it.' It is not our intent at this point to analyse the Basque author's badly distorted interpretation of a liberal and humanist view of the world totally contrary to his own (which, I might add, has much more in common with Quevedo's than with Cervantes's). Others have already carried out that analysis and we refer the reader to their work.[1] We will merely remark that when Unamuno expresses himself in terms of 'life' and 'books' within the literary space of the novel, he seems to adopt the perspective of the plodding realism he had every reason to detest. When life enters a book, it is immediately transformed into literature, and we should judge it as such. Actually, the sixth chapter of Part One ('The Inquisition in the Library')[2] plays a fundamental role in the novel, to the extent that without it, the *Quixote* would not exist. What Unamuno dismissed was nothing less than Cervantes's marvellous gallery of mirrors, that game-playing, at once destructive and creative, with the different literary codes of his time. Unamuno's error once again demonstrates – as if it were still necessary – his total insensitivity to a work both completely different from and infinitely superior to his own.

A novel, let us remember, is not related solely to the social and historical context in which it emerges. It also, and primarily, corresponds to the laws of the genre to which it belongs, to the requirements, that is to say, of its own discourse. Although for an appreciable majority of novelists, critics and readers what is most important is its relation to the 'reality' it pretends to represent – the novel as 'a mirror along the

roadway', characters destined to rival those whose vital statistics are on
file in the civil registry – its connection with the entire corpus of works
published previously is always stronger and more decisive than the one
that links it to 'reality'. The *Quixote* is the best possible proof that a text
cannot be studied in isolation, as if it had come from nowhere or were
a mere product of the outside world, but, rather, must be examined in
relation to other texts, to a whole system of values and meanings that
already exists. As the Russian formalists said in their day, the function
of every work lies in its relationship to all other works. Each one is a
differential sign.

Cervantes's great novel is an extremely complicated literary discourse
which is clarified and ultimately makes sense because of its links with
the literary models of the period. This intertextuality plays a primary
role in the novel, just as it does in the French and English works it
most strongly influenced, from Sterne to Flaubert. Chapter 6 enables
Cervantes to introduce literary discussion into the lives of his characters
and catapult his theory into the space of the novel itself. As is true of an
entire sector of contemporary novelistic practice – which 'cervantizes'
without realizing it – characterized by its mistrust of traditional 'forms'
and 'contents' the *Quixote* is, simultaneously, criticism and creation,
writing and a questioning of writing, a text which both constructs itself
and endlessly evaluates itself.

But the relation of Cervantes's novel to the literary corpus of his
time is not limited, as Unamuno would have us believe, to the highly
important sixth chapter; on the contrary, it manifests itself from the
prologue to the very last page of the work. Américo Castro saw this
clearly when he wrote:

> Much has been said about the literary sources of the *Quixote*,
> and very little about the presence and function of books within
> the creative process of the work. Reading or having read, writing
> or being in the act of writing are occupations of many of the
> characters who people the pages of the *Quixote*, tasks without
> which a number of these figures would not exist [. . .] It could
> thus be said that the *Quixote* is a book forged and derived from
> the active material of other books. The first part issues essentially
> from the books read by Don Quixote; the second part is, in
> turn, an emanation of the first, for it does not limit itself to
> the continued narration of new events, but, rather, incorporates
> into the life of the character the awareness that that life has already

been the subject of a book. The Don Quixote of the second part continues himself, and continues as well the literary interpretation of Cid Hamete.[3]

With his usual keen insight, long before the publication in the West of the formalists' discoveries, the author of *El pensamiento de Cervantes* was able to perceive the decisive role of intertextuality in the *Quixote* and of the play of the written word in the psyche of the characters. As we shall see within the limits imposed by this brief essay, Cervantes's masterpiece illustrates better than any other novel the principle formulated by Shklovsky, which maintains that every literary work 'is created in parallel with and in opposition to some model. New form does not appear in order to express a new content but rather to replace an old form which has lost its aesthetic character.'[4] In the prologue of the novel, Cervantes suggests that we look on it as a new and original literary work which on the one hand activates all or almost all of the latent possibilities of novelistic discourse, while on the other it proposes a unique combination, irreducible to any previous model.

Certain Cervantes scholars, following in the footsteps of Unamuno in his efforts to disassociate the *Quixote* from its creator and consider him an unschooled genius, tell us, as does Rodríguez Marín, that the book contains many excellent features, but 'the father of the work himself was unable to see them [. . .] It has been we readers who have discovered the best of the great book's treasure.' This, of course, is pompous nonsense, and the saddest part is that the author reveals nothing except his own incredible self-importance when he indirectly takes credit for 'discovering' the hidden treasures of the book. Nobody was more aware than Cervantes of the value and the originality of the literary object he was offering his readers. Just as Juan Ruiz boasted of writing 'strange verses' because he was the first poet to use the *zéjel* of the Arab poets with its internal rhyme, Cervantes defines himself as a 'a rare inventor' and takes care to indicate from the beginning that his book is completely different from those which at that time were being published and enjoying public favour. Starting with the prologue, he enters into an imaginary dialogue with the common reader, designed to emphasize the differential sign intended to set his novel apart from the literary system of his time.

The *Quixote* does not reflect, as is commonly said, only the contradiction and the dialectical play between reality and fiction, being and appearance, through the magic prism of its hero's madness.

That opposition – inns/castles, windmills/giants, basin/helmet, noble damsels/harlots, flour mills/fortresses, etc – is, of course, extremely important, but it should not distract us from the capital fact that Cervantes shuts us up in a fantastic gallery of mirrors, a subtle web of signs corresponding to opposing realities. We are reminded at every step of the specificity of the literary phenomenon as we penetrate the book's verbal labyrinth. While in ordinary communication the language code is always taken for granted, to the point that speakers use it automatically and put it, in today's philosophical vocabulary, in brackets, literary language is distinctive in that it offers us some degree of information about its own structure. In the former case, the linguistic structure is simply a mode of transmitting information; in the latter, the literary structure places the emphasis on its own message, rather than on the referent, and the odd thing about it is precisely the information it provides as to its own construction:

> So he decided not to insert any tales, either detached or connected, in this second part, but to include some similar episodes arising out of the actual happenings themselves; and even these should be sparing and no longer than their bare narration required. So, being confined and enclosed within the narrow limits of the story, though he has the skill, the knowledge and the capacity for dealing with the whole universe, he begs that his pains shall not be undervalued, and that he shall be praised not for what he writes, but for what he has refrained from writing. (746)

Like the author – or 'authors' – of the work, the characters of the *Quixote* also show great concern about language and the manner in which facts are related, that is to say the language code, violated by Sancho or the goatherd, and narrative discourse:

> 'Go on with your story, Sancho,' said Don Quixote, 'and leave the road we are to follow to me.'
> 'I tell you, then,' Sancho resumed, 'that in a village in Estremadura there was once a shepherd – a goatherd I should say, for he kept goats – and this shepherd or goatherd, as my story tells, was called Lope Ruiz. Now this Lope Ruiz fell in love with a shepherdess called Torralba, which shepherdess called Torralba was the daughter of a rich herdsman; and this rich herdsman . . .'

'If you tell your story that way, Sancho,' said Don Quixote, 'and repeat everything you have to say twice over, you will not be done in two days. Tell it consequentially, like an intelligent man, or else be quiet.'

'The way I'm telling it,' replied Sancho, 'is the way all stories are told in my country, and I don't know any other way of telling it. It isn't fair for your worship to ask me to get new habits.' (152–3)

Far from being limited to the scrutiny of Don Quixote's library by the curate and the barber, the literary discussion occupies whole chapters throughout the work: in Part One, the innkeeper mentions a valise 'forgotten' by a guest in which two chivalric romances and the history of the Gran Capitán, Gonzalo Fernández de Córdoba, are found. This device, very commonly used in the narrative of the period to insert new stories, gives rise to an extremely interesting discussion regarding the concept of verisimilitude. The debate is reopened later with a defence by the canon of what is artistically credible and a response from the curate which is a subtler version of his earlier point of view. During this exchange, the canon criticizes the structure of the books of chivalry in such a way as to emphasize the contrast between them and the sage and harmonious architecture of the literary object that Cervantes offers us. In Part Two, we find a discussion with the Knight in the Green Greatcoat concerning poetic art and a curious debate about translations and the art of translating when Don Quixote, during his stay in Barcelona, visits a printer's:

'Yet I dare swear,' said Don Quixote, 'that you are not appreciated by the world, which is always loath to reward intellect and merit. What abilities are lost here! What talk neglected! What virtues unappreciated! But yet it seems to me that translating from one tongue into another, unless it is from those queens of tongues, Greek and Latin, is like viewing Flemish tapestries from the wrong side; for although you see the pictures, they are covered with threads which obscure them so that the smoothness and gloss of the fabric are lost; and translating from easy tongues argues no talent or power of words, any more than does transcribing or copying one paper from another. By that I do not mean to imply that this exercise of translation is not praiseworthy, for a man might be occupied in worse things and less profitable occupations.' (877)

The most interesting literary controversy is perhaps the one in chapter 48 of Part One, in which the canon, after finishing his criticism of the unbelievable parts of the books of chivalry, attacks the 'plays being presented these days', that is to say the theatrical works of Lope de Vega. As Vicente Llorens has noted, Cervantes's attack on the books of chivalry would be out of proportion if it did not also imply a critique of Lope's plays, which perpetuated the anachronistic ideals of the *Amadís*, presenting them to the public as actual and applicable values in the context of the time.[5] Moreover, the canon's critique of Lope's popular crowd-pleasing art points out the opposition between Cervantes's subtle literary engineering and the literary canon of the day, affirming, in this way, its specific kind of 'difference'.

The close correlation of the *Quixote* with the literature of its century is evident on all levels of the work, from the most superficial to the most profound. First of all, the book is full of allusions to and quotations from the *Romancero*, the tales of chivalry, the Latin poets, Ariosto, Garcilaso de la Vega, etc. On yet another level, it presents itself to us in its totality as an exclusive literary object, not as a slice of life or of 'reality'. Cervantes does not tell us, as does Benito Pérez Galdós in the prologue to *Misericordia* or Camilo José Cela in that of *La colmena*, that he found the plot of the novel in life, basing himself on observations and studies made of his model on the spot. Cervantes says he found his story in notebooks written in Arabic by one Cid Hamete Benengeli, for which he paid a mere handful of coins and which the last author – that is the say, the compiler – had translated into Morisco Spanish, written in Arabic characters, for 'two pecks of raisins and two bushels of wheat'. The various artifices of the work appear to be enveloped in mist, and it can rightfully be said that the entire fabric of the novel is based on the dialogue of 'the authors who write of this case' (I, 1) with a 'second author' – the compiler – who in turn discovers the work of a third – Cid Hamete Benengeli, who is none the less called the 'first author' – as translated and adapted by a fourth author, since this last one tells us at one point that he does not limit himself to his role of translator and takes on the task of censor and that of exegete as well – whereupon the reader is lost in a labyrinth of conjecture concerning the identity of the narrators as he confronts a text of a text of yet another text: the same technique of infinite inclusion found in nesting Russian dolls or series of Chinese boxes within boxes.

One of the most notable particularities of the novel is that its characters are at once themselves and the literary projections of one of the narrative genres then in vogue. The gentleman of la Mancha has been influenced by literature to such an extent that he becomes a protagonist of the books of chivalry, which means that the norms and the verisimilitude of a very precise and concrete literary code become part of the complex texture of the hero. In his essay on the structure of the *Quixote*, Américo Castro pointedly observes that Cervantes introduces metaphor into the body of the novel not as mere rhetorical figure but as part of the lived experience of his protagonists: 'The windmills are not only giants, but are also the contents of the experience of someone who lives them as such, in close contact with other lives that continue to see them as windmills. The metaphor is no longer what it was for the lyric poet and is transformed into metaphorized existence.' Exactly: when Don Quixote takes the basin for a helmet or the inn for a castle, he is living metaphor from the inside, and something similar occurs, as we shall see, with other characters in the novel.

The irresistible contagion of literature affects not only the gentleman of la Mancha and books of chivalry. In Cervantes's work almost all the characters show themselves to be avid readers of stories and tales: the innkeeper, his wife and Maritornes tell us in passionate terms of their literary tastes and fantasies: other figures inform us about their libraries, as does the Knight in the Green Greatcoat, or confess to us, as does the canon, that they have attempted to write a novel and have 'more than a hundred pages finished'. Literature has addled the brain of Don Lorenzo, as his own father, the gentleman in green, tells us. Some of the characters that Don Quixote comes across are mere projections of the pastoral genre – Marcela, Crisóstomo, Eugenio or Anselmo, for instance. This general receptivity on the part of the heroes of the work to the persuasive magic of reading and their innate propensity for assuming traits of the characters of various literary genres explain the animosity of Don Quixote's niece not only against books of chivalry but against the novelistic genre in general:

He opened one, and saw that it was Jorge de Montemayor's *Diana*, and supposing that all the rest were of the same kind, said: 'These do not deserve burning with the rest, because they do not and will not do the mischief those books of chivalry have done. They are books of entertainment and can do no one any harm.'

'Oh, sir,' cried the niece, 'your worship should have them burnt like the rest. For once my uncle is cured of his disease of chivalry, he might very likely read those books and take it into his head to turn shepherd and roam about the woods and fields, singing and piping and, even worse, turn poet, for that disease is incurable and catching, so they say.' (61)

It must be admitted that the facts bear her out. Momentarily distracted from the business of righting wrongs, Don Quixote is transformed, at the Duke's castle, into a character from an Italian-style novel of love and adventure of the sort that Lope and María de Zayas would later cultivate, and which Cervantes himself tried out in the novelettes inserted in the first part of the book, such as 'The Tale of Foolish Curiosity' or the story of Cardenio and Dorotea. Wooed by the damsel Altisidora, Don Quixote calls for a cittern and decides to respond in verse to her overtures, according to the requirements of the genre. In the same way, at the end of the work when, defeated by the Bachelor Sansón Carrasco, he must renounce the practice of chivalry, he resolves to become a shepherd and live in the countryside, that is, to change from a character of the chivalric genre to one of the pastoral genre and trade in the habits and conventions of the *Amadís* for those of the *Diana*.

In the universe of the *Quixote*, the power of literature is absolute, and nearly all the characters conform to the literary conventions necessary for the credibility of the genre they represent, whether because of their natural inclination or simply because they enjoy playing games: the curate, the barber, Sansón Carrasco and Dorotea disguise themselves as enchanter, damsel, knight errant and spellbound princess and express themselves as would characters in a book of chivalry. The Duke and Duchess, the damsel in distress, Altisidora, and a cast of bit players and servants do likewise in the castle. In this way Cervantes presents us with a sampler of the various literary codes of his time, with the arsenal of techniques characteristic of each, and then proceeds to play the sly game of destroying them in the name of the extraordinary, dazzling literary reality that he creates. The genre of chivalry is continually parodied; we need only remember how the gentleman of la Mancha was dubbed a knight by the innkeeper and two prostitutes. The Italianate genre fares no better: when Don Quixote replies to the damsel Altisidora, accompanying himself on the cittern, his song is interrupted by the racket raised by a bunch of cats with bells tied to their tails, scattering about the room and leaving the hapless knight covered with scratches. In another passage, Don Quixote comes across some shepherdesses framed by the conventional landscape of the pastoral novel; suddenly, a herd of wild bulls with their lead oxen trample the graceful and ethereal characters in the scene and destroy with burlesque violence the unreal atmosphere of that false Arcadia.

The intertextual game that takes place in the work is revealed in a special manner in Part Two, by way of a continuous interplay between what its final compiler tells us and the already published texts of Part One and of the Licenciate Avellaneda. The gentleman of la Mancha and his squire are now characters of Cid Hamete Benengeli's chronicle, printed and sold in thousands of copies, and are recognized as such by the other protagonists of Part Two. The literary discussion, which previously was concerned with genres as diverse as books of chivalry, the bucolic novel, Lope's plays, etc, is now also brought to bear on the first part of the novel. Don Quixote and Sancho often appear to be concerned about the image they are projecting as literary characters in Cid Hamete's chronicle, and other characters, such as Sansón Carrasco and the Duchess, question them about events that occurred in the first part in order to have a clearer picture of confusing or insufficiently explained situations, or to point out contradictions or errors into which the knight and the squire have fallen.

But Cervantes's extraordinary gallery of mirrors acquires a new dimension to the degree that the gentleman and his squire are recognized and recognize themselves not only as characters of Part One but also as characters of the work published by Avellaneda. The latter's attack deeply wounded Cervantes, and in the prologue to Part Two he ironically counters Avellaneda's accusation that his references to Lope were products of envy. He is not content, however, to polemicize from the outside, and following his usual habit, he introduces the debate into the world of the novel itself, beginning a new, audacious and ingenious dialogue between his two heroes and those described by Avellaneda. Thus the Don Quixote and Sancho of Part Two are fully aware of their twofold role as projections, at one and the same time characters of Cid Hamete and of the apocryphal novel, thereby permitting Cervantes to weave a subtle web of relations between the literary projections of the heroes in each of the two works, and in the process point out the manifest inferiority of the one written by his rival.

When Roque Guinart plays host to Don Quixote in Barcelona, he makes clear his preference with regard to the two books, and the knight of la Mancha himself, upon discovering a copy of Avellaneda's work on his visit to the printer's, disdainfully condemns it to the fire that purifies. In Don Quixote's exchange with the damsel Altisidora, she tells him that she saw his enemy's novel consigned to the flames of hell, and the knight replies: 'If it were good, faithful and true it would have centuries of life; but if it is bad, its passage will be short from its birth to its burial' (918). What is even more amazing, the gentleman from la Mancha rebels in a way that today we would call Pirandellian, or in a way reminiscent of Augusto Pérez in Unamuno's *Niebla*, rejects the destiny that Avellaneda has done his best to weave for him, and changes his travel plans in order to deprive the apocryphal author of all authority, clearly showing his story to be false. But the moment when Cervantes's literary game is played most tellingly is in the passage in which Don Quixote and Sancho come across a character from the false *Quixote*:

> 'My name is Don Alvaro Tarfe,' replied the guest.
>
> 'Then I take it,' said Don Quixote, 'that you are no doubt that Don Alvaro Tarfe who features in the second part of the *History of Don Quixote de la Mancha*, recently printed and published by a modern author.'
>
> 'I am he,' replied the gentleman, 'and this same Don Quixote, the principal subject of that same history, was a very great friend of mine. It was I who drew him from his home or, at least, persuaded him to go to some jousts which were being held at Saragossa, where I was going myself. And to tell you the truth, I did him many kindnesses and saved him from having his back tickled by the hangman for his foolhardiness.'
>
> 'And tell me, Don Alvaro, do I in any way resemble this Don Quixote you speak of?'
>
> 'No, certainly not,' replied the guest, 'not at all.'
>
> 'And this Don Quixote,' said our one, 'did he have a squire with him called Sancho Panza?'
>
> 'Yes, he had,' replied Don Alvaro, 'and though he had the reputation of being a comical fellow I never heard him say anything at all funny.'
>
> 'I can very well believe that,' broke in Sancho Panza, 'for it's not everyone that can say good things, and this Sancho Panza you mention, sir, must be a very great knave and a dolt and a thief, all rolled into one. For I'm the true Sancho Panza, and I have more wit than ever rained from the sky.' (926–7)

Cervantes's novel is purely about different stories, discourse about earlier literary discourses which at no time conceals the process of enunciation; on the contrary, it makes it clearly evident. The tale of the character driven mad by books of chivalry thus turns, insidiously, into the tale of a writer driven mad by the prodigious power of literature. If the 'constant play of relations between the parts and the whole on the one hand, and the words and the structure on the other is presented in the form of a spiral in which the number of turns is proportional to the completeness and complexity of the system', in the case of the *Quixote* the helicoidal movement is well-nigh infinite. Cervantes has touched all the keys and played all the registers of the game. For this reason, when today's avant-garde novelists, abandoning the restricting 'realism' predominant in these last centuries, try to return to the genre its possibilities of expression that have been lost or left fallow, they are following, deliberately or not, the path traced by Cervantes.

An analysis of *Three Trapped Tigers*[6] by the Cuban novelist Guillermo Cabrera Infante provides us with an excellent example.

A hurried reading of *Three Trapped Tigers* has led a good number of readers and critics to the mistaken conclusion that is is an uneven work, full of brilliant pages and partial narrative successes, but on the whole chaotic and badly planned. Since its publication, the book has been hailed as a major work, and rather arbitrarily compared with Julio Cortázar's *Rayuela* [*Hopscotch*].[7] These same admirers, after lamenting its verbal juggling, its confused montage, the lack of an overall plan, etc, have often singled out certain passages or chapters, 'She Sang Boleros' or the monologues of 'The Debutantes', for example, at the expense of the rest, considering the remainder of the novel little more than mere fill-in material, an inane joke, a dispensable digression: an opinion admittedly shared by a fair number of readers.

Initially, the facts seem to be on their side: the general structure of *TTT* does not stand out clearly on a first reading. The diffuseness, or better, the strictly controlled disorder of the novel often leads us astray. In a volume dedicated to Cabrera Infante's work,[8] for example, we find an essay containing several important errors: its author confuses Cuba Venegas with Minerva Eros; he fails to see that Ribot, the cartoonist, and Eribó, the bongo player, are the same person; he attributes the brief monologue at the end of the novel to La Estrella, on her deathbed in an oxygen tent, and he judges the dialogue of the last 150 pages between Silvestre and Cué, in which fundamental keys to the book are revealed, to be 'an exercise in tedious inauthenticity', the whole liberally sprinkled with quotes from Mallarmé, Dubuffet, Umberto Eco and other samplings of *à la page* Buenos Aires erudition.

Obscurity, Jean Genet once remarked, is the author's courtesy to the reader. *TTT* is a good example of those works which, instead of obeying the rules of a game known to the reader, invent their own rules as they go along. It is precisely this final victory of the author over the habits of conformity and routine, which in their insidious way slip into every reading, that affords the reader – confused and upset at first, then later on a willing and knowing participant – an aesthetic emotion. As we advance along the tortuous path of the book, we little by little reconstruct the elements that Cabrera Infante has introduced in such a disjointed way. Our reading is thus an active one: it is we, the readers, who must put the jigsaw puzzle together. Cabrera Infante's courtesy consists in his allowing us to collaborate, with our talent and our sensitivity, in the reconstruction of the novel.

In order to attain his objective, the novelist ably plays with 'anachronism' – the relations existing between plot time and the time of the narrative episode within it. Critics have quite correctly pointed out the influence of Sterne: the indirect use of the *excusatio propter infirmitatem*, narration perpetually interrupted by inopportune digression, and in many passages, following the lead of *Tristram Shandy*, the puns, circumlocutions and plays on words become the authentic texture of *TTT*, erasing all vestiges of plot from the novel. In addition, the work's magnificent 'collection of voices' introduces a series of discourses in which intonation, mimicry and audible gesture play a role of the first order. In his introductory remarks, Cabrera Infante advises that the novel be read aloud, a hearing rather than a reading: in this way the rich sonorous wrapping of the word, its acoustic character, acquires a significance independent of its meaning. Often anecdote is less important than miming and gesture, comic or grotesque variations, shocking or peculiar syntactic devices. Cervantes had seen this clearly. He wrote in *El coloquio de los perros*:

> The stories are charming, some of them, in and of themselves; others, in the way they are told; I mean that some give pleasure although they are told without preamble; there are others which must necessarily be clothed in words, along with facial expressions, gestures and changes in the tone of voice, so that something is made from nothing, and a dull spineless piece becomes bold and pleasurable.

The aforementioned features, as well as the influence of the movies, radio, television and the hit parade of the day, have been singled out by the most responsible critics. But *TTT*'s network of connotations does not extend – as is the case, for example, in the works of Manuel Puig – only to the popular culture of the mass media. It also, and above all, embraces the world of books, and like the *Quixote* – in whose footsteps it very often follows, perhaps unwittingly – it is an extraordinary instance of intertextual dialogue.

Cabrera Infante's novel is offered to us as an elaborate and complex literary discourse which is defined and becomes meaningful through its closely woven pattern of relationships with various contemporary models. Bustrófedon's amusing pastiche of the principal Cuban narrators is an opportune reminder that the literary text cannot be judged in isolation, but must be seen, rather, in relation to and in connection with other texts, with a whole system of values and norms that precede it and predetermine its identity, through its imitation, its parody or its rejection of them. Like Cervantes, Cabrera Infante introduces a literary discussion into the body of his novel and creates a work that, as it proceeds, comments on itself, parodies and destroys rival models and erects on their ruins the prodigious framework of its fabrication. The play of correspondences is manifested equally at all levels of the book: *TTT* is full of literary quotations, allusions to writers and works, discussions of the art of translating, etc – exactly like the *Quixote*. The references to Joyce, Hemingway, Faulkner and others are abundant (for example, the jokes and wordplays about 'For Whom the Balls Tell' and 'Beyond-the-river-and-amid-the-trees'). If the world Don Quixote sees is described to us in terms of the *Amadís*, the heroes of *TTT* must also pass through the filter of their literary culture (Conrad, Lorca, André Gide, p. 342; Huxley, and Hemingway again, p. 392, etc). Silvestre and Cué argue as to what literature is or should be, just as the curate and the canon discuss the verisimilitude of the books of chivalry and Lope's plays (357–8). We saw how Don Quixote makes fun of Sancho's repetitive way of telling his never-ending story; in a very funny passage, Cabrera Infante employs a similar technique when he shows us his heroes, during the drive by night with Magalena and Beba, parodying a version of the 'never-beginning story' (419–20). Cervantes's characters frequently talk of their readings and their libraries and, like the canon, confess to us that they have tried to write; Cabrera Infante's trapped tigers seem to be truly obsessed by writing and question each other about their writer's calling: 'Someday I'll write that story,' Silvestre says. The dialogue between him and Cué – an interrupted dialogue, and for that very reason more significant in that it reveals a profound preoccupation – is a good example:

> – Why don't you write? I asked him suddenly.
> – Why don't you ask me rather why don't I translate?
> – No. I think you would be able to write. If you wanted.
> – I used to think so once too, he said and fell silent. (337)

We had been talking. We still were and we ordered a sixth round because the conversation had got around once more, of its own accordion, to what Cué called *El Tema*, and which was neither sex nor music nor even his incomplete Pandects this time. I believe we arrived there on the Gulf Stream of Consciousness, going around and around the subject of words without ever getting to the question, the one and only question, *my* question. But it was Cué who landed first, insisting that I follow him ashore.

> – What would I be then? Just one more average reader? A translator, another traitor? (367–8)

Let us remember that during his visit to a printer's in Barcelona, the gentleman from la Mancha comes upon a translator and discusses the art of translation with him. This topic – translation – is one of the essential ingredients of Cabrera Infante's novel. In the dialogue just cited, Cué answers his friend's question, and then both of them discuss writers and writing:

> [. . .] – Aside from that there is this Montenegro fellow: his *Men without Woman* would be OK if his prose wasn't so underdeveloped; then there are also two or three short stories of Novás Calvo, who is a great translator.
> – Lino? Excuse me! Have you ever read his version of *The Old Man and the Sea*? There are at least three serious mistranslations on the first page alone and it's a very short page. Man, did I feel sorry for him, so I didn't look for more. I hate disappointments but just out of curiosity I looked at the last page. I found that he managed to transform the African lions in the memory of Santiago into *sea* lions! *Morsas*, which is not a morsel but a mouthful of shit! (369)

Later on, Silvestre returns to the attack: 'Ferocious barbarhythms, translated of course from the American. He also says *afluente* instead of *próspero*, *morón* for *idiota*, *me luce* instead of *me parece*, *chance* for *oportunidad*, *controlar* instead of *revisar* and things like that. *Qué horror el Espanglish*. Doctor Esperanglish, I consume. We'll take good care of you one day, Lyno Novás' (399).

At this point, the 'Story of a Stick (With Some Additional Comments by Mrs Campbell)' – a tale inserted in the body of the novel as Cervantes inserts the 'Tale of Foolish Curiosity' or the story of Crisóstomo and Marcela – makes sense: this Mr Campbell, whom we first hear of thanks to the bilingual master of ceremonies of the Tropicana, is the author of a very Hemingwayesque story, of which we are offered two versions in the section entitled 'The Visitors'. The first one, presented second, is a succession of expressions and turns of phrase literally translated from English, which infect the linguistic structure of the Spanish and produce an irresistible comic effect on the reader, while at the same time, and without the tiresome rhetoric we are used to, it tellingly denounces the imperialist penetration of English into the Spanish-speaking world. But the second version – corrected, we later find out, by Silvestre himself – is also, in its way, a betrayal: 'It was terribly hot. There was a low ceiling of fat grey clouds actually more black . . .' ['*Había un techo bajo de gordas nubes grises negras más bien . . .*'] As Emir Rodríguez Monegal says: 'How can one fail to recognize, in the string of adjectives, without a comma, precisely one of the notorious characteristics of the English style of William Faulkner, which his translators (from Novás Calvo to Jorge Luis Borges) acclimatized to Spanish, inevitably betraying the natural course of the language?'[9]

In a very Tristramshandyesque way, Cabrera Infante gives us the key to Silvestre's obsession with the art of translation only in the final pages of the book, an important episode not only because Cabrera Infante slyly inserts himself into the novel as GCI, the editor-in-chief of the Havana weekly *Carteles* – a post he actually held – but also because it motivates the insertion of Mr Campbell's story, an addition that would otherwise have been arbitrary. This obsession follows Silvestre until the last lines of his tale, when, exhausted, he goes to bed: 'dreamiendo soñing of the sea lions on page a hundred and one in the Spanish varsion: *Morsas*: re-Morsas: sea morsels. *Tradittori*' (481).

Faithful to Cervantes's example, Cabrera Infante presents us with a showcase of narrative models with which he wants his novel to be compared, and throws himself into the burlesque game of mimicking them in the name of the differential reality he is creating. The target of these parodies is not books of chivalry or the pastoral novel in this case, but, rather, the works of outstanding Cuban writers. In order to comprehend the purpose of Bustrófedon's pastiches it is indispensable to refer to the already-mentioned literary discussion in the 'Bachata' section, when Silvestre and Cué successively bring up the names Montenegro, Novás Calvo, Piñera and Carpentier, or the passage in the same section in which Silvestre expresses his opinion of José Martí:

> – Is that what it cost to bury Bustrófedon?
> – No, that's what it cost to bury Martí. Sad, isn't it?
> He didn't answer. I'm not a Martian. Neither of us was. I used to have a great admiration for Martí, but there was all this stupid fuss about him, everyone trying to make a saint of him and every politico saying he was his son and sole heir, that I got sick of the sound of the word Martian. I liked the word Martian – or even Marxian – or even, heaven help me, Maritain – better. (437)[10]

'The Death of Trotsky as Described by Various Cuban Writers, Several Years After the Event – or Before' contains imitations of Martí, Lezama Lima, Virgilio Piñera, Lydia Cabrera and Nicolás Guillén. Some are very funny; other are ironically affectionate, such as those of Piñera or Lezama. The cruellest, without a doubt, is that of Carpentier's ornamental style, which often overdecorates the scene as if with cake frosting or papier-mâché, although Bustrófedon admittedly carries the joke too far, and at times it gets away from him.

Even in those passages of the novel that allude to the movies, *TTT* repeats, voluntarily or not, Cervantes's scheme: Silvestre and Cué are transformed into film characters, just as the protagonists of the *Quixote* are converted into characters of books of chivalry or pastoral novels. During his visit to Livia's apartment, Cué identifies with Andy Hardy and David Niven; in the 'Bachata' drive, with Robert Montgomery. At other times, in a spirit of fun, they parody in a very Cervantine way scenes from well-known films, following the lead of the curate, the barber, Sansón Carrasco and Dorotea when they play for Don Quixote the roles of enchanter, damsel, knight errant and spellbound princess: the dialogue of Vincent van Douglas in *Lust for Life*, of Gary Cooper and Katy Jurado in *High Noon*, of *Abbott and Costello Meet the Ghosts*, etc.

The author or authors of Cervantes's novel, like the surname of the protagonist (Quijada, Quesada, Quejana?), are put before us in a dubious and problematic way. The final compiler of the book works with what others have written and the extent of the participation of the different authors is never clarified (Cid Hamete, the translator and those alluded to in the first chapter). As we shall see, the same lack of precision concerning the identity of the person who relates the multiple tales which make up the final structure of *TTT* also affects our reading of Cabrera Infante's novel. To solve the puzzle, we will take a closer look at the section entitled 'Bachata'. Almost all of the 150 pages it takes up – except for the two devoted to the eleventh session of the mysterious woman being psychoanalysed – refer to the drive taken by Silvestre and Cué, absorbed in a long, rambling conversation whose verbal fireworks attempt to hide, without succeeding in doing so, the secret anxiety and anguish of the two trapped tigers. The narrative point of view is that of Silvestre, and the conversation of the protagonists – elusive, full of breaks – little by little reveals the keys – pieces palmed by the author – that will finally permit the reader to put together the whole jigsaw puzzle of the novel (the inclusion of Mr Campbell's story, the personality of Magalena Crus, the end of the story by Cué that figures in 'The Debutantes,' etc).

Cué has recounted a dream to Silvestre (338) and, a hundred pages later, the latter returns to the subject and, in turn, tells Cué the dream of a friend: 'my friend, our friend', 'this cryptic girlfriend [. . .] who's as secretive as yours and almost as obvious' (455). The revelation of the identity of the girlfriend occurs fourteen pages later:

– I'm going to tell you the name of the woman of the dream. She's called Laura.

I was expecting him to hit the ceiling. I'd been expecting it for weeks, I'd been expecting it all day, all through the evening and the early part of the night. I no longer expected it. He didn't even jump up. But I had something you don't: his face opposite me.

– It was she who dreamed that dream.

– So?

I felt like a fool, more than ever.

– It was her dream.

– You've already said it. What else?

I fell silent. I tried looking for something better than the usual pat sayings and catchphrases. A phrase to catch. Words and sentences scattered here and there. It wasn't either baseball or chess, it was a seesaw puzzle. Crisscrosswords.

– I've known her for days. A month or two, rather. We've been going out. Together, that is. I think, I believe, no: I'm going to marry her. (469–70)

In order to understand the secret tension in this dialogue we must go back, in accordance with Cabrera Infante's usual method, nearly three hundred pages, to the story that Cué tells in 'The House of Mirrors' (146–7). In a deliberately elliptical way, Cué mentions the history of his relations with Laura Díaz:

No, there was no love lost between Laura and me that evening, not as yet. There was love, there is, there will be as long as I live, now. Livia knew it, my friends knew it, the whole of Havana/ that is to say the whole world/ knew it. But I didn't know it. I don't know if Laura ever knew it. Livia, sure, *she* knew it: I knew she knew it because she insisted that I come in when I went to look for Laura on June 19, 1957.

I remember now (when the door of Livia's new house opens) another door that closed and the handy, hardy words Laura said and which her suddenly icy tone rendered truly dramatic: *Next time see that you close the door* and she left. I remember her ever-present indifference whenever I went to see her at the TV station and the affectionate coolness in which our relationship ended: phrases like *How are you* and *See you soon* and *So long for now* taking the place of all our previous expressions of warmth, of affection – of love? (153)

The scene in which Laura surprises Cué in a situation of embarrassing intimacy with Livia, and after which she definitely distances herself from him, occurs on 19 June 1957, in other words one year before the late-night car ride during which Silvestre announces his plans to marry her – this is the source of the hidden violence of the friends' conversation. But what is of interest now is a number of scattered elements in the characterization of Laura Díaz, as it appears in Cué's narration: '[. . .] tall girl, *poorly* dressed . . . *simple, down-to-earth* and open beauty . . . she was a *widow* . . . a small blonde and ugly girl. It was *her daughter* . . . today when she is *famous* . . . she works in *television . . .'* (147–53). Let us remember also that Silvestre is a writer, and Laura's dream that Silvestre recounted on page 456, and go on from there to the Mystery Woman's psychoanalytic sessions:

First: 'Did you know that my husband is a *writer*?'
Second: A *dream*.
Third: 'Doctor, do you think I should go back to the *theatre*?'
Fourth: Childhood memory. Implicit *poverty*.
Fifth: Story of the courtship. [What is important is the encounter with the childhood friend, her schoolmate in the *village*, with whom she sat at night on the *sidewalk* of the house. Compare these data with the first sequence of 'The Debutantes' and the two girls' inclination to tell stories, show off and *do theatre* (11–15).]
Seventh: 'I told you a lie on Friday, doctor . . . That boy I was telling you about [the rich one] we never got married. I *married* another boy who I didn't even know.'
Eighth: Another *dream*.
Ninth: 'Didn't I tell you I'm a *widow*?' The dead husband's family took *the little girl* from her, alleging that she lived 'the immoral life of an *artist*'.
Eleventh: Childhood trauma. Another reference to the *husband*.[11]

These scattered data allow us to identify the mysterious woman undergoing psychoanalysis: she is none other than Laura Díaz, Silvestre's future wife. I say *future* because when 'Bachata' ends, Silvestre and Laura haven't married yet. This indicates to us, without a doubt, that the psychoanalytic sessions are set in a time subsequent to that of the plot of the remainder of the novel. Laura is not only Silvestre's wife but has also given up the theatre, as we learn in the third sequence. Referring us in this way to a subsequent period seems to me to be very important since it gives us the key to the structure of the book and the role that Silvestre plays in it.

In the 'Bachata' section, Silvestre – like a character in Cervantes or in *La Lozana andaluza* – looks about for paper and pencil to jot down an anecdote (324), or affirms: 'Someday I'll write that story,' and Arsenio – likewise as if he were a character in Cervantes or in the Delicado novel – alludes to his future condition as a character. After a reference – one far from being coincidental – to Don Quixote, as 'a perfect example of an early contradictory personality' we read:

– What about you and me?
I thought of telling him to be more modest.
– We aren't literary characters.
– And when you write up these nighttime adventures?
– Even then we won't be. I'll be a scribe, just another annotator,
God's stenographer but never your Creator. (442)

As we see, in this passage Silvestre characterizes himself, defining his later work in terms of being a scribe, annotator, God's stenographer, 'but never your Creator'. The observation seems fundamental to me since, like any coherent literary text, *TTT* provides us with information about its own structure:[12] the role of the novelist in it will be that of a scribe, annotator, stenographer – not the nineteenth-century-style omniscient narrator, Jehovah, God and Creator. The time following that of the action set forth in the work thus includes the stage of Laura Díaz's psychoanalysis and of Silvestre's work as scribe, annotator or stenographer, while he constructs or deconstructs for us the admirable edifice of the novel. Silvestre's privileged role is first revealed to us by way of his frequent references to the act of writing ('. . . and I'm taking more time to write it than he took to do it'); moreover, he is the only character to conceive of the work as a volume, a printed novel, with numbered pages, published or ready for publication ('*Titles by commentator*', 348).[13]

The identification of Silvestre as *editor* or compiler of the work is still more precise when he refers to the definitive pagination of the novel that we, the readers, have in hand: 'He told me everything. Or almost everything. The story is on page 53'; 'I was sleeping dreamiendo soñing of the sea lions on page a hundred and one in the Spanish varsion' (481).

The story that Cabrera Infante 'omits' – the quintessential piece necessary in order to complete the puzzle and decipher its disorderly order – is none other than the process of structuring the novel at a time later than that in which the plot unfolds, just as the 'omitted' story of the *Quixote* is the one which could have clarified for us the process of its successive fragmentary creation. By so stating I do not mean to infer that the repetition of the devices of the *Quixote* in *TTT* is always conscious. In my opinion, it is not, as my experience with *Don Julián* proved to me. I didn't discover until later, after the book was finished, that the episode of the flies in the library of Tangier played a role in the internal structure of the book similar to the function of the scrutiny of the gentleman's library by the curate and the barber; in other words, it is possible to 'cervantize' without being aware of it. No doubt this is owed to the fact that Cervantes implicitly explored the latent possibilities of the genre in which he had chosen to express himself, and whoever conceives of the novel as an adventure, no less problematic for being necessary, is obliged to refer to the immense field of stratagems that he explored. If to this we add that – thematically (*Tiempo de silencio*) or structurally (*Juan sin tierra*) – some of we Spaniards are intentionally continuing along the lines of his 'rare invention', it is proof that, by way of Borges or of Américo Castro, the lesson of the *Quixote* has finally forged a path and on both sides of the Atlantic presides over the contemporary resurgence of our novel.

In *TTT*, Cabrera Infante has presented us with facts in a scattered form that none the less fosters the effort to order them. He has cleverly shuffled the materials like a cardsharp and, with a truly praiseworthy courtesy and respect for our intelligence and sensibility as readers, has afforded us the exquisite pleasure of reconstructing them.

Notes

1 See Carlos Peregrín Otero, 'Unamuno y Cervantes', in *Letras* I, Barcelona: Seix Barral, 1972, pp. 172–90.

2 Miguel de Cervantes Saavedra, *Don Quixote* (J. M. Cohen translation), Penguin, 1950, pp. 56 ff. All following citations from the *Quixote* are from this edition, with corresponding page numbers noted in the text [*translator's note*].

3 Américo Castro, 'La palabra escrita y el *Quijote*,' in *Hacia Cervantes*, Madrid: Taurus, 1958. [My translation – H. L.]

4 In *Théorie de la littérature: Textes des formalistes russes* [collected, presented and translated from the Russian by Tsvetan Todorov; introduction by Roman Jakobson], Paris: Seuil, 1965, pp. 76–97. [My translation from the French – H. L.]

5 Vicente Llorens, *Literatura, historia, política*, Madrid: Revista de Occidente, 1967.

6 Guillermo Cabrera Infante, *Tres tristes tigres*, 1967. English translation by Donald Gardner and Suzanne Jill Levine in collaboration with the author (New York: Harper and Row, 1971). The citations that follow are from this edition, with corresponding page numbers noted in the text. The abbreviation *TTT* refers both to the original Spanish title and to that of the translation, *Three Trapped Tigers* [*translator's note*].

7 Although I am not in agreement with the severity of Juan Benet's criticism of Cortázar, expressed in an interesting interview published in the Uruguayan weekly *Marcha* (later closed by government order), there

is no doubt that he is exactly on target when he points out some of the defects and shortcomings of this lengthy novel. In any event, the critics' inadequate comparison of the two works serves only to emphasize the indisputable superiority of *Tres tristes tigres*. Cabrera Infante can rightly claim kinship with Cervantes and Sterne; the laborious construction of Cortázar's *Rayuela* – some brilliantly successful sections notwithstanding – is more in line with the experimentalism of Gide's *Les faux monnayeurs* (*The Counterfeiters*).

8 Julián Ríos, ed., *Guillermo Cabrera Infante*, Madrid: Fundamentos, 1974. See in particular the excellent articles by Emir Rodríguez Monegal and Julio Matas.

9 In Julián Ríos, ed., op. cit.

10 Something of the sort is happening today in Spain with the process of beatification of Antonio Machado, 'the Good' – a beatification which demonstrates a total lack of understanding on the part of its well-intentioned promoters of the teachings of Mairena. How long will our so-called literary historians persist in the typical, caricatural Spanish custom of dividing writers into Bad Ones and Good Ones?

11 My emphasis throughout in the two sections above [J. G.].

12 We find the same structural information and, ultimately, indirect references to the process of their own creation in two fundamental Spanish novels of the postwar period: Camilo José Cela's *La familia de Pascal Duarte* and Luis Goytisolo's *Recuento*.

13 It is true that on page 290 Códac refers to himself as 'this anonymous scribe of latter-day hieroglyphics,' but we know that it was Silvestre who gave him Bustrófedon's 'memoirs' to copy, and we can deduce that, once transcribed, they returned to the hands of their former owner.

Terra nostra

I

I believe it was André Gide who established a distinction between those literary works which, on first appearing in print, find a ready-made audience all prepared to appreciate their value, and those which must create, laboriously and at times extremely slowly, their own audience in order to be understood. These latter works – especially those which by virtue of their boundless ambition, their attempt at total synthesis, or their radically new mode of expression fail to fit the categories and canons of the criticism of the time – very often give rise to a sort of uneasiness and anxiety that is betrayed by two reactions long familiar to psychoanalysts: violent rejection or absolute silence. In a world such as the Spanish-speaking one, barren of any genuine critical spirit or tradition, where the literary work is, so to speak, a monster born of the cultural limbo, the usual response of the so-called 'powers that be' is to play deaf and dumb. So it was with the one great Spanish novel of the nineteenth century: I am referring, it need scarcely be said, to Clarín's *La Regenta*. So it has been and so it will always be in our world every time that our 'critics', with their puny, miserably inadequate arsenal of critical weapons, are confronted with a work that does not conform to the supposed laws of their rhetoric. Literally disarmed, powerless and helpless, the reviewer – or rather, the penny-a-liner, since no other term properly describes the scribbler who is the victim of a cruel lack not only of culture but of the true spirit of criticism – prudently takes refuge in silence. As proof of this, one need only leaf through the annals of Spanish literary life in the last ten years, a veritable telephone book of lists of authors and prizes in which, as though by sheer happenstance, there is no mention whatsoever of the few rare innovative works published during this period, thus bearing out the truth of José Angel Valente's astute observation concerning the cultural atmosphere of the Hispanic Peninsula: in the face of the idle prattle, the vacuity, the mutual back-scratching that is the general rule, it is silence and only silence that has any meaning.

Another way of dealing with the censored work – a work, that is to say, which the penpushers cannot or do not care to analyze – consists of condemning it *ab initio,* of dismissing it out of hand. To do so, a few phrases of the work will be pounced on and cited out of context, whereupon the author will be demolished in the name of a supposed intellectual or moral superiority, from the stronghold or behind the bulwark of a seemingly 'ideological' position. Or better still: the work will be anathematized on the basis of the writer's political stance; the latter will be roundly repudiated in order to free the hack reviewer of the painful, irksome necessity of examining the former. It will be said of the author, for instance, that he is 'a young man brought up abroad who nostalgically creates imaginary ties to the mother country by way of European interpretations of Mexican mythology'; that 'he has chosen to be a high-ranking and highly-favoured civil servant, having at his entire disposal the prestigious, publicity-garnering platform provided by his Government'; and finally, there will be a reference to 'his latter-day lameness as an independent writer.'[1] Such a method, which is perfectly valid as a way of evaluating Carlos Fuentes's political trajectory, providing that it is employed with a modicum of fairness and common decency, becomes downright impertinent if it is used as a weapon or a battering ram to demolish a work as rich, as substantial, and as thought-provoking as *Terra nostra.*[2] To condemn the novel merely on the basis of the fact that its author holds an official post awarded him by Mexico's single-party government would be as absurd as it would be to summarily dismiss Quevedo's *Sueños* on the sole grounds that it was a work written when he was an agent of the Duke of Osuna, or to reject, as the Spanish Right recently did, the admirable criticism of Manuel Azaña simply because of its author's wholeheartedly detested secularism. Rather than being genuinely critical, such an attitude has all the earmarks of a familiar brand of critical terrorism, although in this case, fortunately, it does not have behind it the evident powers of the State.[3] The violence of a great number of 'ideological' attacks scarcely conceals the totally irrational, visceral nature of their perpetrators' reactions. Reason, as Jonathan Swift once remarked, is a skittish steed that can readily throw its rider. To judge *Terra nostra* to be 'the traditional interpretation of the mother country by a colonial country', one of those *romans de pays chauds* that are an integral part of 'culture for export', or to characterize the work of the novelist as being an expression of the 'culture of despotism in which the writer is a solitary petty dictator incapable of conversing' is not even to undertake an ideological – and hence reductive – interpretation of a vast, complex and frequently self-contradictory novel. Such a priori judgement totally disregards the specificity of the literary work it claims to analyse, turns it into the OK Corral of a vicious settling of accounts disguised as an ideological battle, manipulates it, and endows it with an irreducible prior essence that will be used as the *deus ex machina* of the demonstration. By going about their task with such Manichaean rigidity, the so-called critics do not define or characterize either Fuentes or *Terra nostra*: they define only themselves, and characterize only their own method.

One of the usual tactics of critical terrorism (whether or not it is backed by the power of the State) is to create a grotesque image of the author (I know from personal experience what that means) or of the work, making it out, for instance, to be an impenetrable, confused, chaotic hodgepodge (the tactic successfully employed by literary critics in the case of Góngora's poetry, and unsuccessfully in the recent case of Lezama Lima's *Paradiso*) – so that the potential reader comes to associate it in his mind with the label 'unreadable'. The ambition, difficulty and deliberate excesses inherent in *Terra nostra* thus make it the ideal candidate for transformation into a scarecrow-image of a work, which is quoted from (in order to tear it to pieces) but not read, and the mausoleum of an author whom the hack critics would like to see buried in it once and for all. But these overeager gravediggers forget that *Terra nostra* belongs to that category of novels which, like *Ulysses* or *Under the Volcano*, little by little create, through the text alone, an audience of fanatically devoted readers. 'A great creative work', Maurice Nadeau has written with reference to Malcolm Lowry's novel, 'is not easily opened to the four winds: it looms up as a closed world, bristling with defences and surrounded by towering walls, that can be penetrated only by attempting again and again to scale its ramparts and by 'breaking and entering'. The notes I shall now put before the reader are intended to aid him in his attempt to scale the ramparts and to 'break and enter', to guide his first steps within Fuentes's disturbing and fascinating fortress through which it is necessary to make one's way with the utmost caution, on tiptoe, testing the ground inch by inch in order not to land in the pitfalls, traps and snares that the novelist has treacherously set for us. The total occupation of the castle, the safe arrival at the end of the perilous journey will convert, I am certain, the successful perpetrator of the crime of breaking and entering into yet another aficionado, yet another passionate devotee of this difficult and demanding novel that is related both to the radical experiments of our contemporary literary avant garde (Guillermo Cabrera Infante, Severo Sarduy) and to the ambition to stand as a total synthesis that marks the most outstanding works of fiction in Spanish that have appeared in the 1960s (Mario Vargas Llosa's three major works; Lezama's *Paradiso*, García Márquez's *Cien años de soledad* [*One Hundred Years of Solitude*].

II

According to the author of the review previously cited, *Terra nostra* presents an image of Mexico as

> a tropical country [. . .] that cannot and must not change its history but, rather, accept the mythology that present-day world capitals have assigned it, [that] will never aspire to democracy because its colonial essence is surrealism, schizophrenia, superstition; [whose] political life has nothing to do with class struggle, as in countries with a human face, but instead is rooted in sempiternal Azteco-Hispanicism [. . .] Criticism, dissidence, independent thought [. . .] would therefore be undesirable things: emissaries of the bloodthirsty gods of destruction because they do not respect 'National Unity', without which everything is apocalypse.

In a word: what Fuentes purportedly proposes to his readers is 'despotism as inescapable destiny'.

To extract from a work a few paragraphs or sentences setting forth ideas which are then attributed to the author himself as representing his philosophy is an undertaking as misleading as it is dangerous. The elements constituting a novelistic work take on their true meaning in the inner dynamics of the narrative circuit and are the transmission line, so to speak, of a message that transcends, limits or contradicts – depending on the circumstances – what is conveyed by the words or phrases that have thus been artificially isolated. Hence an ideological interpretation – or reduction – of the text of the narrative meets with a series of stumbling blocks that frequently are the undoing of the

critic whose intention is to enlighten the reader: it is as improper to
impute to the author the thoughts or opinions of his characters as it
is to take for the expression of reality what may in certain instances
be no more than a stylistic device. The components of a novel find their
justification and demonstrate their validity not as static elements that
can be isolated and analysed independently of the whole of the work,
but rather in their living, ever-changing, dynamic interaction with each
other within the work. This by no means excludes the possibility of an
ideological interpretation of the narrative text – though it is incumbent
upon anyone who undertakes such an interpretation to proceed with at
least a minimum of logical rigour and plain common sense. The task
is even more complicated in the case of a novel such as *Terra nostra*
because of the continual shifts of narrative perspective and the splitting
of personalities or changes of identity of the 'persons telling the story'.
Hence, without attempting in any way to be exhaustive, we shall extract
with a pair of tweezers the most significant reflections of the narrators
or speakers on the theme of History, and endeavour to establish the
existence of various trends of thought, some of them contradictory,
with regard to it.

The fatalistic vision of the past that our critic decries is indeed quite
apparent at certain points when the narrator – in this particular case
the chronicler Fray Julián – rejects the 'ingenuous and mendacious
chronologies' of linear history and stoutly maintains that 'true history
is circular and eternal': 'Men learn nothing. Times change. Settings
change. Names change. Passions are ever the same. None the less the
enigma of the history I have recounted to you is that, despite the fact
that it repeats itself, it has no end' (658), or again when this same
chronicler – who should not be confused with Carlos Fuentes – insists
that even though the earth may not be mad 'the men who inhabit it are;
and their madness is a movement such as you describe: ceaseless and
circular, forever ending up at the same tired, well-worn starting point,
though they are persuaded that they have reached some new shore'
(305). A vision which, proceeding from the general to the particular,
from the abstract to the concrete, may be summed up in the bitter
reflections of the leader of the guerrilla band fighting the Yankees, after
he has brought into focus on the film screen and in his imagination the
sombre images of the history of Mexico:

> [. . .] all that just for this, you ask, so many millennia of struggles
> and suffering and refusal to yield to oppression, so many centuries

of invincible defeat, a people rising up again and again from its own ashes, to wind up with this: the ritual mass murder of the beginning, the colonial subjection of the start, the blithe lies of the end, yet another time?' (737)

But as we shall see, Fuentes alternates the expression of a historical pessimism on the part of his characters and a much more nuanced vision which, while taking into account the repeated failures of the past, none the less does not resign itself to fatalism or passivity (and in this regard it is significant that despite the gloomy reflections on his part that we have just cited, the guerrilla leader continues the struggle against invasion by the US). Ideas, the elder of the One-Way-Street Synagogue says, 'never become fully realized. From time to time they go into seclusion, they hibernate like certain animals, they await the opportune moment to reappear . . .' (545). From the point of view of the narrators, the repetition of the cycles of history is not necessarily absolute or inevitable: the need for revolution, for the material and moral progress of mankind continues, as strong as ever, despite the failures, the errors, the bloodbaths that it has everywhere left in its wake. To call them to mind is not a sign of helpless resignation, but precisely the contrary. As one narrator, Guzmán, remarks: '[. . .] nothing is forgotten more quickly than the past, nothing is repeated as often as the past' (514). The awareness of this is therefore an indispensable step to be taken on the steep, arduous path that will one day permit history not to repeat itself. To point out, as the Lord and Master does, that 'on the day when all of you will be seated on my throne, you will be obliged to learn everything all over again starting from zero, and will hence commit the same crimes in the name of other gods: money, justice, that progress of which you speak' (327) is not an invitation to the reader to stand by with arms folded and do nothing: it helps him, rather, to understand the downfall of idols enthroned by those very persons who refuse to learn the lessons of history, and rather than purging it of its sins and crimes, stubbornly continue to put their grim, rational abstractions before us with a sort of smiling, complacent fatalism. Today, when the political vanguards of the most advanced societies face the need for a revolution that will avoid at all costs the errors of so-called authoritarian socialism, such a warning from the past takes on an eminently cathartic and constructive purpose. In this regard, the aim of the rebellion that Pedro dreams of, by contrast to Celestina's shining utopia, is instructive: 'to forget our own code of brotherhood and actively destroy those who are not worthy of it' and to justify doing so by the argument that 'we must defend ourselves, for if we are destroyed we will be unable to offer any sort of example' (123), or in other words, to champion the conquest of freedom through precisely those methods of tyranny against which one is fighting is the kind of perverted logic that has led, as we realize today, to the horrors of the Gulag and psychiatric clinics for devationists, is it not? To remind us – as did Rosa Luxemburg in her celebrated polemical exchange with Lenin – that if the new society for which men fight 'could be established without rivals it would soon degenerate into a reign identical to the one that you are combating' (483) strikes me as rather less pessimistic than the attitude of certain Marxists of the old school, who persist in putting the present system of the Soviet world before us as the sole possible model of revolution (an attitude as fatalistic and as resigned as that of those pertinacious Catholics with whom I consorted in my early years, stubborn believers who were apparently happy in their knowledge that, because of original sin, their descendants would be, *in saecula saeculorum*, as wretched as they were). Moreover, there is another troublesome question that is all too familiar to those of us who have at one time or another excused the crimes of 'institutionalized' revolution in the name of a supposed historical necessity: '[. . .] will not that oppression have been even worse than mine', the Lord and Master asks slyly, 'since I am not obliged to justify my acts in the name of freedom whereas they on the other hand are so obliged?' (623) – words that take us to the very heart of the controversy that has been raging within the worldwide leftist movement ever since Khrushchev's traumatic revelations in the face of the spectre of Stalinism that could not be conjured away.

The ideological debate that runs through the pages of *Terra nostra* cannot leave us indifferent, inasmuch as it takes up many problems that those of us who believe in the ideals of justice and progress must necessarily confront. The attentive reader will glimpse between the lines a subtle denunciation of the compensatory mechanisms employed by those who justify today's avoidable evils in the name of imaginary future paradises. Over and against the familiar – and false – assertion that 'new worlds are born only through sacrifice' (209) and that 'there have always been men who have been sacrificed', there rings out, like a cry of hope, the impassioned invocation of the *hic et nunc* by the rebel leader: '[. . .] my history, neither yesterday nor tomorrow but today I wish to be my eternal time, today, today, today' (737). Justice and freedom here and now, won painfully, step by step, without allowing

a single inch of them to be given up in the name of some supreme
later perfection; taking as the point of departure the fact that the
real, concrete man is irreplaceable; living and glorifying the instant,
through the daily struggle for an immediate terrestrial heaven that
does not waste and destroy human beings for the good of future
generations; abandoning the Christian notions of guilt and sacrifice
in favour of the reappropriation of the body and the attaining of a
social order whose aim is to promote physical, material and moral
well-being for all rather than the conquest and monopoly of power
for the benefit of a few. Saying *no* to stoicism disguised beneath the
mask of the 'new man': proudly proclaiming, rather, that one is just
another '*Epicuri de grege porcum*'.[4] The historical thought in which
the episodes of the novel are steeped – set forth from the shifting,
contradictory points of view of the various characters who alternately
take on the role of narrator – appears to oscillate, as we have seen,
between two diametrically opposed ideas – the necessity and the failure
of revolution – without ever definitely opting for either one. No one,
least of all in the intellectual world, can sincerely claim to be unaware
of the abysmal gap that separates the revolutionary undertaking whose
aim is to abolish the fundamental injustice of the capitalist world and
the more or less oppressive reality of the new revolutionary societies
that have thus far been created. This dilemma is still with us, and we
shall resolve it (as Jean-Paul Sartre stated in an interview I had with
him for *Libre*, a review that has now disappeared) only by way of a
long and difficult struggle against the world based on the exploitation
of the human being, wherever that exploitation makes its appearance
– whether it be in the name of the old idols of the world from which
we are emerging, or in the name of those that await us on the road to
the longed-for future revolution.

III

The meditation on History in the pages of *Terra nostra* is not limited
to the sort of abstract ideas and principles that we have just considered.
The novel is above all a cruel and penetrating vision of Spanish history
and its prolongation in the New World through the Conquest. Here
too the accusations of pessimism and fatalism – reality seen as a 'sick
dream' – that have been levelled against Fuentes would appear to have
some foundation. The perspective of the novelist that emerges from the
various shifting focuses of the narration is proof, as we shall attempt to

demonstrate later, of the seminal influence on our literature of the ideas of Américo Castro and his interpretation of a land – Spain, Hispanic America – 'exhausted by so many battles, so many crimes, so much heroism, so much unreason'. According to the novelist's detractors, Fuentes paints far too dark a picture. But let us consider a few examples and judge for ourselves. The history of Spain: 'the chronicle of inevitable misfortunes and impossible illusions' (257); Spaniards: 'heroes only because they would not disdain their own passions but rather, would follow them through to their disastrous conclusion, masters of the entire realm of passion but mutilated and imprisoned by the cruelty and the rigidity of religious and political reasoning that turned their marvellous madness, their pure excess, into a crime: their pride, their love, their madness, their dreams – all punishable offences (253); our appointed destiny over the centuries: 'to purify Spain of every plague of infidels, to tear it out by the roots, to mutilate her limbs, to have nothing left save our mortified but pure bones' (101); the ruling principle of our leaders: 'servitude, slavery, exaction, homage, tribute, caprice, our own will sovereign, that of all the rest passive obedience, that is our world' (300); the reality for their subjects: 'Give us your lives, your paltry treasures, your arms, your dreams, the sweat of your brow, and your honour so as to keep our pantheon alive' (79); Spain: 'look at how it closes its doors, expels the Jew, persecutes the Moor, hides itself in a mausoleum and rules therefrom through the names of death: purity of the faith, purging of the blood, horror of the body, prohibition of thought, extermination of the incomprehensible' (568); Spain again: 'century upon century of death in life, fear, silence, the cult of sheer appearances, hollowness of substance, imbecilic deeds of honour, look at them, these miserable realities, look at them, hunger, poverty, injustice, ignorance: a naked empire that imagines itself clad in golden raiment' (ibid.); the Conquest: 'let Hell be built in the New World; let its necropolis rise on the ruins of pagan temples; let Spain congeal outside of Spain' (511); Hispanic America: 'the same social order translated to New Spain; the same rigid, vertical hierarchies; the same sort of government: for the powerful every right and no duty; for the weak, no right and every duty' (743); our past: 'luxurious marble prisons for the dreams of the dead, but never enough chains for the dreams of the living' (276); our future: 'a blind, stubborn and painful return to the fantasy of the future in the past as the only possible future of this breed and of this land, of Spaniards and of Spain, and of all the peoples descended from her?' (659).

Let us interrupt this enumeration at this point and take a look, if only a very brief one, at the historical context within which the gestation of this novel took place. When *Terra nostra* was published in 1975 the panorama offered by the Spanish-speaking world was not one that inspired much hope. Let us refresh our memories a bit. Spain: dictatorship, repression, censorship, the total absence of any of the timidly progressive institutional structures that had been permitted by even the most conservative governments of the past century; Latin America (with the exception of Cuba): hunger, wretched poverty, exploitation, illiteracy; Spain: execution by firing squad of the five revolutionary militants, mass demonstrations by Spaniards, one arm upraised in defence of our sacrosanct values, the interminable death throes of the dictator (orchestrated by epigoni of Goya and Valle-Inclán at their very best); Chile, Argentina, Uruguay, Paraguay, Bolivia, Guatemala, the Dominican Republic: legalized violence, terror, assassinations, torture; Chile: Pinochetism is reborn and adopts as the government's programme the Falangist cry of *Viva la muerte!* Argentina: the poverty of the political thought of a Left capable of pinning its hopes for revolution on the return of Perón, who is looked upon as an instrument of the future Marxist revolution, leads to a situation that even within the perspective of this outlandish doctrine is without precedent, whereby the destiny of the country is entrusted to a nightclub performer and an astrologer (another grotesque episode reminiscent of one of Valle-Inclán's *esperpentos*); Peru: the thwarting of the revolutionary aspirations of the masses by the new military caste that is ruling the country; Mexico: corruption, demagoguery, the concentration of power in the hands of a very small minority; the Caribbean countries (including Cuba): one-crop agriculture, bossism, the army as the only institution, political and economic dependence on a great power (the US or the USSR); throughout the Spanish-speaking world: the arbitrary power described in *Tirano Banderas* (Valle-Inclán yet again!), humiliations, powerlessness, lack of freedom, the impossibility for the masses of determining their own destiny. This is the naked truth, and the objective existence of an immense revolutionary potential (against which the International of repression is mobilizing its forces all over Latin America) or of genuine hope for the future (as is demonstrated by the case of Spain since the death of Franco) does not prevent a certain amount of pessimism from being not only excusable but indispensable. A national awareness of their wretchedness on the part of the Spanish-speaking peoples is not a recent phenomenon: to limit ourselves to the Hispanic Peninsula, the work of our best writers, from Blanco White and Larra to Cernuda and Luis Martín-Santos is steeped in it and nourished by it. As one of their number, the poet Jaime Gil de Biedma, mournfully noted:

> Of all the stories in History
> the saddest is surely that of Spain
> because it ends badly . . .

Fuentes lapses into this sort of pessimism, but his acute awareness of misfortune does not stifle his hope of vindication: '[. . .] in all of history, your grace, there cannot be nations more in need of being what they were not than those that speak and will speak your language' (568). When Valerio Camillo reminds us that 'by knowing what was not, we know what cries out to be', his words foreshadow the conclusions of the character (Polo Febo, the chronicler, the shipwreck victim, Cervantes?) who is addressed in the familiar form by the anonymous voice that takes up the narration of the last sequence, dealing with 'the least fulfilled, the most miscarried, the most latent and longed-for of all histories: that of Spain and Spanish America' (775). Everyone knows of this longing, hears this outcry, but what is so desperately sought is not to be attained within the framework of a work of literature, but in the daily struggle of our peoples for justice, progress and freedom.

To scoff at Fuentes's historico-poetic vision as being evasive and unrealistic is to fall into the error of accepting the canons of a shallow and mechanistic realism which continually confuses life and literature, thereby demonstrating that it does not understand either of them very well. The 'total alliance of imagination and reason beneath the deceptive appearance of delirium' that was attained and transmitted to us through the genius of Goya apparently continues to disturb an entire school of critics – those who remain entrenched behind the precepts and prejudices of nineteenth-century realism. (So-called socialist realism is probably the most reactionary aesthetic doctrine of our time and its enthronement as official dogma in the USSR reduced the rich literature of that country during the 1920s to the frightful desert of fanaticism and conformism with which we are all familiar.) To say that in *Terra nostra* 'the words are interchangeable, the facts reversible, [and] mythologies turn into a drug trip', that in the end 'the whole thing may or may not be a dream or an insane vision', or that it is 'a hallucination or a nightmare recorded as nightmares presumably ought to be recorded: confusedly, chaotically, irrationally' does not serve to enlighten the reader as to the aims of the novel; in fact it does precisely the contrary.

Since drugs are mentioned in general and abstract terms – as though the reviewer in question were passing on mere hearsay – I shall permit myself to describe my own very limited personal experience with one specific drug: *kif*. After inhaling a few pipefuls of this herb – and I am referring to the leaves of *cannabis sativa* and not to its concentrated preparation in the form of *maxún* or hashish – the smoker begins to apprehend reality in a different way than usual, though without losing touch with it, as happens with *maxún* or with hard drugs, of which I have no knowledge. His objective, then, is not to substitute an artificial relationship to the herb for his normal relationship to social reality. It is not an attempt to escape. In the *kif*-smoker's modification of the real, he is seeking a new vision through the alteration of his visual and auditory perceptions. But the 'normal' relation does not disappear; it remains as a fixed point of reference throughout the experience; it is always possible to resume it whenever the smoker chooses. *Kif* does not replace or blot out reality; it confirms and gives a new dimension to our experience of it. This ambivalent and enriching relation makes our enjoyment of *kif* very much akin to the pleasure we sometimes receive from literature.[5] Naturally our stern 'ideologues' are completely unfamiliar with such sensations, thereby resembling those pitiable married couples who limit their erotic play to the swift and utilitarian act of procreation.

Let us take another look at Carlos Fuentes's novel with this in mind. As the reader makes his way through the fascinating hall of mirrors that reflect both the world and each other, he never loses sight of real history. Though the novelist has thoroughly assimilated the admirable lesson of Goya and put it to striking use, he none the less remains scrupulously faithful to the rational and objective vision of the historians. Even though it takes on the appearance of a dream or of madness, his historical nightmare never employs these latter as a substitute for real past history. At each step of the way the reader is able to return to real history, and then plunge once again into the novelist's deliberately distorted and often grotesque perception of things. Even in the most delirious and most dreamlike passages – the magnificent scenes, for instance, with the Madwoman, the dwarf Barbarica and the doltish Prince in the rotting-chamber of the Hapsburgs – there appear, at times as a sort of sudden brief powder-flash, at times in the form of parody or incantation, reminders of a real and specific history with which the novelist – as well as the Spanish reader – is perfectly familiar.

I mentioned previously the influence of Américo Castro – one of the very few Spaniards to have possessed that analytical imagination of the past without which the historian becomes a pedestrian compiler of meaningless trivia. 'History shares the methods of science and the vision of poetry,' Octavio Paz has written. This fundamental vision or intuition of Castro's has demonstrated its seminal power not only in the field of historiography but also in that of literary creation.[6] When I say this, the first case that naturally occurs to me is my own, but that of *Terra nostra* is even more obvious. In no way does the novelist's stimulating and unconventional method of confronting our past, his interpretation of tradition, at once critical and creative (thanks to which one and the same 'linguistic character' sums up in his person the physical traits of an entire dynasty and consorts at will with the chroniclers of the Indies and Cervantes, with Don Juan, the Comendador, and Celestina), preclude our interpretation of real history: as in the case of the *kif*-smoker, it serves Fuentes as his basic point of reference. As proof, here is a brief list of the extraordinary sequences in which, by way of the discourse of one or another of the characters, the author reminds us, if perchance we need reminding, of the continuing existence of our 'normal' relation to the past, which is in no way distorted – complex, yet clear, almost dazzling history lessons on the crisis of the nobility (147–8); the birth of the new bourgeois class (322, 507, 518); the two sides of the coin (Cortés and Las Casas) of the Conquest of the New World (661, 662, 708); the historical role of gold in the Indies (710); the different directions taken by Spain and England as the result of the differing scale of values of the two peoples (650–1); the intellectual persecution of the Jews, unleashed by the Holy Office (504, 512, 513); the genesis, development and failure of the Communes of Castile (637–56), etc. By contrast with the grim Spain which, after having subjugated the Moor, expelled the Jew, and crushed the freemen of the towns, will stubbornly cleanse its soil of 'traitors, queers, blasphemers, infanticides, murderers disguised as physicians, poisoners, usurers, witches, profaners of the Holy Spirit' (515), Fuentes offers us a timely reminder of the existence, beyond the walls of its necropolis and its gloomy, austere façade of unity, of another Spain, 'an age-old, original and varied Spain, the work of many cultures, plural aspirations, and different interpretations of a single book' (624). The character Mijail ben Sama, the Lady's lover, who is found guilty of the 'abominable sin' (sodomy) and sentenced to be burned at the stake, is a symbolic personification of that common, multidimensional space in which the coexistence of creeds and cultures permits the development of a free and democratic society: the antiphony he chants before the Lord and Master in the last pages of the novel counterpoints the concepts of community, tolerance, doubt, diversity and life on the one hand, and power, repression, faity, unity, death on the other. The sinister image of what was does not exclude the presence of what might have been and may one day be if we Spanish-speaking people resolve to work towards that end – lucidly, energetically and unremittingly. An active reading of *Terra nostra* does not take us on a drug trip that does away with our relation to the real: on the contrary, it offers us the larger-than-life double vision, at once 'normal' and distorted, of the *kif*-smoker.

IV

It goes without saying that the novelist can allow himself to take a number of liberties with the past that would be unthinkable in the case of the historian. Hence *Terra nostra*'s author performs sleight-of-hand tricks both with chronology and with the real-life existence of historical figures. Philip, the Lord and Master, builder of the Escorial and champion of the faith, is the son of Philip the Fair and the hapless recluse of Tordesillas, and assumes by turn the physical features of various monarchs of the Hapsburg dynasty down to Charles the Bewitched; Joanna the Mad is transformed at one point into Mariana of Austria and at another into the Empress Carlota of Mexico; the discovery and conquest of America are presented as contemporary with the Comunero movement and the construction of the pantheon of the Escorial, etc. The confusion is further compounded by the fact that these symbiotic characters, whose physical features constitute a composite portrait, are all alive at the same time, consort with each other, and are dealt with on the same level of novelistic reality as such purely literary creations as Inés, Don Juan, the Comendador or Celestina. As Mario Vargas Llosa has remarked, speaking of Martorell: 'The novelist creates from *something*; the total novelist, that voracious being, creates from *everything*.'[7] For Fuentes history and literature become one: history can be read as literature and literature as history. By weaving the fabric of his novel with threads from both, the novelist demonstrates to us 'his wish to use, with no exceptions and no scruples, all of reality as a work tool'. This extremely free use of the imagination to further an aesthetic purpose invariably enrages or irritates those self-styled philosophers who seek to extirpate from the human mind the faculty that leads us to paint invisible worlds' and who would gladly 'convert us into a species made of rough stone and mortar, on which only a hammer would make a dent or an impression'.[8] The liberties Fuentes takes with our cultural patrimony are the sign of an omnivorous creative appetite. His imaginary museum impartially houses novels and chronicles, paintings, legends, sciences, myths. But these liberties are much less gratuitous than might appear at first glance. The normal relation with history, we repeat, is always present as a point of reference, in the form at times of what would seem to be the most trivial novelistic details. Let us skim off one example from among a hundred: the fact, recorded in the annals of the period, that the young emperor Charles was greeted in Spain on his arrival from Flanders with the shout: 'Close your mouth, dolt!' turns up in the novel in the form of Fray Toribio's remark to the Lord and Master: 'Close your mouth, Your Highness, for Spanish flies are most insolent.' The novelist's uninhibited play of imagination thus disguises the care that he has taken to copy the historical reality down to the smallest detail, with a patience worthy of a miniaturist of the old school. All the precepts of realism are applied with great felicity in the novel, though they are incorporated and juxtaposed in such a way as to be unrecognizable to those who refuse to stray from the well-worn path of hackneyed literary convention. Fuentes's meticulous reconstruction of historical reality takes as its point of departure not only chronicles and annals but also literary texts and above all certain major or minor Spanish, Flemish and Italian paintings. We will find the best example of this 'unreal realism', as we shall now see, in the extensive passages in the novel devoted to the necropolis of the Escorial and the hallucinatory cortege of the spectres of kings and queens belonging to the dynasty and the fierce, monstrous, or ridiculous figures in their retinue.

The cult of death, the fatalism disguised as serenity of spirit, the stiffness of movement, the frozen, motionless ceremonial in which the Hapsburg dynasty slowly immures itself, are described by Fuentes with the pen of a master. When Joanna the Mad asserts that 'there is no decadence possible when the will to lose predominates over the will to gain' (189) or when the Comendador remarks to Guzmán that 'the dynasty of the Lord and Master confuses honour and loss, [. . .] like the magpie which, without profit to anyone, steals every glittering object it spies and hides it in its barren nest' (507), when the phantoms of the royal mausoleum dream of a universe entirely given over to mortification and death, 'power and loss, honour and sacrifice, nothingness – we will vanquish [our foes], we will impose the reign of nothingness there where they turn their eyes full of hope, for each step forwards that they take we will take two backward, we will trap the icy expanse of the future in the icy expanse of the past' (510), what might be taken to be a lugubrious invention of the novelist is in fact the literary expression of a historical reality. 'Spanish history was made by passionate enemies of life,' Luis Cernuda has written. Let us leaf through the pages of *No importa de España* by Francisco Santos (1639–1700), for instance, and stop for a moment to contemplate his awesome portrait of Philip II:

> He was enjoying peace and tranquillity when Fortune clamoured: 'Behold, Sire, a kingdom has risen up in arms against you and those who swore fealty to you have proved to be traitors.' What mortal would not be moved by this news to vengeance and wrath, which are the passions that cause one to be beside oneself? But with that fixed expression peculiar to him and in an unusually stern tone of voice he said: 'Thanks be to God; let a forty-hour litany be recited in my chapel . . .' 'Have you taken leave of your senses, Sire?' 'No.' 'But the Armada has been lost.' 'Thanks be to God; let the chapel be informed of the forty hours, and let the convents hold a rogation.'[9]

An arbitrary creation on the part of the novelist? No, for the Spanish past frequently defies all reason and surpasses our powers of imagination. The monarchs of the Hapsburg dynasty appear to have had a secret obsession: to build 'a hell on earth' in order 'to ensure the need of a heaven' so as to compensate themselves and their wretched subjects for the paralysing horror of their lives. When the Madwoman says to Philip: 'Take good care of your corpses, my son: let no one rob you of them; they will be your descendants' (222), the Lord and Master is already that 'inverted father' who 'disengendered us', of whom José Angel Valente speaks in his eloquent 'Corona fúnebre' dedicated to our last absolute sovereign.[10] The extraordinary monologue of the Queen Mother – who has suddenly been transformed into Mariana of Austria – on the subject of the dolt seated on the Gothic throne ('[. . .] crown him forthwith, so that his head may become accustomed to the weight of the crown, he is five years old, he cannot yet walk, his nursemaid must still carry him about in her arms, he has not yet learned to talk, he can communicate only with dogs, dwarfs and buffoons, he is becoming torpid, rigid, a stammerer, a helpless weakling') (712), is the

terse, condensed transcription of the contemporary accounts of Charles
the Bewitched referred to in Sarrailh's book on the Enlightenment. As
for the minutely detailed portrait of the Lord and Master – jutting jaw,
thick pendulous lower lip, leaden eyelids, lifeless eyes, as motionless
as a wax figurine – it is proof of the scrupulous care with which the
novelist has followed the written testimony of chroniclers even though
he shuffles the order of facts and events with the hand of an expert
prestidigitator. Let us compare, for example, the portrait of Philip II
left us by the French traveller Antoine de Brunel:

> [. . .] his demeanour is customarily so grave that he moves about
> and comports himself as though he were an animated statue.
> Those who have had an audience with him assert that during
> the time that they have spoken with him, they have never seen
> him shift position or change place; that he received them, heard
> them out, and answered them with the same set expression, there
> being nothing mobile about his person.[11]

We thus discover that, as in Goya's painting of Charles IV and María
Luisa, Fuentes has not used too dark a palette at all: sheer fidelity to
reality has permitted both painter and novelist to enter the realm of the
fantastic and the hallucinatory.

Fuentes's fascination with the spectres of the House of Austria is
accompanied by an equal or even greater fascination with the edifice
that serves them as their tomb: the Escorial, as so admirably evoked
by Cernuda in his poem 'El ruiseñor sobre la piedra' ['The Nightingale
atop the Stone'] and the 'ragged and burning' tableland that supports,
surrounds, enhances and magnifies it. The palace 'conceived in the mortified mind of the Lord and Master' (85), the temple of the Eucharist,
the citadel of Faith, the fortress of the Holy Sacrament, the tabernacle
of stone, the necropolis of princes, the marvel of the ages which, in
accordance with Philip's vow, was to be 'the work of my entire lifetime,
the pantheon of my ancestors, and the mausoleum of my own mortal
remains' (192) is described in great detail, its implacable austerity, its
perfect frozen symmetry the symbol or the concrete realization of the
dream or the nightmare of the history of Spain:

> [. . .] a granite quadrilateral, as tall as it is wide [. . .] like a
> Roman camp, severe and symmetrical, or like the grill on which
> St Lawrence was tortured to death [. . .], a fortress of straight

lines that forever recede in the distance on the boundless plain and the endless horizon without a single concession to caprice, like a dressed block of grey granite set on a platform of polished white stones whose contrasting alabaster gleam would cause the structure to appear even more sombre. (99)

As a background for this abode of the phantoms and mummies of the dynasty, the Castilian *meseta* that the Madwoman traverses with the catafalque of her lecherous husband does not correspond to the idealistic and uncritical image of it created by Menéndez Pidal, Azorín or Unamuno, but rather to the much more penetrating and realistic vision of a George Borrow or his translator Manuel Azaña as they divest it of its mythical aura of grandeur – as Martín-Santos was also to do in his *Tiempo de silencio [Time of Silence]* by showing it to be a mask or a disguise for wretched poverty, neglect, melancholy, monotony. A rotting-chamber, a necropolis, a pantheon, a mausoleum, the beauty of the Escorial is intimately linked with the obscene cult of death and its works which from the reign of Ferdinand and Isabella onwards slowly stifled Spanish culture and culminated in that Fascist cry of *Viva la muerte!* that we have already mentioned. The agony of Lord and Master Philip is recounted in *Terra nostra* with an awesome wealth of detail that betrays both the horror and the fascination it holds for the novelist:

> [. . .] once the abscess had been lanced, the physicians removed a great quantity of matter since his thigh had become a great pocket of rot that extended more or less down to the bone. Because of its enormous size Nature, not content with the opening that the physicians' art and steel had made, made other holes herself through which the Lord and Master expelled such a quantity of pus that it seemed a miracle that a subject so badly wasted away had not drowned in it [. . .] When he was not vomiting, he was seized with a flux of the bowels resembling goat excrement, that flooded the black sheets of the bed with green faeces [. . .] Thus that bed turned into a putrid manure pile, which continually gave off the most noisome odours: the Lord and Master was lying in his own dung. (748–51)

This preciseness of detail, not unlike that of a medical bulletin, will doubtless cause Spanish readers to call to mind certain more recent events in their country, though in point of fact these latter had not yet taken place when Fuentes penned the following prophetic lines:

> [Philip] opened his eyes and gazed at [the relics] placed next to the bed, the bone of St Ambrose, the leg of the Apostle Paul, and the head of St Jerome; three thorns of the crown of Christ, one of the nails of His Cross, a fragment of the True Cross, and a shred of the tunic of the Most Holy Virgin Mary; and, leaning against the bed, the miraculous cane of St Dominic of Silos. (749)

For that very reason the thinly veiled allusion to Franco's Valley of the Fallen – which Jean Genet also had in mind in *Le Balcon* – is not at all gratuitous. The 'homunculus, the mandrake root, the offspring of gibbets and stakes' that Philip will discover seated on the Gothic throne is a historical constant that the genius of Goya and of Valle-Inclán brilliantly captured in their works. Fuentes's historical imagination is not simply an oneiric game that masks reality and perpetuates myths, as our incorrigible defenders of a superficial, one-dimensional reading have written of García Márquez's *Cien años de soledad*. Many crimes have been committed in the past, are being committed today, and will be committed in the future in the name of ideology, and perhaps the gravest and most infamous of these lies in the fact that – just as patriotism is the last refuge of scoundrels and the priesthood frequently that of fools – it is used as a shield or a bunker by zombies in order to conceal from the eyes of the public their abysmal lack of ideas and their insufferable lack of sensibility.

V

Fuentes's creative imagination – like that of Lezama in *Paradiso* – is often nourished by a vast imaginary museum of oil paintings, frescoes, engravings. Some of these are readily identifiable: El Greco's 'Dream of Philip II', Signorelli's 'Last Judgement', Hieronymus Bosch's 'Garden of Delights', Goya's 'Royal Family of Charles IV'. Others belong to that common heritage or store of memories shared by all of us whose day dreams or reconstructions of our history were first inspired by the plates and reproductions that customarily illustrate grammar-school textbooks. Once again, the novelist's pen, sketching in as it does a wealth of minute particularities intended to create an 'unreal realism', succeeds in portraying a series of unforgettable scenes in which the prose seems to take on the concrete texture of a fabric, becoming a canvas saturated with colour, light, movement, sensuousness. There are descriptions, for instance, of Joanna the Mad, most likely seen through the filter of Padilla's portrait of her: '[. . .] and behind her, drawn by six slow-moving horses, escorted by another company of halberdiers, the huge, forbidding, black funeral coach, like a vulture on wheels' (65); of Philip, the Lord and Master, as in the grave and noble portraits of Velázquez: '[. . .] lips and jaw thus masked by the beard and silky moustache and by the folds of the high ruff that hid the neck and separated the head from the trunk; above the throat the head was reminiscent of the body of a trapped bird' (155); of the Lady, a prisoner of the frozen ceremonial of the court: '[. . .] ten years of speaking in phrases prepared for the occasion, of learning to walk tall and straight, as rigid as a hunting hawk poised on my fist (unfailing symmetry: as countrywomen walk to the fountain with a pitcher on their heads, so it is with my falcon and me)' (166); of a court page, likewise a figure out of Velázquez, black hose, black leather pumps, black gloves holding the sticks of the black drum, and a face which 'gleams, in the midst of so much blackness, like a golden grape' (66).

Fuentes's pictorial prose and his appeal to the visual memory of readers are particularly noticeable in the hunting scenes and in his many evocations of a bestiary whose plastic values are once again reminiscent of the genius of Lezama: portraits of the mastiff Bocanegra lying at the feet of the Lord and Master; of a pack of famished hounds, 'a river of glistening flesh, with tongues glowing like sparks'; of the Lady's mind-haunting falcon: 'Such is the union of the avian feet with the woman's gloves that the bird's talons appear to be an extension of the greased fingers of the gauntlet' (49). In other passages, the phantasmagorical discourse of the narrator transports us to the canvases of Velázquez and El Greco, to Goya's *caprichos*, and to Buñuel's films (scenes with the dwarf Barbarica, dressed in a tattered wedding gown, drunk and surly, belching and farting), or into the company of the grotesque courtiers and royal mummies conjured up by the cruel hand of Antonio Saura (whom the novelist ironically transforms into the surgeon who first operates on the putrid body of the Lord and Master and later autopsies the rotten corpse).

The richness and variety of resources of *Terra nostra* would merit a separate chapter. In the face of the impossibility of discussing all of them in detail here, we shall limit ourselves to calling the reader's attention to just a few of them.

One of the most striking and most successful devices is the abrupt shift in narrative point of view (at times without the unwary reader's even noticing), passing from first-person narration to second, and even to a personal narration (since in the final analysis that is what the recounting of events from the point of view of the novel's 'he' is equivalent to), and simultaneously rendering objective and subjective reality in one and the same passage with patent scorn for the rules of discourse that ordinarily govern expository prose:

> And the father pushed Celestina away from the little girl, daughter, sweetheart, what's happened to you? who hurt you? look at your mouth, that bastard of a butcher? no, this witch here, this sorceress, this woman in rags, hey, all of you, grab that wicked woman, look at my little girl's mouth, get her, run, Celestina, tear down canopies, trample pigs underfoot, a house, a stairway, dogs are barking at you, flies are buzzing at you, damp rooms, chamber pots full of shit, madmen are screaming at you, I've just seen the devil, straw on the floors, conceal yourself, hide, they're going to burn you, witch, run, wait, night is falling, the marketplace gradually empties, they forget the incident, through the little peephole of your hiding-place you gaze at the city on the promontory [. . .] (543)

In this passage, the rapid shift of narrative points of view is achieved through an accelerated rhythm in which the words seem to run, to hurtle along, to flee on and on, like Celestina herself, sweeping up everything in their path in a great flood that carries off pell-mell even the most firmly-rooted linguistic and literary conventions, leaving in its wake the destruction and death of all canons and rules, a catastrophe without precedent in the eyes of the wretched priests and guardians of the basic principles of language and the sacrosanct grammatical conventions of fictional narration.

The description of the siege and sacking of the heretical city by the troops of the Lord and Master (54–6), the shipwreck victim's ride in the Madwoman's funeral coach (84), the arrival of the latter, with the corpse of her husband, at the necropolis of the Escorial (186–91), offer us other examples of this pluridimensional narrative that situates us simultaneously inside and outside the consciousness of the characters, a narrative that achieves its greatest success and reaches its high point in the pages devoted to the rebellion of the *comuneros* (633–56) – a multidimensional space in which different voices converge and speak in turn, assuming one after the other the task of relating events from different perspectives, a transition from Euclidian geometry to the geometry of Einsteinian space, from a motionless narrative universe to the relativism of Copernicus, from the laws of conventional harmony to the fruitful exploration of atonality: a polyphony of voices, the recounting of all sorts of events, historical chronicles, the superimposition of grammatical persons, Guzmán, the workers and craftsmen of the Escorial, the Lady, Philip, Don Juan, Sor Inés, the *comuneros*, the Madwoman, inside the subjectivity of the characters and outside, acceleration again, the trampling underfoot, the flood that levels, devastates, totally destroys canons, laws, principles. The multiple perspective, the story that reflects itself and appears to contemplate itself brings us back once more to Velázquez, whose seminal influence is transparent in one of the most highly charged and meaningful moments of the book – the sequence entitled 'Todos mis pecados' ['All My Sins'], devoted to the contemplation of a painting from Orvieto (in reality Signorelli's 'Last Judgement'):

> The group of naked men turn their backs on the Lord and Master and the Lady to look at Christ; the Lord and Master looks at the downcast gaze of the Christ and the Lady looks at the little tightly constricted buttocks of the men. And Guzmán will look at his master and mistress who are looking at the painting. Ill at ease, he will look upward: the painting is looking at him. (96)

As the secret painter of the canvas, Fray Julián, says: 'I paint in order to look, I look in order to paint, I look at what I paint, and what I paint, on being painted, looks at me and in the end looks at you who are looking at me as you look at my painting' (343). The novel, like the friar's composition in the style of Velázquez, is a gallery of mirrors in which the intruder – the reader – is reflected and lost in the vertigo of an infinite duplication of his own image.

In other passages the speeded-up narration, reminiscent of Delicado's dialogues or of silent films, allows Fuentes to sum up the entire history of Mexico (736–7) with a violence akin to that found in several chapters of another Mexican novel which has been unjustly neglected: *José Trigo*, by Fernando del Paso. The rich repertory of narrative resources that Fuentes sets before us with such bravura is almost never employed gratuitously: the novelist does not dissociate what, for mutual understanding (though with little conceptual rigour), we ordinarily term 'form' and 'content' by resorting, as do so many mimetic avantgarde writers, to the use of complex narrative devices to express simplistic ideas devoid of either daring or vitality. *Terra nostra* is a synthesis, achieved by a form of writing that makes no distinction between the two terms: a work that emerges and takes shape, as Pere Gimferrer notes in his discerning review of the book, through the active intervention of a literary architect of a new type: the *voyeur*, the intruder, the reader.[12]

VI

Who will remember a single act that has not been set down in writing?

One of the most fascinating characters in *Terra nostra* appears to be obsessed by that fetishism of the written word, so common in Arabic poetry, which makes no distinction between the thing and the sign. For the Lord and Master, the mere recording of a fact suffices to make him believe in its autonomous existence: only what is written remains; reality becomes identical to writing. 'Write,' he orders Guzmán: 'nothing really exists unless it is consigned to paper; the very stones of this palace are smoke so long as its history is not written' (111). The monarch exercises absolute dominion over his subjects, a reflection of that exercised by God over the universe. A symbol of the unity and the immutability of the theology professed by Scholasticism, Philip clings to a rigorous code of certainties, a single fixed vision of the world and of objects: '[. . .] all words and all things have a set place, a precise function, and a perfect correspondence in the Christian universe. All words signify what they contain and contain what they signify' (673). Confronted with this idolatrous cult of the written text, the chronicler envisages the possibility of a Copernican reading, in which the text would cease to be the fixed and flat world of narrative before Cervantes and instead become a tissue of relations, a vast warp and woof of correspondences, attractions and repulsions, centrifugal and centripetal forces – author and readers, reality and writing:

I then thought of that knight whom Ludovico and his sons chanced to meet inside a windmill and I began to write the story of a gentleman from la Mancha who continues to believe in the laws of certainty. For him nothing would be uncertain, yet anything and everything would be possible: a knight of faith. That faith, I said to myself, would come from reading. And that reading would be a form of madness. The knight would stubbornly cling to what he believes is the one possible interpretation of the texts and would apply it to a reality that has become multiple, equivocal, ambiguous. (673)

The reference to the *Quixote* is neither fortuitous nor pointless. Fuentes's ambitious novelistic exercise is a deliberate exploration of the literary space opened up by Cervantes. The man from la Mancha, Fuentes reminds us, is not only a hero in a novel born of the reading of books of chivalry: he is also the first character in fiction who knows that he is read and who changes his behaviour as a result of this reading.[13] Literary works – and this is the great lesson of the *Quixote* – thus cease to be closed, untouchable worlds, constituted once and for all and mummified for the convenience of hordes of scholars: later readings and interpretations modify them. If the reading of Cervantes has left its mark on Borges, there is not the slightest doubt that Borges has left his mark in turn on our reading of Cervantes today. Works of literature influence other works, and this influence is reciprocal, operating in two directions: if the past acts on the present, the reverse is also true, and once the present has in turn become the past, it will both influence and be influenced by the future. Summing up the literary discovery that the *Quixote* represents, the chronicler tells us that 'it will leave open a book in which the reader will know himself to be read and the author will know himself to be written' (674).

Like *Paradiso*, *Tres tristes tigres*, *Recuento* and other works that are clearly descendants of the *Quixote*, Terra nostra contains numerous references and statements of the author regarding the structure of the novel that he is writing – a characteristic which, as we have said elsewhere, distinguishes literary language from everyday language governed by norms that we automatically obey. The novelistic space in which the action of *Terra nostra* unfolds is that new world evoked by Fray Julián, 'where knowledge can be reborn, rid itself of the immobility of the icon, and reach out to infinity, in all directions, over all of space, toward each and every era of time' (617). Rejecting the convention of the linear story, marked out on a flat narrative plane, in which events are presented in the order in which they occurred, fixed for all eternity (its characteristic verbal tense: the preterite), the Lord and Master, overcome by one of his fits of diabolical rebellion against the order that he has respected and that has enslaved him, counsels his scribe: 'Sow doubts, Guzmán, recount all the histories possible and ask yourself again why we choose only one version from this deck of possibilities [. . .]' (207). These doubts and possibilities will be spread out in a fan before the reader's eyes, spurring him to intervene, to abandon the passive role of the person obliged to accept one and only one version of the facts, of what has really happened, against which he is powerless. The new reader discovered by Cervantes will retain his total freedom of choice, selecting whatever interpretation he likes, reconstructing in any way he pleases events and episodes presented in an incomplete and confused fashion; in a word, he will participate in the process of construction of the novel by way of multiple contradictory readings. To assert that the novelist behaves like a 'despot' towards his creatures or is 'a solitary petty dictator incapable of conversing' are words that aptly describe Ian Fleming, Corín Tellado, and the authors of so-called 'popular' or mass-market books in general, but not, I need scarcely add, Carlos Fuentes. The narrative space of *Terra nostra* is a free space, open to dialogue and the intervention of the reader aware of the fact that 'nothing is beyond belief and nothing is impossible for profound poetry that relates everything to everything' (310). Like García Márquez and the authors of books of chivalry, Fuentes believes in the pleasure of improbable fantasies that allow a mouse to gnaw away the restored virginity of the Lady or the members of the Hapsburg dynasty to turn into members of the animal kingdom and to fly, as Isabella does, with bits of various corpses in her beak. Metamorphoses, transformations, anachronisms which, instead of controverting the order of the real, confirm it and enlarge it – a 'total' realism, in the sense in which Vargas Llosa employs the term: objectivity and subjectivity, acting and dreaming, reason and miracle. In one of the conversations between Fray Julián and the Chronicler, the former urges the latter to write a book in which there will be allied

the real and the virtual, what was and what could have been. Why should you tell us only what we already know, without revealing to us what we still have no knowledge of? Why should you describe to us only this time and this space, instead of all the invisible times and spaces that ours contain? Why, in short, should you content yourself with the thin trickle of the successive, when your pen offers you the fullness of the simultaneous? (659)

An empty pride in the sheer powers of invention? A freedom which, by dint of proclaiming itself absolute, becomes merely a hollow boast and an airy caprice? No, for as Fray Julián offers us the timely reminder, the writer is forever 'bound to the earth by the chains of accursed reality, which imprisons, diminishes, weakens and levels everything'. But this is far from being an evil – as Cervantes and his perspicacious admirer Blanco White are well aware – since 'without the horrid gravity of the real our dreams would lack weight, they would be gratuitous, and hence of little worth and scant conviction. Let us be thankful for this battle between imagination and reality that gives weight to fantasy and wings to fact, for birds cannot fly without the resistance that the air offers them' (660).

In the manner of Picasso and Joyce, as described by Hermann Broch,[14] Fuentes engages in a systematic 'sacking' of the whole of Spanish culture. For one thing, he borrows entire phrases from Fernando de Rojas, Cervantes or the chroniclers of the Indies and incorporates them in his own narrative (a trick typical of the author of the *Quixote*); for another, he transforms the world of the novel into an imaginary museum in which the paths of all manner of disparate literary characters meet and diverge (thus bringing us back once again to the *Quixote*): Celestina has a chance encounter with the Knight of the Mournful Countenance, takes up with Dulcinea and Don Juan, brings about a meeting between the latter and Sor Inés, and so on. In his literary voracity, Fuentes does not scorn the use of age-old devices characteristic of storytelling in all times and places, but – and herein lies the difference as compared with conventional novelistic narration – he employs them to weave a radically new overall pattern, a sort of dizzying *summa* of storytelling. Manuscripts found in a sealed bottle are used, for just one instance, to interpolate a story of the same type as The Story of the One Who Was Too Curious for His Own Good inserted by Cervantes in the *Quixote*; and above all there is Fuentes's vast gallery of storytellers, whose function consists of extending to infinity the Chinese-box technique of the story within a story within a story (like the series of men on the Quaker Oats box, each holding a box with a man of ever-diminishing size), with the tale of Celestina ('This is my story. I wish you to hear my story [. . .]') apparently functioning (though this is by no means certain) as the frame story for almost the whole of the novel, into which there are interpolated tales told by the Lord and Master, Fray Julián, the shipwreck victim, the blind flautist, etc, until the narrative loses itself and the reader in the vertigo of its endless, all-embracing proliferation.

As in the *Quixote*, once again, the one possible reading offered by traditional works of fiction is superseded by alternative or multiple interpretations that preserve our freedom of choice and judgement, thus conferring on what would appear to be merely an aesthetic undertaking a profound moral justification that quite obviously goes beyond the limits of literature.

VII

A few words, finally, concerning the plot of *Terra nostra*. As in an entire sector of the contemporary novel, the most significant and most dynamic one, the story line takes the form of a deliberate, intricate tangle, thus entrusting to the reader the arduous but exciting responsibility of disentangling its many threads. Corollary number one: the abandonment of the conventional paternalistic attitude on the part of the writer, who 'orients' and indoctrinates an audience, offering it everything in a fabricated, premasticated form, in favour of an attitude that is much more respectful of that audience's intelligence and sensitivity. Corollary number two: the writer takes for granted the existence of a free, mature reader capable of figuring out the rules of the game proposed and competing with the author in the enjoyable match play of 'reconstructing' the work.

Terra nostra begins in Paris, on the eve of the year 2000. A fictional character, Polo Febo – who is maimed in one arm, as is the Chronicler who will dream of writing the *Quixote* – is present at the birth, amid most unusual circumstances, of a child with six toes on each foot and a mark in the form of a red cross on his shoulder. A mysterious missive, signed 'Ludovico and Celestina', announces the child's coming into the world, an event which has been awaited for centuries, and orders that he be baptized Iohannes Agrippa. After having witnessed a veritable epidemic of similar births, Polo Febo meets Celestina by chance on a bridge spanning the Seine. She appears to recognize him, though she addresses him by the name of Juan. The young one-armed man falls into the Seine and as he is drowning in its waters, the woman throws a sealed green bottle into the river, and suddenly turning into a Scheherazade, tells us the thousand and one stories that will constitute the novel.

Let us follow some of the main threads of the narrative. The principal story line of Part I of *Terra nostra* centres on the arrival at the Cape of Disasters, some five centuries ago, of three shipwreck victims – all of whom have twelve toes and a red cross on their shoulders – who have been washed up on those deserted shores by the tide, along with three sealed green bottles, each containing a manuscript. The first of the three shipwreck victims (Iohannes Agrippa?) is rescued by Isabella, the virgin wife of Philip, the Lord and Master (44–5), who hides him in her bedchamber and takes him as her lover (163–73); he is then transformed into Don Juan (291), seduces servant girls and nuns, obtains the favours of Sor Inés, kills the Comendador in a duel (534), and finally is turned into a stone statue inside the royal mausoleum (345). The second twelve-toed shipwreck victim, cast up by the sea on the shores of the Cape of Disasters wearing an odd mask of feathers, is rescued by the Madwoman, Philip's mother (65); transported to the funeral coach of her lecherous husband, he is next seen dressed in the latter's garments (as meanwhile the dead monarch appears clad in the shipwreck victim's rags and wearing his feather-mask (83–4), and eventually he becomes the cretinous Prince sequestered in the apartments of his benefactress; proclaimed the royal heir by the Madwoman and her female dwarf, he chooses instead to slip into one of the sarcophagi in the royal rotting-chamber and repose there, alongside Don Juan and the corpse of the Lord and Master, amid the other spectres of the dynasty (301–2). The third shipwreck victim, found on the shore by the pageboy-drummer (in reality Celestina in disguise) is taken by the latter, along with the sealed bottle, to the mausoleum-palace where the other two have ended up (255–8); he lives there with Celestina and the blind flautist until he is one day seized, along with the two of them, and enlisted in the corps of guards of the Lord and Master (316); brought into the monarch's presence, he relates the story of the voyage to the New World that constitutes all of Part II of the novel (the idyllic society of the Siboneys; Aztec myths, cruelty, blood sacrifices). As we have said previously, Fuentes recounts events in bits and pieces, completely rearranging the chronological order and shuffling the details about as though he were doing card tricks, with the deliberate intention of keeping the reader on the alert and forcing him to remain on the *qui vive* at every moment as he reads, as though the slightest distraction or lack of attentiveness on his part might cause the thread of the artist's narrative to be lost (or his very lifeline to be severed). The meetings of characters as perfectly identical as his shipwreck victims allow the novelist to apply the most effective technique of the mirror-image narrative (an *I* seen as a *you*, a *you* seen as an *I*) already employed in two of his earlier novellas, *Aura* and *Cumpleaños*. A vast accumulation of miraculous happenings and odd events, the action of Part I of *Terra nostra* could be summed up in the question: 'Why three of them? Why the cross? Why six toes on each foot? And, above all, why in this whole strange wide world the three of them here?' (269).

The answer is forthcoming in Part III. But in order to find it, readers must first patiently tie up the many loose ends that lie strewn throughout the space of the novel (for a purpose that is the exact opposite of that of the pebbles that show the way in the tale of 'Tom Thumb') and fill in as best they can the gaps in a narrative that, to employ an expression used by English-speaking critics, we might describe as 'unreliable'. The identity of the three shipwreck victims is revealed to us little by little, in fragments, and despite the silences or the omissions of the narrators (as in Celestina's story, and even more particularly, in the Lady's story). The first of the three (and here I am reconstructing an order of events that is not the same as that of the novel) is the son of Celestina and the lecherous king, who is the husband of the Madwoman and the father of Philip: on the day of the young girl's wedding with a blacksmith, the king demands the *droit du seigneur* for his son, and when the latter proves incapable of exercising it, the monarch himself deflowers the virgin bride (116), who later gives birth in the Jewish quarter at Toledo to a son who bears the mark of a red cross and has six toes (527). The origins of the second, the offspring of a female wolf, whose birth has been witnessed by Celestina (140), are not revealed to us until much later in her tale, when she recounts the fornication of the king (who robbed her of her virginity) with the animal, which has been caught in a trap (545–6, 665). As for the third and last, the presumed son of the Wandering Troubadour, it will be necessary to follow the trail through the veritable jungle of flashbacks, deliberate omissions and false accounts of events in the stories told by a number of characters: the child discovered by Azucena in the buffoon's bed of straw (115, 339), who is later rescued by Ludovico and Celestina as Philip's troops are about to slaughter the rebel forces and takes refuge with the two of them in the Jewish quarter of Toledo (523, 525, 571), also turns out in the end to be a son of Philip the Fair, by Isabella, his future daughter-in-law, whom the monarch has raped when she was still practically a child. Hence the three shipwreck victims turn out to have the same father and to be half-brothers thanks to the lechery of Philip the Lord and Master; Isabella, left a *virgo intacta* by her spouse, whose hymen is broken by her future father-in-law and repaired by a procuress (Celestina?) before it is gnawed away by the mouse, thus knowingly sleeps with her own son (or with one of his two half-brothers who look exactly like him) when she makes love to the shipwrecked lad whom she hides in her bedchamber; Celestina, who has caught the 'French disease' from the sovereign when he violates her, will in turn transmit it to her offspring, young Prince Philip, the heir to the throne and future ruler. Transmutations, caroms, multiple encounters ricocheting like cannon shots round about the three lads and their corresponding sealed bottles, from the Jewish quarter of Toledo to Mexico to Spalato and Venice, where Ludovico and the Lord and Master's three bastards attempt to decipher their fortuitous shared fate in the 'memory theatre' of Valerio Camillo.

The origin of the mystery involving the number three is revealed to us in one of the scrolls sealed inside the two bottles covered with sand that Philip finds in his spouse's bedchamber (the third bottle has been left behind by one of the three survivors of the shipwreck in a cell in the palace, when Guzmán, organizing his own hunting expedition, came to fetch him) (757), entitled 'The Manuscript of a Stoic'. During the last days of the reign of Tiberius, we are told, the slave Clement, the servant of Tiberius's rival Agrippa Posthumus, is metamorphosed into the latter after having assassinated the emperor and been flung in turn to his death from the top of the cliffs of Capri. Before dying, the Roman despot put the following curse upon his enemy:

> May Agrippa Posthumus be one day born again, multiplied by three, from the wombs of she-wolves [. . .] and of the three sons of Agrippa, may nine other sons be born, and of the nine, twenty-seven; and of the twenty-seven, eighty-one until unity shatters into millions of individualities [. . .] And since the cross of infamy will prevail over these future lives, as it prevailed over the death of the Jewish prophet El Nazir, may the sons of Agrippa, who will bear the cross on their shoulders, be called by the Hebrew name of Yehohannan [. . .] (702)

The scribe Teodoro – who also happens to have six toes on each foot – has drawn up the chronicle in triplicate and placed the scroll in three large green bottles, sealed with Tiberius's imperial signet.

The beginning and the end of *Terra nostra* thus represent the working-out of a curse or a prophecy whose fulfilment is at once the cabalistic key of all of history and the organizing principle of the novel. I am here anticipating the outcry that will be forthcoming from ideologues who cling to the certainty that time is progressive, linear – as they have a perfect right to do. But scornfully to dismiss the 'circularity' imposed on real history for the purpose of constructing a work of literature that 'bites its own tail' – an artistic convention likewise employed most effectively by García Márquez in the final pages of *Cien años de soledad* and by the author of the *Divine Comedy* long before him – as simply an attempt to 'erase from the reader's mind all recollection of reality' and to 'perpetuate ignorance and myth', as has been written of the Colombian novelist's work – is to be hopelessly blind to the distinction between reality and novelistic technique.

Our reading of *Terra nostra* has admittedly left a fair number of loose ends: some of them can be tied up by attentive readers after their own assault on the imposing fortress of the book by escalade and by stealthy breaking and entering; others in all likelihood can never be neatly tied together and will linger in the mind of the breacher of its walls or the intruder as an insoluble enigma. As Carlos Fuentes says by way of one of his characters: 'Every human being has the right to take a secret to the grave with him; every storyteller reserves the right not to clear up mysteries, in order that they may remain mysteries; and anyone whom this displeases may ask for his money back.'

Notes

1 José Joaquín Blanco: 'Más allá de la lectura, las intenciones monumentales', in literary supplement of *Siempre*, Mexico City, 1976. We refer to this attack throughout the present essay.
2 Carlos Fuentes, *Terra nostra*, Mexico City: Joaquín Mortiz, 1975. Numbers in the text are keyed to this original Spanish edition, and all translations in this essay are my own. The complete translation into English is Margaret Sayers Peden's *Terra nostra*, New York: Farrar Straus and Giroux, 1976. [H. L.]
3 One wonders why the criticisms levelled against Fuentes do not appear to apply to other high-ranking, highly favoured civil servants who, thanks to their governments, have at their disposal a far more prestigious and powerful platform (in so far as it allows them to silence all criticism) – as is the case, for instance, with Nicolás Guillén and even Alejo Carpentier. The obvious differences that exist between the two 'institutionalized' revolutions in Latin America are not a sufficient justification for this phenomenon. Or

can it be that the independence of the intellectual, so passionately defended by the critics when it is a question of Mexico, is of no concern when it is a question of Cuba?

4 'Pig belonging to Epicurus's herd'. Horace's description of himself in his Epistle to Tibullus – his way of poking fun at the stern language of the Stoics [*translator's note*].

5 We find a good example of this in the fine novel of the Mexican writer Luis Carrión, *El infierno de todos tan temido*, Mexico City: Fondo de Cultura Económica, 1975.

6 The final monologue of the protagonist of Martín-Santos's *Tiempo de silencio* is also proof of its author's well-assimilated reading of Castro's *La realidad histórica de España*.

7 Mario Vargas Llosa, *Carta de batalla por Tirant lo Blanc*, Madrid: Alianza Editorial, 1969.

8 José María Blanco White, 'Sobre el placer de imaginaciones inverosímiles', in Vicente Llorens, ed., *Antología de obras en español*, Barcelona; Labor, 1971.

9 Julio Rodríguez Puertolas, *De la Edad Media a la edad conflictiva*, Madrid: Gredos, 1972.

10 J. A. Valente, 'Corona fúnebre', in *Cuadernos de Ruedo Ibérico*, Enero 1976.

11 Julio Rodríguez Puértolas, op. cit. The same rigidity and statue-like appearance is noted in the descriptions of Fernando VII by Blanco White and of Alfonso XIII by John Dos Passos.

12 Pere Gimferrer, 'El mapa y la máscara', in *Plural*, Julio 1976.

13 See also Fuentes's interesting essay, 'Cervantes o la crítica de la lectura', Mexico City: Joaquín Mortiz, 1976.

14 'James Joyce et le temps présent' (French translation), in *Création littéraire et connaissance*, Paris: Gallimard, 1966.

The Erotic Metaphor:
Góngora, Joaquín Belda and Lezama Lima

'Writing about *Paradiso*', Julio Ortega says, 'is an undertaking doomed
from the start to fall short of the mark, for this enormous novel is
practically irreducible to the image of a process or a structure that
criticism claims to reveal in texts.'[1]

The observation could not be more exact: the essayist confronted
with Lezama Lima's monumental work comes up against an obstacle
of the same sort that the novelist himself points out in the case of his
master Luis de Góngora. 'The approaches to Don Luis', he says, 'have
always been those of learned fools. They do their best to apply critical
cleverness to his succession of words, and whitewashed seriousness
to his sly tricks. They endeavour to read him critically and miss his
deliberate confusion, his commotion, his verbal parading.'[2] For the
usual reader of novels, *Paradiso* is a verbal magma, a work with
neither head nor tail in which the plot gets lost in a sea of words
and extraordinarily long sentences, which stretch out like interminable
lianas or ramify till they take on the leafy luxuriance of a jungle. Such a
reader is ordinarily content to read the renowned Chapter VIII and then
decides that the rest isn't worth the trouble. Some of the commentaries
I have heard remind me of those that three and a half centuries ago
greeted the appearance of a work with which *Paradiso* has many
features in common: Góngora's *Soledades*. Let us listen, for instance,
to the humanist Francisco Cascales: 'O diabolical poem! For what has
our poet's intention been? I will tell you: to destroy poetry [. . .] In
what way? By returning things to their original chaos, so that thoughts
are not understood, nor words recognized, such is the confusion and
disorder that reigns.' From Cascales's point of view, so close to that of
those doing battle with today's avant garde, *Soledades* is a sort of Babel,
a delirium of language motivated by the poet's incorrigible vanity. His
allusions, images and syntactic artifices strike them as 'useless and

frivolous'; they serve only 'to strangle understanding to death'. 'The Góngora of *Soledades* and of *Polifemo*', Cascales concludes, 'is the Mohammed of Spanish poetry.'[3]

The denseness of Lezama's prose, his apparent impenetrability have aroused similar reactions in recent years. When faced with works such as *Paradiso*, realist-conservative critics inevitably speak of 'chaos' and argue that the novel itself is in danger – identifying the type of novels that they defend and esteem with the novel as a genre, as bourgeois commentators speak of 'confusion' and 'disorder' whenever they refer to the struggle of revolutionary groups, and instead of saying that the latter are endangering bourgeois society, maintain that they are endangering Society itself. This identification of the conservative-realist critic with the Novel and of the bourgeois with Society is, naturally, simply a reflection of their fear of new realities that they can neither understand nor control and that represent a mortal threat to their small or great capital of knowledge or material goods in the name of a different, and in the final analysis, a vaster and more fruitful cultural or social reality.

An infinite number of interpretations of *Paradiso* are possible; from one that centres on the spiritual 'content' of the text to one that focuses its attention on the allegorical 'figures' that can be made out from an oblique reading – like those engravings whose structure emerges only from one definite angle of vision and in which we discover a 'scene' or 'picture' where at first glance there had been nothing but a jumble of lines. In view of the limits imposed by this brief essay, I shall pay particular attention to the primordial element of the novel, that is to say, language, though I shall not wholly disregard the existence of a system different from that of language, situated at the level of the plot line – what, in other words, goes by the name of narrative discourse.

At this level, *Paradiso* gives the appearance of being a hybrid of *story* and *discourse*, in which the author, like a typical nineteenth-century novelist, goes back and forth between one system and the other with the greatest naturalness in the world, intercalating comments, opinions, digressions that reveal at every turn his omniscient presence, so much so that, even though the novel is written in the grammatical third person, Lezama unconcernedly violates the rule of remaining faithful to the narrative point of view chosen and sticks his nose or his whole head into the story by means of frequent appearances in the first person singular or plural. He often interrupts the tale to offer us this or that bit of information concerning the narrative episode that will come next: 'Rialta's brother, who will now demand, as is his peculiar habit, to enter the novel all of a sudden [. . .]'; 'That night [. . .] which we are about to mention because it deserves a special accompaniment [. . .]'; 'José Cemí's father, whom we saw in previous chapters from within the order of command and ceremonies appertaining to his rank as colonel, we shall now proceed little by little to discover in his childhood, up until his meeting with the Rialta family [. . .]' These 'authorial signs' are obviously intended to be ironical: the deliberate use of a long-familiar, threadbare device, as though Lezama wished to show us that a novelistic plot is a mere pretext and that what interests him is something else entirely. None the less, the numerous elements characteristic of the nineteenth-century novel are intermingled with others marked by the opposite sign: thus, rather than hunting around for a realistic motivation of the 'chance' meetings of the characters, he employs the pre-Cervantine narrative procedure of the purely functional meeting, as required by the plot. In Chapter XIII, Martincillo Vivo, Adalberto Kuller, José Cemí and Oppiano Licario 'happen to meet' aboard the same bus, all of them having arrived at this point of convergence via a different route – although in this case the functionality takes on a symbolic aspect: Cemí's encounter with his own fate. At other times, Lezama presents the characters through a deliberately anti-realistic prism. All the heroes of *Paradiso*, from Juan Izquierdo the cook to Oppiano Licario, seem to be possessed by the same metaphorical, euphuistic and baroque passion as the author. Criticizing Lezama for this would be as impertinent and ridiculous as it would be to reproach Melibea for her florid Greco-Latin erudition in the scene in *La Celestina* in which she commits suicide, or upbraid the characters of Shakespeare, Calderón or Racine for expressing themselves in verse.

A poet who took up the novel, Lezama endlessly reveals the existence of communicating vessels between the two genres. Let us take, for example, the notion of the 'novelistic hero': instead of the transitive characters in ordinary novels, the protagonists of *Paradiso* almost always play a passive, merely receptive role. Their destiny is decided from outside, by way of enigmatic forces beyond their control. The events that rain down on them have a twofold meaning: they are at once literal and allegorical. Cemí's quest is a search for the secret code that guides his steps towards his birth as a writer. Everything that happens in his life will thus have, inescapably, a suprareal dimension that he will be forced to interpret. If we examine *Paradiso* carefully, we will discover that the attitude of its heroes is totally divorced from the active voice of the verb: Cemí, Fronesis, Oppiano Licario are swept along by mysterious currents that lead them to fulfil a destiny of which they have no knowledge. The predominant causality in the novel – that is to say, the logic behind its actions – is neither psychological nor factual but symbolic. Although Lezama uses the grammatical third person and the past tense that are conventional features of the novelistic genre, as a character Cemí is much closer to the 'I' of the poet than to the 'he' of the narrator: 'he felt that a magnetic force was guiding his gaze [. . .]'; 'A three-storey house [. . .] lured him towards it with its sibylline spell [. . .]'; 'He felt that the driving force of the courtyard of his house had been dispelled in him, but that at the same time there had been born, to replace the previous one, a force of absorption, especially constituted so as to attract him to its engulfing or magnetizing centre.'

The fluid communication between the two genres is even more evident in Lezama's characteristic use of language. In his novel, he avoids the verbal Malthusianism inherent in ordinary communication in favour of the deliberate opacity of poetic language. In the face of the 'transparency' of purely denotative language, the poet's tropes and images reaffirm the existence of a linguistic expression perceptible in and by itself and not as a mere vehicle of its meaning. The owl will not be an owl, but 'a grave globe of indolent feathers'; the falcon, 'the swift whirlwind of Norway'. As Lezama himself says of Góngora, 'he inherited, principally from the Arabs, the secret desire [. . .] of sensualizing verse, transforming it into a minute sensory receptor'. The poet thus replaces transparent language by a figurative language so as to command respect for the presence of words – and common language with literary language so as to command respect for the presence of things.[4] As we shall see, the expansion of the language of *Paradiso* rivals reality and substitutes a verbal body for it; that is to say, it appropriates the exterior world by means of the proliferating mechanism of metaphor. In a strikingly beautiful passage of the novel, Lezama explains to us the origin of this mechanism in the mind of Cemí as a youngster, when his father shows him two copperplate illustrations representing respectively the holder of a bachelor's degree and a knife grinder:

Avid curiosity outstripped the time needed to examine each plate, and in his anxious haste José Cemí placed his index finger on the plate showing the knife grinder, as at the same time he heard his father say: 'That one is the bachelor' [. . .] Thus when some days later his father said to him: 'When you're older will you want to have a bachelor's degree? What does it mean to be a *bachiller*?', he answered with the assurance of one who has sought and found verification of his visions. 'A *bachiller* is a wheel that gives off sparks; as the wheel picks up speed, the sparks multiply till they light up the darkness.' Since at that moment his father could not pin down down the relation between the exchange of images and the voice that was explaining, he was amazed at his son's rare gift for metaphor. At his prophetic and symbolic way of grasping the meaning of different occupations.

Lezama's analogical obsession proceeds in two ways: usually, it starts with a dissimilarity so as then to bring together, thanks to the connective power of words, two completely disparate semantic series, or, less frequently, he has recourse to metonymy, through association by contiguity, appropriating as in this case the nearest object:

The breeze had a touch of shadow about it, the shadow a touch of leaf, the leaf with its edges nibbled by the iguana cradled the night once again. Night grabbed the clock on the wall in its arms, supported it in its fall, divided the body of the flour with its obsidian pendulum. Cemí felt the moon's brightness ahead, fluttering like the silhouette of the Pong bird, from the sea to the shell of the black tortoise.

Metonymies and metaphors proliferate with splendid baroque sumptuosity and acquire an autonomous existence in the course of their accelerated progress. Lezama himself has astutely described this irresistible advance of similes when he examines Oppiano Licario's cognitive mechanism:

He took Cartesian mathematical progression as his point of departure. The analogy of two terms of the progression led to the unfolding of a third progression or advance until the third point that was unknown was reached. In the first two terms a great deal of nostalgia for extensible substance still survived. It was the discovery of the third unknown point, that at the same time recaptured the one that he was visualizing and slowly extracting from the extension the analogy of the first two expressions.

In *Paradiso* one word calls forth another and the meeting of the two of them generates a third. As Julio Ortega has grasped very well, this metaphorical process sums up and exemplifies the method of composition: 'one character presupposes another and the two of them a third. A person's gaze moves one object closer to another and they interpose between them a new figure, [. . .] one episode gives rise to another in a successive hyperbolic transformation.' Every happening, we were saying, has a literal sense for José Cemí and another that is allegorical. Lezama does not suppress one of the terms of the opposition, but, rather, maintains them in a perfect simultaneity that negates the laws of logical thought. Cemí's mind embraces both terms and extends a metaphorical bridge between them. Like Don Quixote, he lives the metaphor from within – that is to say, he metaphorizes himself.

The use of the excess value of words as signifiers – of their verbal surplus value – allows Lezama to establish a semantic compatibility between signs not previously related to each other: the dead words of the dictionary take on life, form sensual clusters before our eyes, trace exquisite figures on the blank page, are transmuted into a 'body' as in Arabic poetry.[5] Thanks to this extensive mechanism, even the most trivial phrase forms infinite ramifications. Lezama's ability to transpose is truly prodigious: he mixes temporal relations with spatial ones; he suppresses or modifies the distance that separates one object from another by fusing them in dazzling metonymy or by breaking them down into brilliant synecdoche; he turns temporal succession topsy-turvy and projects the past into the future or the future into the past. The order of priorities of the novelist also undergoes a profound alteration: while the death of Uncle Alberto is described in three lines, the folk ballads of the guitarist which precede it take up several pages. This subversion is a compositional factor of the first order in the total structure of *Paradiso* and manifests itself in a new configuration of the characters as well:

Old Mela extended a gorgon's head above the nodules of time [. . .] Her ninety-four years seemed like tiny canes in the hands of gnomes raised by Count Cagliostro. Like objects in certain painters that move forward to their proper location in space, time had escaped from its succession in order to situate itself in favourite, tyrannical planes, as though Proserpina and the present-day hoi polloi were exchanging personalities with such domestic cordiality that they did not manifest the asymmetries of their extraction, the laments of their evaporated errant life.

In Lezama, every simile generates a causal series in which the link is more important than the objects that it connects, to the point that it very nearly effaces them. *Paradiso* creates a system of elective affinities that embraces at one and the same time the world of nature and the world of culture. The register of his figures of speech is vast, since the novelist almost always makes singularities of objects as he wrests them from their own semantic series and projects them on to a heterogeneous series. This mechanism leads him to appropriate elements from any number of cultures – to pillage, so to speak, facts, dates, realities drawn from geography, painting history and natural sciences. There does not yet exist, to my knowledge, a detailed inventory of the rhetorical figures and tropes of *Paradiso*. In the only one I know of,[6] its author lists: metaphors and images related to the classical world; those that have some connection with what she calls 'historical cosmopolitanism'; those that refer to an 'exotic geography'; and lastly those that are linked to the animal world and go to make up the magnificent bestiary of the novel. In general, the classification seems to me to be adequate, even though it might be better to include the first two groups in a single vast historico-cultural repertory. I for my part would add yet another series: that of the completely unusual, striking associations characteristic of surrealist poetry, although in this case they can be traced back, with greater exactitude, to Góngora's universe.

In the first three groups of the new classification, the novelist's tropes reveal that his poetic imagination would appear to have been nurtured in large part by plates in history textbooks and manuals of 'picturesque geography', illustrated art books, drawings in encyclopaedias. These works, read in his school days, doubtless awakened young Lezama's sensuality and eagerness to learn as they later did mine – though in my case the erotic impression left by plates illustrating the natural sciences and their references to the animal kingdom was much greater than that produced by what to me were the cold, vapid nudes of Greek art. Plates, probably in colour, from textbooks on history or painting:

His right hand raised, as in an eighteenth-century allegory [. . .] as if in one of those occult societies of the Age of Enlightenment, the secret sign were being given when it was visited, incognito, by Benjamin Franklin [. . .]

Puffing like the hand bellows of an alchemist belonging to the school of Nicolas Flamel [. . .]

Time [enlarged] the figure till it took on the solid bodily build of a Desmoulins, of a Marat with his fists clenched, lashing out at the factional differences, the repetitiousness, or the boredom of a Thermidorian meeting.

She descended the stairs with the majestic determination of one who must fulfil a fateful obligation, with her grandson a few steps ahead of her and her two grandsons at her side. A composition straight out of Velázquez.

At certain tables young ladies with prominent potent bosoms exchanged smiles and simpers with young men who seemed to be waiting in ambush to hunt down the unicorn, between the fountain and the petticoats of a little princess of Westphalia.

The mild early days of winter caracoled like a sorrel ridden by the young Infante Baltasar.

Unexpected bagatelles, suddenly opened like a parasol at an imperial landing in Tunis[. . .]

or of textbooks on human geography:

he looked like one of those giants of Eastern Europe, dressed in executioner's tights, who lift up lengths of iron railroad tracks in circuses and placed on one of his outstretched arms a working-class couple with their daughter as she ate a vanilla ice cream.

[. . .] as hieratic as a seller of cooking pots in Iran.

[. . .] all the garments on his right arm seemed to turn Alberto into a petty thief from a market in Smyrna.

[. . .] to turn the scorpion into a pigeon eating grain from the palm of the hand of a Venetian.

[. . .] so as to free himself of a following grown larger and larger, like an entourage of devoted disciples in Bombay[. . .]

or of animals shown in a schoolbook on zoology:

> [. . .] his lying in wait was that of a feline separating the pampas grasses with amazing slowness so as to pounce upon her prey.

> [. . .] mysterious and rare as the blue fox running across the Siberian steppes.

> [. . .] in a drowsiness similar to that of a lazy bear cub in a London zoo.

This visual influence is not merely a personal impression of mine, and Lezama Lima himself appears to be referring to it when, on commenting on the pictorial art of Van Eyck and Simone Martini in one of his essays, he writes: 'from all these plates we have taken natural presences and cultural data – that act as characters, that participate as metaphors'.[7]

A fourth group of tropes – I emphasize the fact that this is not meant as an exhaustive classification but as a grouping to orient the reader – includes all those based on an odd, deliberately paradoxical association: on the creative spark brought into being by the contact of two elements belonging to completely heterogeneous series. Lezama's metaphor – Severo Sarduy says in his magnificent 'Homenaje' to the author – [8] bridges such a distance between its terms that it gains a freedom that only Góngora attains in Spanish. Here the distancing between signifier and signified, the gap that opens up between the faces of the metaphor, the range of the *as if* is maximal:

> [. . .] he felt as if a comet governed by the booming voice of a Burgundian dwarf were passing through the region of his cerebellum [. . .]

> [. . .] little whiskers of a seal that on an Ottoman table displaces, with its androgynous Pythagorean nose, the Swedish balls, the skullcaps of the thief from the mosque.

> [. . .] clutching a compact in which a lovebird appeared to be boiling [. . .]

> [. . .] night fell interminably as if it had dismounted from a Norman draft horse.

[. . .] the cat twitching its whiskers as if it were about to put two words together.

The extensive mechanism likewise operates, in the case of these unusual associations, even in the discourse of one or another of the characters of the novel:

The escort went dragging along, his calfskin boots stirring up dust and spittle, aimed at the centre of cleverness and downfall and drove in the drill bit as with the muleta of a momentary umbilical serpent. One of the prisoners launched an attack; they let out shouts like Japanese fishermen driving back a squadron of nobles, and the ruined drill bits, with their sacred lymph returning to the Thebes of their first sowing, saw their ruin through the chips in the paint, where very soon the arrival of the sun's rays ordered their mysterious transmigrations, as a peacock in Ceylon, or a sloth in a London zoo.

The abundance of images, similes, circumlocutions, figures of speech is essentially Gongorist. When Lezama describes the university demonstration against the dictatorship, he does so in terms of a combat between Achaeans and Trojans, and the student leader is named, indirectly, by means of a series of paraphrases. Michelena's Chinese manservant is 'Golden Doughnut', 'Swift Honey-Coloured Steed', 'Surefooted Fountain Leaper', 'Grasshopper Tray'; Uncle Alberto's coachman 'Clever Auriga the Charioteer'; Oppiano Licario, 'the mediator, the one who waylays fate'; the revealers of the infamy of Baena Albornoz the athlete, 'the glossers of Ulpain, Gallus and Modestinus'.
'Góngora' – Sarduy writes – 'is the absolute presence of *Paradiso*: the entire discursive apparatus of the novel, complex as it is, is nothing but a parabola whose centre – an ellipsis – is Spanish euphuism.' His observation could not be more exact: the Cordovan poet is, in fact, the referent of *Paradiso* and the whole novel illustrates the verbal mechanism of the greatest creator of the Baroque. A few years before Lezama, the Spanish novelist Luis Martín-Santos had begun the same intertextual dialogue with the works of Góngora in a number of passages in his *Tiempo de silencio*. But in Lezama this dialogue becomes systematic. The allusion to the Cordovan poet is in some cases literal or very nearly literal: 'this monstrosity of sea wrack and

slime'; '[. . .] whose tooth was unforgiving of grape clusters, even on the brow of Bacchus, and all the more so on their vine'.

Still gongorizing, the novelist describes objects not with the usual names of the elements that enter into their composition, 'but with words taken from the description of corresponding parts in other objects'.[9] The more remote the similarities between the two series, the more unexpected the common denominator invented by the poet, and the more the images or series of images that he uses are dislocated and ramified. On other occasions, the Gongorist metaphor successfully creates that 'verbal polyhedron', that 'swimming verbal body' that will allow José Cemí to be reconciled with the world through language: 'The practice of poetry, the verbal search for an unknown ultimate purpose, little by little developed in him a strange ability to perceive words that take on an animistic relief in spatial groupings, seated like sibyls in an assembly of wraiths.' For a better understanding of his narrative-poetic art, we shall imitate Lezama's unduly hasty readers of the year 1966, focusing our attention on his odd use of erotic language and comparing it to that of an ingenious author of risqué novels at the turn of the century, the Spaniard Joaquín Belda.

II

The erotic literature of all times and places enjoys an abundant repertory of euphemistic formulas intended to avoid the vulgar name for sexual parts of the body or the act of copulation, either through indirect and oblique reference, or through recourse to a figure of speech. Very frequently the writer proceeds to single out the object, separating it from its own series and mapping it on to a heterogeneous structure, or else he describes it with feigned innocence, as if he hadn't the least idea what it was and was seeing it for the first time. In the *Cancionero de burlas provocantes a risa*, and above all in *La Lozana andaluza*, we find numerous images of this sort: the male member is a 'lance', 'spear', 'unicorn', 'pestle', 'paschal candle', 'reed pipe'; the female organ a 'swamp', a 'toll house'; semen, 'whey', 'paste'; the testicles, 'buddies'; the sexual act, 'to enter the arena', etc. With these euphemistic figures of speech, Delicado devises metaphors such as 'the ferret' which 'hunts' in the 'thicket', or 'to say two words with the dingle-dangle'. In other passages, the protagonists of the 'portrait' refer to sex in a tangential way by resorting to the use of periphrasis, demonstrative pronouns or adverbs of place.

In a famous essay,[10] Roman Jakobson astutely observed that the form of euphemism employed varied, depending on the context: whereas in a milieu accustomed to obscenity the use of tropes fulfils the obvious function of singularizing an object or an act and thus makes a greater impression on an audience, in a 'highbrow' cultural milieu – that of the readers of a literary text – the sudden intrusion of a vulgar word has much greater impact. If, on the one hand, the repertory of popular vaudeville makes it a rule never to mention things by their name, the bard may purposely violate the harmony of poetic language and write, as Miguel Hernández does, 'in the soul's balls'. In both cases the crude epithet and the euphemism transport the reader or the spectator to another semantic series and give the displaced term a new outer container, forcing the public to pause and pay attention to it. A comparative examination of the similes and erotic paraphrases of *Paradiso* and those of Belda's novel will help us to understand the determining role of the context.[11]

The leafy luxuriance of Góngora's language – his violent syntactical distortion combined with a striking talent for metaphor – is the principal axis of the process of erotic singularization in *Paradiso*. The high ratio of dislocation of the Cordovan poet, his slithering, serpentine verse, allow the twentieth-century novelist to take possession of the complex world in which he lives through the creation of a living verbal body and, consequently, a sensual one. In the same way that the erotic game postpones the moment of orgasm for as long as possible, the literary game is meant to prolong the sensual pleasure of our reading as an end in itself. Eroticism and baroque writing thus coincide, as Sarduy has observed, by virtue of a common playful tendency; typical Cuban 'teasing' infiltrates Lezama's metaphors and spans the distance between two disparate series with a bridge of comicalness, organizing surprising, offbeat elective affinities. The erotic similes of *Paradiso* are taken from the same general area as his other figures of speech – that of illustrated school texts on history, geography, painting or the natural sciences that marked the omnivorous imagination of the young Lezama with their imprint, there being a notable predominance of metaphors related to the animal and vegetable world. But the violently 'rhetorical' nature of the text brings about a subtle change in the use of this device: Lezama's novel is not addressed to a popular audience, in the habit of calling things by their names, and for whom the author's cleverness is measured by how well or how badly he handles periphrasis or euphemism; the reader of *Paradiso* moves in a strictly cultural universe, at the opposite pole from 'realism', and for that very reason the introduction of the sexual term used in ordinary language causes an abrupt break, a sort of short circuit:

> [. . .] the school yard was supervised by a pupil of the preparatory class which at that time was the end of a student's primary education: one Farraluque, the offspring of a semititanic Basque male and a languid Havanese female, a cross-breeding that ordinarily produces a leptosomatic adolescent, with a rather melancholy face and dark circles under his eyes, but endowed with an enormous cock.

Throughout the novel, in the middle of a supra-rhetorical, purely literary structure, Lezama craftily sows words such as phallus, penis, glans, foreskin, vulva or scrotum. More frequently, when he makes use of a trope, he does not entirely eliminate the referential subject since the latter remains present in the form of an adjective: 'phallic candle', 'ascending spiral of the phallic column', 'phallic cornelian', 'phallic tail', 'phallic serpent', 'phallic rod', 'phallic colossus', 'phallic dolmen', etc. At other times, a characteristic Lezama metaphor takes off from a common noun to trace an unpredictable parabola, which catapults the subject of the sentence to a predicate entirely its own, taken either from the natural world or from the objects created by man:

> [. . .] Fronesis's penis was as limp as a pod dried in the sun.

> [. . .] Vivo's phallus, like a rolled-up parasol [. . .]

> [. . .] the retracted glans revealed the outlines of a tiny cupola [. . .]

or, as is more often the case, it catapults it into an artistic-cultural, historical, or mythopoetical perspective:

> [. . .] the phallic potency of Leregas the peasant reigned like an Aaron's rod.

> [. . .] Leregas took out his cock – with the same majestic indifference as in the Velázquez painting where a key is handed over on a cushion – as stubby as a thimble in the beginning, but then, as if driven by a titanic wind, it grew to the length of the forearm of a manual worker.

[. . .] placing on his rod three good-sized in-octavo books, which moved like tortoises urged on by the expansive force of a fumarole. He was imitating the Hindu legend recounting the origin of the worlds.

On certain occasions, Lezama inverts the terms of the poetic equation, and instead of tracing the comparative arc with the sexual expression as his point of departure, he uses it instead as a predicate of the metaphor: '[. . .] the sword inserted in the ground like a phallus; '[. . .] little mushrooms, poisonous only to man, resembling phalluses with an albino glans'. But, like Góngora, Lezama particularly favours the use of the substitutive image. Sexual euphemism, especially if it concerns the phallus, at times draws from the rhetorical arsenal of authors of pornographic novels: taper, spur, earthworm ('the stupefaction of the supple advances of his rose-coloured earthworm'), fang, goad ('the plump length of his goad'), cock's beak, fruit ('Lupita did not hesitate to hide in her body the fruit that she had made hers'), lance, column; at other times, it employs periphrasis: 'the penetrating instrument', 'germinative spirit', 'germinative endowment', 'germinative attributes', etc. The image links us now and again to the historical or mythological world: '[. . .] that impromptu Trajan's column', '[. . .] the bedazzlement of the peasant's Alexandrian lighthouse', '[. . .] the Luxor column', '[. . .] Pompeyan lance at the ready', '[. . .] the seminal Augustinian reason', '[. . .] the excited Gorgon dripping with sweat brought on in the depths'. At still other times, the circumlocution writhes like a serpent, with annulated Gongoristic lubricity: '[. . .] the outpouring of the joyful liquid', '[. . .] the weeping that wound about his tusk', '[. . .] the other limp, lengthy theory', '[. . .] the two algae entangled in a nest of toucans', '[. . .] the conical casque of the cornaline', '[. . .] the serpent's somniferous muscular strength', '[. . .] the cascade of supreme energy', '[. . .] the interrupted transfiguration'.

The elision characteristic of the Cordovan poet flourishes in the sylvan vegetation of *Paradiso* with a richness and a prodigality unknown to our language for more than three centuries: the beds where Farraluque's 'little sexual chain' adds one link to another will be, successively, 'a foamy square', a 'festive square'; passive homosexuals 'movie fans with a congenital megacolon'; Roxana's caresses 'her endless artisan's task'; Lucía and Fronesis kissing each other 'two caterpillars questioning each other with their antennae'; the anus is 'a copper circle', 'a Joculus crater', 'a Sneffels crater'; the scrotum, 'a shadow marked with rings by Scartaris';[12] the lord with the mask sodomized by Farraluque, 'his concise contrary', 'powerful incorporator of the exterior world', 'a recently initiated subject'; coitus, 'suspension wherein the contraries are inundated in the One and Only', 'a central touch set aflame'. The female sex is described to us either through images from the animal world: 'fat spider', 'swollen spider'; or from the vegetable or the inorganic world: 'coarse horsetail or esparto grass pecked by a night bird', 'bearded grotto', 'undulations of a carboniferous terrain', 'delicate Venerian grasses', 'a cave alongside the dark meadowland', etc.

The extension of Lezama's language, his hard-fought pursuit of 'a resistant substance embedded amid a metaphor that is moving forward' and 'a final image [that ensures] the survival of this substance',[13] flexibly prolongs the comparative mechanism beginning with the initial substantive term, raising it to a supra-rhetorical level – the rhetorical squared – through which, as always, a slight aftertaste of laughter, of discreet irony comes through: '[. . .] when he stated in precise terms that the hole in the canvas covered the circle through which one entered the river of the female, the cock of Eros announced the arrival of dawn with his possessive goad'; '[. . .] the coarse grasses, the excoriations, the mossy shoots where the new coil of the eighth day turned into a little mushroom with a small planetary crown round about the glans of a colloidal ivory'; '[. . .] in the hostelry of rotten Boards, in the lover of fiestas, a cylindrical drawer, wood louse, grotto welling forth, camphor stalactite, pumice stone for the tense beak of the sleeping cock'; '[. . .] the energy, ranked by rancour, turned over several times in the bays, quite exposed, of the enigmatic desiress'.

> That amorous encounter was reminiscent of the incorporation of a dead serpent by the hissing victor. Ring upon ring, the extensive limp theory little by little penetrated the body of the victorious serpent: monstrous organisms that still called to mind the indistinction of the beginnings of the tertiary in which digestion and reproduction were a single function. The relaxation of the tunnel to be traversed was demonstrable proof in the petite Spanish woman that the visits of the sea serpent to her grotto were frequent. Farraluque's phallic configuration was extremely propitious to this retrospective penetration, for his spur had an exaggerated superiority in length to the bearded root. With the quickwittedness of a Pyrenean pickpocket, the petite Spanish woman divided the length to be taken in into three zones, which

gave rise, rather than to pauses in the dream, to genuine panting breaths of proud victory. The first additive segment corresponded to the hardened casque of the glans, joined to a corrugated, extremely tense fragment extending to the inferior contour of the glans and the penis stretched taut like a string to enhance the resonance.

To conclude, let us take a close look at an example of Lezama's *ars combinatoria* which will help us decipher, as in a Baroque pictograph, his distinctive process of singularization as it relates to his unconscious Gongorism.

The second addition contributed the support of resistance, or the stem properly so called, which was the part that had the most responsible role, since it would give the sign as to whether the incorporation would be abandoned or would be boldly pursued to the end. But the petite Spanish woman, with the tenacity of a classical potter, who with just two fingers opens the entire mouth of the jug, succeeded in uniting the two little fibres of the contraries, thus reconciled in those dark shadows.

III

Among the novels of Joaquín Belda we shall choose the one that describes the life and miracles of 'the renowned and incomparable Coquito, queen of the rumba and empress of the popular song'.[14]

Its author belongs to that group of writers at the beginning of this century who, taking advantage of the relative liberalism of censorship under Alfonso XIII with regard to sex, tirelessly cultivated, at times with great talent, the so-called 'risqué' novel, a number of which enjoyed enormous popularity. In my opinion Belda ranks first among them because of his discreet satire of Spanish society, and as we shall see, because of the particularly baroque nature of his images and euphemisms. Although the social intent of *La Coquito* is less obvious than that of other works by the same author,[15] the reader can glean from it a series of observations that, with a refined sense of humour and without the dramatic overemphasis of the Generation of '98, are none the less definitely related to the problems posed by the writers of that generation and their general criticism of the country.[16]

The plot of the novel is very simple: la Coquito, the star of the Salón Nuevo in Madrid – a theatre specializing in a repertory of farces and a great many dance numbers with titles that could be interpreted as having a double meaning – sells her body to the highest bidder when the show is over, thanks to the Celestine manoeuvres of her own mother, the pragmatic and Galdosian Doña Micaela. Among those who ardently seek her favours is Julio González, known as Julito, a poor student who for months, at the cost of great sacrifices, manages to put aside, peseta by peseta and duro by duro, the amount of money, an astronomical sum at the time, that the bawd demands. Meanwhile, the young man feeds the flame of his passion with sporadic visits to the Coliseo, where the beauty ends her performance with a dance number that is a predecessor of the striptease. 'I solemnly declare' – Belda writes – 'and if I am mistaken may History place upon my shoulders all responsibility for the statement, that we are witnessing, in this matter of the rumba, an event equal in importance and transcending ordinary experience to a far greater degree than the Battle of the Pyramids.' Confronted by this glorious vision, the lad's 'vital river' overflows its banks and floods the 'countryside' of his thighs with 'incendiary inundations'. Finally the night so eagerly awaited arrives and the rumba dancer and the student surrender to the arduous, almost liturgical exercise of a passion that occupies approximately a third of the novel, in a crescendo which, although it does not involve a change of *partenaire*, calls to mind Farraluque's exploits in Chapter VIII of *Paradiso*. The drama reaches its climax at the moment when la Coquito, armed with 'a strange object' of German manufacture, attacks the young man's 'virgin fortress', and as he experiences 'an impression that his flesh was splitting apart, as if an automatic umbrella had opened within [his] organism and was determined to make its way outside without closing', Belda merely comments: 'A new means of communication had just been opened for later travellers to Spain, a country, so it is said, that has such a dearth of them.'

Belda's language is extraordinarily inventive and brilliant: like the authors of the theatrical repertory of the Salón Nuevo, it is addressed to a public whose inexhaustible appetite for scabrous situations is complemented by a no less ravenous relishing of paraphrases and euphemisms based on a single rule: never calling a spade a spade. This principle obliges the author of salacious works to make continuous use of similes and tropes, meant to focus the attention of the reader or the spectator on the exquisite art with which the writer gets round the obstacle of crude, common expression. As in theatrical works of the 'Don Juan Tenorio' type (in which the drawback of the lack of dramatic tension, in view of the fact that the plot is familiar to the audience beforehand, is counterbalanced by diverting the spectator's attention to the staging and the acting), the artistic verisimilitude of a genre as conventional and rule-bound as the one cultivated by Belda allows him to display to excellent advantage, on the other hand, his brilliant exploitation of a rhetoric which is thereby transformed into the dynamic factor of the work, that is to say, into its 'differential sign'. The standardization and strictness of the code consequently leave ample room for improvisation in which the 'what' is much less important than the 'how'. Although Belda chooses to apply his storehouse of tropes to the human body and the sexual act, it is interesting to note that his predilection for metaphor infects the remaining descriptions in the novel. Often his similes bridge an immense abyss separating two terms belonging to heterogeneous series: '[. . .] she [the black woman] looked like a huge piece of ebony furniture [. . .] a little as though Cybele had taken a bath in ink'; '[. . .] her sweat, thick and smelling of a spinster custard apple, ran down my body like sacramental oil'; '[. . .] two resounding kisses, one on each shoe, fell at the feet of the performer, like two white roses thrown from a theatre box overlooking the stage'.

Because of the fact that it was written during the First World War, the work abounds in military similes and images or allusions to the course of events during combat: 'He, invaded from the back, like the Tyrol and the Trentino'; 'Clausewitz said that one of the most difficult war manoeuvres was to harry the enemy's rearguard'; 'compared with what the body of the young girl would be forced to go through [. . .] the taking of Liège by Von Kluck's army would be a lunch at the Bombilla'; etc. The fearful 'object' with which la Coquito sodomizes her young suitor is likewise alluded to in military terms: 'as long as the Kaiser's people had in their arsenal arms such as that, it could mortgage the future of the world with cannon shots'.

Unlike Lezama, Belda carefully avoids direct mention of the sexual act or the genitals, inasmuch as these elements are always present in his readers' minds and are, in all truth, the real protagonists of the work. His euphemisms ordinarily take the form of paraphrase: 'the hemispheres of the façade', 'the nutritive little button', 'the cordillera that encircled the sexual vertex', 'certain generative folds belonging to the hostess', 'the flower bud that rose in the middle of the rock', etc; transformed into an image, they frequently come to be, as in Lezama, the subject of a metaphor whose predicate seems to stretch like elastic –

a mere pretext on the part of the novelist to fill out the verbal material: the breasts of a popular singer are 'two plums pecked clean by the beaks of birds', and la Coquito's are 'two divine little lemons, as white as the spikenard [that] rose stiffly heavenward and with the button of the vertex as threatening as the horn of a Miura bull'; or yet again, 'two little half-grown melons, of the same size, dark, with a slight swaying movement when she walked, which set the little buttons at the vertex, as pink as the bald head of an immaculate senator, to trembling'.

The various aspects and components of the sexual act are described in metaphorical terms, at times by means of sinuous circumlocutions with convoluted Gongoristic syntax:

[. . .] a mouse that had gained entry – smelling of Roquefort cheese – through the seamstress's narrow sexual passageway.

[. . .] the violet furrow of the circles under his eyes [. . .] indicated that the youth had endeavoured to console himself for the slights of the beloved being by disturbing the silence of his nocturnal ego with Hindu manipulations.

[. . .] the lightning rod also tapered to a sharp end and possessed a bare smoothness resembling the floor of a dance hall with a little pointed mound in the centre.

[. . .] she hoped that [. . .] like a pilot who guides the ship between the reefs at the entrance of the port, he would bring to light his categorical imperative,[17] which resembled a vigilant beacon amid ocean storms.

[. . .] his categorical imperative [. . .] obeying the law of gravitation surrendered to the ground like the panache of a wounded cavalier.

[. . .] the widow turned on the light and saw that, coming through the roof, acting like a drill, was a strange object, tapering to a point, though a bit blunt, that she remembered having seen now and again before she had been left a widow. The object rose and fell in peristaltic movements, until it finally disappeared.

In this last case, Belda pretends to have no knowledge of the reality of the penis, describing it as something altogether strange, that he is seeing for the very first time, thereby imposing on us, in accordance with Shklovsky's precept, a 'vision' of it, not a 'recognition'.

For a clearer understanding of the method chosen by Belda, we shall chose a few paragraphs and passages from the 'variations on a theme' which the student and the cabaret performer engage in over a space occupying more than sixty pages of the work.

[. . .] Would she be able to keep in the divine jewel case of her body that precious gem seemingly fashioned in the land of giants? Would the elasticity of her judgement have no limit? [. . .] As the Indian kneels before an idol on the shore of the Ganges, so she was prostrate before Julio [. . .] Coquito slowly stretched out her hands, and gently took hold of that sceptre of the empire of the world.

Once the act has been consummated, Beldo writes that Julio

[. . .] threw himself at her feet, like one of those greyhounds in English paintings [. . .] and there on her patent-leather slippers, left kiss upon kiss as an offering; at times he mounted with his kisses as high as her knee, but then descended almost immediately, like a humble pageboy who in a moment of daring enters the private apartments of his queen, and then dashes out like a fallow deer on hearing the slightest noise [. . .] timidly, as one who fears profaning the sanctuary of an image, he raised her dressing gown with both hands and contemplated the inner panorama [. . .] With an attentive eye and directing his line of sight downwards, what could be seen was a tenuous channel, like a rivulet trickling down amid mountains, and although its end could not be seen, it could be envisaged as a divine pool of splendour [. . .] it was labour for an engineer expert at sapping to clear the path of obstacles; there were not many of these; only the trousers and the dressing gown but for the labour of a miniaturist that he intended to perform, a cigarette paper would be coarse cotton cloth.

Beldo then devotes himself to an elliptical description of cunnilingus, crammed full of images, figures of speech and similes of all sorts, with a display of imaginative and poetic richness that we find in none of the Spanish writers of his time, with the exception, naturally, of Valle-Inclán:

With the devotion of the pilgrim who after a long journey reaches the holy altar, Julio knelt before the body of Coquito [. . .] It was first a peaceful stroll along the two thoroughfares that from the knees led to the central palace of pleasures; that stroll was like a gentle massage with vaseline that smoothed the way, or like those thorough wettings that are done twice a day on the roads of the Basque provinces by means of a little cart carrying a tank sprinkling water at the back.

But during this stroll, wherever the wanderer came upon a pleasant and propitious place to pause to rest, he did so with the greatest pleasure, and those places were the ones in which the terrain was broken, doubling back on itself, as in the little valley of each groin, or in other plains where the skin, because it is less exposed to the sun and to the air, is infinitely softened, sensitized. There the weapon renewed its attacks, increased its velocity and its fiery ardour, to resume again immediately thereafter in a pianissimo, which was like a truce, his usual pace along the rest of the way [. . .] There is a grove at the entrance of certain of a woman's narrow passages, where the shade is pleasant and a stop to rest is an orgy; in it: why not?, the student halted, after having properly inspected all the environs.

In the shade of its little trees, chestnuts with silky reddish foliage, the artist fought a battle that was reminiscent of the interminable one or ones of the Argonne, in which the combatants do nothing but weave and unweave as they pass again and again across the same stretch.

In all likelihood the explorer, making bold advances, appeared in the deep valley that divided the wood down the centre; but he did no more than look quickly about, then retreated immediately [. . .] The vanguard of the invading army was advancing through the northern part of the wood; it appeared that it was there, the most dangerous site, as those who are intelligent know, that the attack in depth would take place; but that was simply a false alarm, for very soon the enemy withdrew so as to go on with their reconnaissance sorties [. . .] That youngster was a master: experience, the eternal teacher of love and life, had been supplanted in him by a delicate instinct that produced in his buccal appendage the vibrations of an aeolian harp. The invader penetrated that cavity with the timidity of a beginning student at first; with the boldness of a Norwegian master pilot later on.

He found himself face to face there with one of those spots that it has pleased Nature to locate in certain regions close to the sea or to humid areas, a veritable cave of stalactites, in which the water, weary of dripping for centuries, marking the monotonous flow of life, has paused to form polyhedral crystallizations that because they end in abrupt points are very reminiscent of the majority of Bernstein's dramas. Poetry has made of these places chapels of their idolatrous cults [. . .] That grotto, the property of *La Coquito* through which, without exaggeration, one could be certain that more than a thousand tourists had passed, seemed like a recently discovered place, a mystery whose veil had just been rent at the entreaty of a tenor aria, as in mythological operas. The coolness inside, the very narrowness of the place spoke of something virginal, of a primeval fountain that is hidden amid the branches of a wood – the wood where the pilgrim had marauded shortly before – and that for the traveller is a surprise and a blessing. And it is true that imagination and water of this sort sometimes work these miracles.

Whether it was new or old, pristine or known from antiquity, a first endeavour or a *reprise*, the traveller began a thorough inspection of the most secret recesses of the miraculous cave, that promptly had its effect. There was not one twist or turn, one arabesque tile of that marvel of Moorish art that failed to yield before the insistence of the stiletto that Julio kept for such occasions and for wetting the edge of the Jean paper he used for rolling his cigarettes.

There was a place, at the very top of the ceiling there where the latter began to curve so as to form the back wall, which stood out and shone more brightly than the rest, a bit like those grains of pure gold which the miners of California spend a life of slavery in the hope of finding, and for which, once they are outside the mine, men fight each other to death, as for a female who gives herself only to a lover with bloodstained hands. Julito, or rather, his appendage, stared fixedly at it, and realizing that that was the enemy's weak point, went straight to it like a bullet and began a fight in which all the probabilities of victory were on his side.

The final 'surprise' of the fear-inspiring rumba dancer also offers us a *morceau de bravoure* in which the verbal pyrotechnics and the humour which the figureheads of the Generation of '98 so cruelly lacked are delightfully combined in the account of the opening of a new tunnel 'to the civilization of the world':

[. . .] the product of German workshops began an advance between two promontories [. . .] Getting lost in a shortcut, which no one else has ever taken before, has its drawbacks [. . .] but it also has its charms, and not least among them is that of taking in panoramas that no other eye has ever contemplated and that offer themselves to us with all the enchantment of the virginal [. . .] The young man [. . .] felt a very strange thing within himself, [. . .] an impression that was as if, while taking a bath, by virtue of a physical phenomenon, all the water of the sea were beginning to enter his organism [. . .] It was an introspection: his skin drawing inwards, like an umbrella that is closing, never to open again [. . .] Only one cry of complaint was heard; all the rest were frank voices of delight, like a chorus of angels [. . .]; the product of German manufacture had completely disappeared – it measured no more than twenty-six centimetres – from the sight of mortals and it would have been futile to look for it on the floor, or underneath the furniture. Where was it? A riddle [. . .] The truth was that, since the human body did not suddenly dilate, creating new organs, nothing more could have been done there than had been done.

IV

We shall conclude this diptych contrasting Belda's little book and Lezama's extraordinary creation by clearly stating that what we have here is in no way a case of influence, as the learned bookworm, in his eager search for souces, would hasten to assert, but, rather, a coincidence occasioned by the internal process of writing. For form's sake, I none the less consulted Lezama and received a written reply, of which I shall quote the following brief, significant lines:

As regards the other subject of your letter, I have never read the work you mention, nor do I believe that anything more is needed for the reading of that Chapter VIII than what is set forth within it. A few verses from the *Laws of Manu* and above all the *Kamasutra* (the chapter devoted to the Opoparika or buccal union) read at an early age and retained in sensual relief by memory. The only pornographic books I have read are the Bible (Genesis) and Plato. In all truth literary influences are not what is fundamental in my work, but, rather, the appearance of something sudden, a suddenness of empowerment and realization.[18]

To sum up: whereas the great Cuban writer uses Góngora as the referent which will allow him to appropriate reality – of which eroticism is a part – through language, the ingenious Spanish novelist gongorizes *despite himself*, from the moment he finds himself obliged to have recourse to the use of ellipsis and euphemisms in order to leave his 'personal imprint' on his readers. The different nature of the publics to whom the two authors address themselves explains the employment or the rejection of the crude word in accordance with the particular – and apparently paradoxical – logic of the context. Above all it reveals to us that the encounter with Góngora – whether deliberate or unconscious – can play a role in the Hispanic narrative of the twentieth century not unlike the influence of Joyce in the English-speaking world. Along with the rediscovery by Borges of Cervantes's prodigious literary game, it is the valid demonstration of the fact that, after an eclipse of over three centuries, the novel in Castilian has again found the lost crossroad, the unforeseen conjunction marking its resurrection: the one exemplified by Góngora and Cervantes, each in his own way – a bold raid on the reality of the world mysteriously transmuted into an adventure of the creative process of the writer.

Notes

1 *Relato de la utopía. Notas sobre la narrativa cubana de la Revolución*, Barcelona: La Gaya Ciencia, 1973.
2 'Sierpe de don Luis de Góngora', in *Orbita de Lezama Lima*, Havana: UNEAC, 1966.
3 *Cartas filológicas*. It would be superfluous to point out that the reference to the prophet of Islam was the greatest possible insult in the perverted Spanish context of the period.

4 Cf. Tzvetan Todorov, *Théorie de la littérature*, Paris: Editions du Seuil, 1966. Spanish translation – Buenos Aires: Signos, 1971.

5 On 'second-degree' metaphors in Andalusian poetry, see Ibn-az-Zaqqaq, *Poesías*, edited and translated by Emilio García Gómez, Madrid, 1954. See also James T. Monroe's enlightening pages on Ibn Zamrak's *qasidas* in *Hispano-Arabic Poetry*, University of California Press, 1974, pp. 65–7.

6 Esperanza Figueroa Amaral, 'Forma y estilo en *Paradiso*', in *Revista Iberoamericana*, XXXVI, no. 72 (julio–septiembre 1970), pp. 425–35.

7 'Mitos y cansancio clásico', in *La expresión americana*, Madrid: Alianza Editorial, 1969.

8 *Escrito sobre un cuerpo*, Buenos Aires, Sudamericana, 1969. (English translation to be published by Lumen, New York, 1990.)

9 Victor Shklovsky, 'L'art comme procédé', in *Théorie de la litterature*, op. cit.

10 'Du réalisme artistique', in *Théorie de la littérature*, op. cit.

11 In Joaquín Belda's *La Coquito* we find numerous examples of this type of vaudeville or farce so popular in the Paralelo theatres in Barcelona or the renowned Blanquita in Mexico City. 'The repertory of the Salón Nuevo was made up of works with ambiguous titles which lent themselves to double entendre interpretations by those with 'dirty' minds. *El hijo de Pura*, *Tres noches sin sacarla*, *Tomar por el atajo*, and the biggest hit of the season, the epitome of the genre, the inspired *Tortilla de almejas*, a performance in six scenes, reputedly written by an official of the State Council, in which one of the characters was a ruined banker, who in a scene with a decided tragic flavour stood stock-still at centre stage and declaimed the following lines:

> Me persigue la justicia.
> Todas las gentes me escupen.
> Quieren chuparme la sangre?
> Pues bueno, ¡que me la chupen!

> (Justice pursues me.
> Everyone spits in my face.
> Do they want to suck my blood?
> Well then, let them go right ahead!)

See also the scenes of the same work on pp. 86–7, 90–2 and 94–5.

12 Julio Cortázar has analysed these cryptic references to Jules Verne in the essay devoted to Lezama in *La vuelta al día en ochenta mundos*, Mexico City: Siglo XXI, 1967.

13 Interview with Armando Alvarez Bravo in *Orbita de Lezama Lima*, op. cit.

14 *La Coquito, novela picaresca*, Ediciones Alegría, n. d. Belda's novel was forbidden in Spain, and I acquired the copy of the edition I have cited in a sex shop on 42nd Street in New York, apparently frequented by a Spanish-speaking clientele.

15 The peripatetic old lady in *Las noches del botánico* is a type who

brings to mind Galdós's Benina, a witness to the miseries and penury of the petty-bourgeoisie in Madrid. The final speech of the parish priest extolling their penny-pinching 'virtues' is a piece that appears frequently in anthologies.

16 *La Coquito*, pp. 77–8 and 146.
17 In *Juan sin tierra* I have used this image in homage to Belda.
18 The original of Lezama's letter is included in the collection of my papers preserved at Boston University.

From *Count Julian* to *Makbara*:
a Possible Orientalist Reading

Before turning to the analysis of the part played in my novels by the Arab world – and, more concretely, by Morocco – I find it indispensable to refer to Edward W. Said's observations on Occidental discourse concerning the Orient,[1] and what he quite aptly terms the strategic position of the author with regard to the material he handles. He states:

> I use the notion of strategy simply to identify the problem every writer on the Orient has faced: how to get hold of it, how to approach it, how not to be defeated or overwhelmed by its sublimity, its scope, its awesome dimensions. Everyone who writes about the Orient must situate himself with respect to it: translated into his text, this location includes the sort of narrative voice he adopts, the type of structure he builds, the kinds of images, themes, motifs that circulate in his text – not to mention his deliberate manner of addressing the reader, approaching the Orient, and finally, representing it or speaking in its behalf. None of this takes place in the abstract, however. Every writer on the Orient (and this is true even of Homer) assumes some Oriental precedent, some previous knowledge of the Orient, to which to refer and on which he relies. Additionally, each work on the Orient *affiliates itself* with other works, with audiences, with institutions, with the Orient itself. The set of relationships between works, audiences and some particular aspects of the Orient therefore constitutes an analysable formation – for example, that of philological studies, of anthologies of extracts from Oriental literature, of travel books, of Oriental fantasies – whose presence in time, in discourse, in institutions gives it strength and authority.[2]

Although the citation is lengthy, it merits our pausing to examine it. Orientals, Arabs or Moroccans, objects of the discourse of the Occidental writer, have a perfect right to confront him with the problem of his strategic position with respect to his chosen theme. If we look back to the past, as Said does, and examine Occidental discourse on the Orient, and especially on Islam, from the Middle Ages to our own day, we can arrive at a certain number of conclusions that will help us to situate the literary work – mine in this case – in a proper perspective. Given the impossibility of adequate treatment here, I shall limit myself to mentioning only a few aspects of the question, directly related to my own research and practice.

1) The Orient as a theatrical performance, spectacle, *tableau vivant*. From the *Chanson de Roland* and the *Cantar del Mío Cid*, including Dante and the *Romancero* and a series of significant works from the last two centuries, the Orient and the Islamic world appear to be a closed stage on which actors and their company of supporting players give visible form to a series of symbols and stereotypes familiar to the audience and to the author alike.

2) Empirical reality, direct observations, and confrontation with the facts play a secondary role. What counts in the aforementioned discourse is an antecedent vision of the subject which shapes and forms it, contains and frames it. This vision, as may be supposed, structures the corpus of earlier works on the East and on Islam. There exists, in fact, a natural predisposition to prefer the authority of a canonical text to the disorientation and uncertainty of a personal focus that lacks points of reference. When it comes to a choice between the wide and alien world and the text that purportedly describes it, as a general rule we consult the latter. When this written corpus embraces several centuries and disciplines, it gains formidable power, and the textual vision obscures or completely eclipses the reality. 'In the system of knowledge with respect to the Orient,' Said writes, 'this is less a place than a *topos*, an interplay of references [. . .] which apparently originate in some quotation, the fragment of a text, a passage from some earlier work on the Orient, some preceding idea or imagining, or an amalgam of all of these.' That is to say, the East and Islam are represented according to a totality of concepts and images that are not related to reality or to a concrete experience but to a vast concatenation of desires, repressions, fears, spectres, rivalries, prejudices.

3) Because of the threat which Islam (whether Arabic or Turkish) signified for the Christian world between the eighth and the seventeenth

centuries, the Muslim world occupies a central position with respect to this latter, one qualitatively different from other non-European civilizations (Buddhist, Hindu, etc). This explains, as the Tunisian historian Hichem Djait has astutely perceived, the persistence of an acute and tenacious 'anti-Islamic sensibility on all levels of the European subconscious'. By virtue of the well-known dialectic of identification between the ego and the world, the I and the non-I, Islam has played for the Occidental Christian world a consciousness-raising role, expressed in terms of opposition and contrast: that of otherness, of the Other, that 'intimate adversary' too close to be totally exotic and too resistant, coherent and compact to be domesticated, assimilated or diminished. As a consequence there exist a history, a tradition of thought, a legend, a rhetoric, a collection of images or Islamic clichés created by and for Occidentals which establish an unbridgeable gap between what is 'ours' (and viewed, naturally, with a conscious attitude of superiority and self-satisfaction) and what is 'theirs' (contemplated with hostility or scorn). Thus, both abstract entities, the Occident and Islam, reinforce and reflect each other, creating a dialectical interplay between their mirror images. Islam is the hollow mould, the negative of Europe: what it has rejected, and at the same time what has tempted it.

4) All European literature which attempts to come to grips with the Arabic or Islamic world emphasizes (independently of the sympathy or the personal affinity of certain writers towards it) its foreign, irreducible, alien character of a simple object created by and for the eye of Western man, or, as Said says, 'incorporates it schematically on a theatrical stage whose audience, manager and actors are for Europe and only for Europe'. The East and Islam thus become a mere pretext for the pen of the writer – whether his name be Lope, Shakespeare, Flaubert, Nerval, Loti, T. E. Lawrence, Gide or Duvert – to carry out his creative project, illustrate his obsessions, seek his own identity, invent plots, develop fantasies, forge metaphors, etc. In no instance do the ideas, visions, discoveries, images act for the benefit of the human beings who evoke them, nor do they even elaborate any sort of truthful discourse about them. What counts (let us be brutally frank) is the personal, selfish operation of the writer and its effect on the European public, no matter whether it be illuminating or on the other hand redundant and negative, reinforcing its clichés and prejudices.

If we reflect on these observations and considerations in the light of such novels as *Don Julián*, *Juan sin tierra*, and *Makbara*, we can trace a series of co-ordinates that will permit us to situate them within the historical, ideological and cultural framework in which they should be read. Even if in the essays that I have devoted to Spanish colonialism in Morocco, to the imbroglio of the Sahara, and to the sociological and cultural affinities of our two countries (largely the fruit of my assiduous readings of Laroui and other contemporary Moroccan thinkers), I have approached the problem of the real Morocco and the Moroccan of the twentieth century from a clearly anti-colonial, democratic and emancipatory perspective, the Morocco and the Moroccans present in my novels none the less offer entirely different particularities. This is not simply owing to the specific nature of the work of literature (to its essential ambiguity, to its inherent and therefore irreconcilable contradictions, to the creative tension aroused by the clash between two opposing ideas or emotions). Literature does not correspond to logical and rational discourse alone: it has neither the clarity of the essay nor the simplicity of the pamphlet: it has its areas of shadow, its obscure motivations, its secret vibrations. It oscillates between reality and dreams, moral criticism and the opacity of instinct, human beings and the spectres interiorized in their subconscious: it may be read in the light of Marx or Bakunin, but also in that of Sade or Freud. From my own experience, I know that the whole of my novelistic work is based on a certain number of contradictions and ambiguities, but any attentive reader of it will probably notice that being contradictory is in no sense synonymous with being incoherent. On the contrary, the persistence of certain contradictions throughout the work of a given author may be a revealing indication of his profound internal coherency.

But the specificity of literary creation only partially explains the subject to which I am referring: the role played by this historical, geographical and human entity called Morocco in three of my latest novels (*Count Julian, Juan the Landless, Makbara*).[3] To understand it, it will be necessary to reread the Occidental discourse on Islam and analyse these works in the light of its principal characteristics.

With the aid of this prism, we may risk a few generalities which I shall endeavour to make more specific later on. First: the Muslim world, and more concretely, the Moroccan, are incorporated in these novels within a mental world wherein empirical reality and direct observations nearly always make their appearance on a secondary level. Second: the actors and supporting players who cross the imaginary spaces of Tangier, Fez or Marrakesh are not (or not *only*) 'flesh and blood' Moroccans, but shades or masks created by a Western tradition steeped in repression, fear, desire, enmity and prejudice. Third: the traditional Europe/Islam antinomy (though situated on a different and even inverse scale of values) none the less maintains its irreducible character. Fourth: paraphrasing Said, the audience, director, and actors of this mental staging 'are for Spain and only for Spain'. But now that I have established my strategic position with respect to the Moroccan material, I shall attempt to show that this position (while indispensable for the Arab reader in so far as it allows him to measure the distance separating the real from the imaginary, being from fantasizing, yet at the same time causes him to lose interest in what he may reasonably take to be a simple 'internal quarrel') does not put an end to the problem posed, as least as far as the prejudiced Spanish or European reader is concerned. To tell the truth, the personal procedure of the author – my own in this case – is based on these premises, and its effect, whether repressive or liberating, should be evaluated in connection with them.

From the vast quantity of Occidental works having to do with the Near East and the Maghreb, there emerges a vision of the Islamic world that invariably involves a certain number of negative judgements: it is taxed with barbarousness, eccentricity, indifference, despotism, cruelty, mystery, habitual lying, etc. Among these characteristic traits, sexual fantasms or images constantly play a primordial role, as we shall see. On the one hand, 'Oriental fantasies' are pervaded by harems, female slaves, handsome youths, princesses, veils, erotic dances, unbridled sexuality – elements, that is to say, beyond the reach of the well-off but guilt-ridden and frustrated European writer and reader. On the other hand, this promise of sexual bliss (in reality, a simple projection upon the Other, the Oriental, the Arab, the Moor, of a 'libertine' conduct severely repressed by Christian and middle-class morality) appears on the horizon as a latent threat and even a punishment. If the first-mentioned aspect predominates among Romantic and Modernist writers (it will suffice to cite the examples of Flaubert and of Gide), the second – that of sexual terror – suffuses Spanish literary tradition, and in more general terms, the collective Hispanic subconscious, for a variety of reasons.

In my novel *Count Julian*, I set myself the task of undergoing a national psychoanalysis through a reading of the collective traditional discourse on Islam embedded in our literature and in our history. The *Vindication of Count Julian*[4] is not (as the title might suggest) a historical novel in the sense in which the term is generally used. The narrator is an anonymous being who contemplates the Spanish coast from Tangier and identifies himself with Count Julian, the Visigothic governor of the region, the Great Traitor who, according to legend, opened the portals of the Iberian Peninsula to the Muslims. This narrator (a fugitive, it must be remembered, from forty years of order under Franco) dreams of another invasion of his fatherland, whose effects will also last for eight centuries. That is, the destruction of the values and symbols on which the Spanish personality has been constructed through opposition to the threat and rejection of the temptation of Islam: the exploding of the myth of the Christian knight, ever ready to do battle, striking good clean blows with his cross as a crusader of the Faith; of belief in Spain's singular and privileged destiny, what Américo Castro ironically calls 'the Hispanic Essence, triumphantly resisting the ordeals of millennia'; of the exaggerated and hypocritical notion of super he-man masculinity and of feminine virginity; of the metaphysics of the Castilian landscape forged by the writers of the Generation of '98, etc.

The greatest historic tragedy of the Peninsula – the Saracen invasion and the consequent 'destruction of sacred Spain' was blamed *ab initio* by our chroniclers and poets on a sexual crime: the illicit love of the last Visigothic King for the daughter of his vassal, Count Julian. From the first half of the eleventh century (the approximate date of the Pseudo-Isidorian chronicle) down to the mid-nineteenth century (in the work of outstanding Romantic poets such as the Duque de Rivas, Espronceda and Zorrilla), we find ourselves in the presence of a tradition composed of hundreds of chronicles, tales, poems and dramas which interpret the collapse of the Visigothic monarchy through the lens of a hostile, condemnatory attitude towards sexuality. Satisfaction of the carnal appetites of King Rodrigo is the direct cause of a punishment – the Islamic Conquest – which was to humiliate Spain for eight hundred years. This legend and its general acceptance over the space of centuries are woven into a systematic discourse, or if you prefer, into a 'textual vision' (poetic, narrative, dramatic, etc) in which successive creators illustrate or represent (frequently introducing variations and new elements into the earlier literary corpus) a conglomeration of wishes, longings, frustrations, anxieties, fantasies, animosities and prejudices interwoven with a mass of clichés and *ideés reçues* having no connection whatsoever with actual history. We are thus confronted with an authentic mental extravaganza of the relationship between Spain and Islam, whose action, audience and actors are 'for Spain and only for Spain'.

Popular insistence on attributing the 'fall' of Spain to the sexual 'sin' of King Rodrigo circulates throughout a discourse of many centuries' duration in which the experience of writers and readers is determined by what they have read; this discourse in turn reinforces later textual experiences. Tradition thereby creates not only acquaintance with the facts but the facts themselves. In his compilation of the legends dealing with the theme of King Rodrigo and the treason of Count Julian, Menéndez Pidal has most pertinently traced the genesis of the collective discourse in which the myth of the sin of the conquered King and divine punishment in the form of the Arab invasion unfolds:

> At each step the developing legend brings to mind the *nihil novum*. Every legend, no matter how original it may appear to be, has an antecedent, an embryo whose novelty is an almost imperceptible form before opening as a showy flower. The most daring individual innovation is undoubtedly, on the one hand, an act of breaking with the past, but on the other, it is a traditional and collective act as well; born within a minority in order to oppose a majority, it rests upon a restricted, possibly occult, tradition, so as to divorce itself from divulged tradition [. . .] The paths leading from one author to another may be half erased and perhaps even difficult to conjecture or to comprehend. But we cannot for that reason ignore the tradition that unites them. The frequent polemics with regard to plagiarism are usually founded on a total lack of acquaintance on the part of modern 'traditionalism' with certain themes, or with the great collective role played in any individual psychic labour [. . .] To sum up, the work of a modern author, precisely like that of a medieval writer, no matter how personal it may be, contains a great many elements of collective art, even though the author may gainsay them, and even though contemporary critics may not take the trouble to track them down [. . .] There is, even if unknown, a modern traditionalism which naturally has very different characteristics from the ancient version, but which it is necessary to study and analyse as a form of traditionalism in order to recognize the degree to which poetic creativity is a collective phenomenon.[5]

It is not my intention to examine here the birth, development and variations on the Hispanic discourse concerning the presence of Islam in the Peninsula, and I shall limit myself to indicating two aspects thereof that impress me as being worthy of attention. In the first place, we find ourselves before a variant of the fable of Original Sin and Paradise Lost in which, instead of the apple, the bait of the Evil One was said to be the beauty of a damsel, and the role of Adam fell to the last of the Visigothic kings; through the fault of the latter, Spaniards supposedly lost their innocence for ever, and in their eyes the Moorish invader would come to symbolize evil, sin and punishment. In the second place, from the *Refundición de la crónica de 1344* on, there appeared a new factor which was to have tremendous repercussions on later tradition: I am referring to the penance imposed on the King and to the introduction of the serpent into the legend, not in the form of temptation but as part of the punishment, or in other words, of temptation metamorphosed into a heavenly sanction of the act of lust. In order to expiate his guilt, Don Rodrigo is condemned by the monk who hears his confession to shut himself up in a cave in the company of a serpent who will devour him 'there where his sin has been greatest'. As the *Crónica sarracina* recounts it:

> [. . .] at the end of the third day after he had entered there, the serpent raises himself up beside him and mounts his belly and his chest and begins to eat his privates with one head and [the region] to the right of his heart with the other. At this time the jailer appeared at the peephole and inquired how it was going, and he replied that 'thanks be to God' all was well and the serpent had begun to eat him. And the jailer asked where, and he told him in two places: one to the right of his heart, with which he had thought of all the wrong he had done in this world, and the other his privates, which had been the cause of the great destruction of Spain.

It is not necessary, of course, to have read Freud to note in the mental scenery of the Hispanic subconscious the sexual connotations of terms such as cave (vagina) and serpent (phallus), as well as their displacements and transmutations (censorship). Beyond the punishment of the King, the enduring consequences for Spain (guilty let us not forget, as the ninth-century *Chronicón* stresses, of 'living in licentiousness' in imitation of the monarch) also bring onstage the spectre of a cruel and lascivious Moorish invader, the image of that which is repudiated by Spain but is none the less the object of fascination. From the time of the *Primera crónica general* of Alfonso X onwards – 'What evil or what tempest did Spain not suffer? Suckling babes were smashed against walls; those who were worthy of respect and far along in years were thrown into a vile fount by the cruelty of the Moors; the younger women were kept in order to dishonour them and their beauty cast in chains and violated' – poems, novels, chronicles and dramas, supporting each other, nourishing each other, persist in characterizing the Moor as ferocious and lustful, an involuntary instrument of divine anger. Although the literary elaboration of the myth slows down in the nineteenth century (the period's few productions based on this theme are, as Menéndez Pidal himself notes, of little importance), the mental picture does not take its leave altogether from the Spanish subconscious, as is shown by their abrupt updating of the myth in 1936 to justify the 'African punishment' inflicted on a Republic guilty of every crime and libertine excess. The subject is highly unpleasant, but we cannot omit or avoid it, though for various reasons it may be as painful to our Right as to our Left.

Legends are difficult to erase, no matter how forcefully reality may demonstrate their inconsistency. Here too we encounter the phenomenon of the rejection of sociopolitical analysis in favour of myths and fictions when it comes time to recount a real experience, an actual fact. The spectre of the Moor as a pitiless rapist, repeated and introjected by writers and readers for nine centuries, reappears in all its crude bluntness in our political literature when the government of Gil Robles had recourse to the unit of Moroccan Riffs attached to the Spanish Army to quell the uprising of miners in Asturias. In 1934, the leftist press initiated an indiscriminate campaign against the 'Moors', and in the northern zone of the Protectorate the parties of the Popular Front were still, a year and a half later, providing for the enlightenment of the 'protected' in Er Rif and Djebala such paragraphs as the following: 'They say that they [those belonging to the Rightist Coalition] are Spain, but they took Moors to Asturias to raid decent Spainish homes and to satisfy their most obscene and filthy appetites.'[6] Following Franco's revolt, the Republican parties, instead of strengthening and consolidating the alliance existing between the democratic forces in Spain and the Moroccan nationalists, launched into xenophobic and openly racist propaganda, saturated with clichés and the same images that had been repeated century after century by the bards, chroniclers, dramatists and narrators of the *Romancero*, in which, making no distinctions whatsoever between manipulators and manipulated, they tarred all Moroccans with the same brush, in tones more suitable to the defenders of 'racial purity' than to those who proclaim (or proclaimed) themselves followers of Lenin, Engels and Marx: 'Savage Moorish hordes, drunk with sensuality, who pour forth to wreak horrendous violations of our daughters and our wives; Moors brought from the backward encampments of Morocco, from the most uncivilized mountain villages of Er Rif.' It would have been logical to inquire of the person proffering these enormities (I refer to Dolores Ibarruri, 'la Pasionaria', the former president of the Spanish Communist Party) what the Republic had done or was planning to do to civilize these 'savages' and to bring a decent standard of living to their encampments and villages. Nothing, absolutely nothing – and the delegation of Nationalists dispatched to the Republican camp to propose the provoking of an uprising against Franco in Er Rif, in exchange for a formal promise of independence, met with incredible delays and evasive answers which in the final analysis were equivalent to a rejection.

When forced to choose, that is to say, between a statistically verifiable reality (the fact that the crimes, abuses and rapes committed by the Moroccan regulars were no more numerous than those carried out by Spaniards during the war against Abd el Krim) and the collective anti-Moorish discourse produced by the textual vision discussed earlier (from the Alphonsine *Crónica* down the the nineteenth-century Orientalist Francisco Javier Simonet), our Left decided – with rare and honourable exceptions – in favour of legend, fantasies and stereotypes.

Like the greater or lesser creations of the *Romancero*, sketches by the socialist Luis Quintanilla show quite simply, with their caricatural racism, the phantoms of the mental scenario firmly implanted in our subconscious. The socioeconomic opinions of our Marxists – with their supposed sympathy for the Moroccan victims of the misery and humiliation imposed under the Protectorate – are obscured and ultimately nullified by the centuries-old prejudice against the Moors embodied in our traditional discourse. One of the few authors who has had the courage and the honesty to tackle the subject writes:

The arrival of a *harka* [an auxiliary unit of native Moroccan troops] provoked a wave of sexual terror that acts alone did not justify – in wartime everybody rapes – but something more profound, obscure, ancient and popular [. . .] The Moors were not there to wage war but to 'violate' the women of the Spanish people. It is quite certain that those wretched peasants sold into Franco's army for a few miserable coins were totally unaware of

the tremendous sexual fear they aroused [. . .] The whole thing
was made possible by ancestral terror. We have already seen what
the 'memory' of the Spanish people is concerning the Arab: he is
the punishment for a particularly 'filthy' misdeed.[7]

The 'Moors' depicted by Republican literature and propaganda coincide
in fact with the ones who populate and illustrate the works of the
Romancero: in neither case are the authors inspired by real people,
seen or known by the writer who describes, portrays and interprets
them, assuming even their voices; they are monsters and phantoms
from a mental stage production created by and for us. Between the
flesh-and-blood Moroccan who lives the tragedy of underdevelopment
and colonization of his country and the 'Moorish rapist' who persis-
tently lurks in Spanish fantasy, there is the same distance as between
the 'Moorish' character of Othello and the actor who portrays him. The
Morocco of Dolores Ibarruri, Luis Quintanilla and their cohorts ceases
to be a historical, geographical, cultural and human reality to become
an 'Oriental *tableau*', frozen and encapsulated in a hermetic space, our
subconscious. Once again, the internalized textual vision imposes itself
and cancels out reality.[8]

Curiously, the rebirth of the old legend justifying the Islamic presence
in our Peninsula during the Civil War did not attract the attention or
the critical scrutiny of our writers. It none the less offered an excellent
opportunity to reread the traditional Hispanic discourse on Islam and
to undertake a psychoanalysis of the literary corpus on the subject
capable of exorcizing its ancient terrors. The timeliness of this had been
understood even by one so unlikely to be suspected of Arabophilia as
Menéndez Pidal when, on alluding to the lack of interest on the part of
his contemporaries in the legend of Don Julián and the 'loss' of Spain, he
mourned the absence of the 'vatic gaze of poetry' and lamented the fact
that a series of mental padlocks should seal 'the door to this enchanted
palace of the imagination'. 'We are still awaiting', he added, 'the artist
daring enough to break the locks and enter the secret enclosure to reveal
the ancient mysteries guarded by Hercules.'

The response to that invitation, to its creative challenge, was one of
the fundamental incentives leading to the genesis of my *Count Julian*.
It was difficult to live even for short periods in Tangier, just across from
the Spanish coast – facing a Spain governed by a regime as oppressive as
that of the Visigothic monarchy – without evoking the mythical figure
of Don Julián and dreaming of a betrayal as grandiose as his. Since

my projected invasion could not be material (that is, the conquest of a real space, by men of flesh and blood) but had necessarily to be cultural and symbolic, it should attack and destroy the whole of the anti-Islamic discourse in the *Romancero*, turn it inside out like a glove, giving the betrayal a dynamic and positive content and extending it to language, inverting the hallowed scale of values, possessing the legend from behind, sodomizing the myth; what the Hispanist Annie Perrin, on studying the internal functioning of my novel, most aptly termed the 'sodo-mito', the sodomyth.

This somewhat sacrilegious inversion of legendary values – of the traditional discourse embodied in several centuries of textual vision – is nevertheless confined within certain limits: those indicated at the beginning of this essay. Morocco and the real Moroccans described in the first pages of the book fade litle by little into the familiar mental staging or 'Moorish *tableau*' of our collective unconscious. The role they play in it is undoubtedly different, and even diametrically opposed: the castrating, punishing serpent of the myth becomes a tempter once again; the once-feared phantasmagoria is accepted and provoked; sex fulfils a regenerative, stimulating, dynamic function. But at the same time the Spain/Islam dialectic retains its irreducible Manichaean opposites intact: values turn into anti-values and vice versa. The novel is not the fruit of unblinkered observation (the only observation capable of abolishing the prejudices of 'otherness', of a basic distinction between cultures and peoples); on the contrary, the personal gaze of the author in his stroll through the streets of Tangier is diluted in a textual corpus of quotations, recollections, motifs, rhymes, fictions, images conveyed down through the years by Spanish literary tradition. This is, of course, deliberate: the author's battle is *against* tradition, but he acts from *within* it. The potential Moroccan reader who is not acquainted with our Islamic phantasmagoria might rightly decide to pay no attention to something that obviously does not concern him, and he might even feel offended. Although the reality of Morocco today seeps in through a few interstices, the Morocco and the Islam of the book are not the Morocco and the Islam of reality.

When the new Don Julián summons to his side

you warriors of Islam, you Bedouins of the desert, you instinctively cruel Arabs! I offer you my country, invade it, sack it plunder it: its fields, its cities, its treasures, its virgins are yours for the taking: destroy the tottering bastion of its personality, sweep away the debris of its metaphysics: collective animal aggression is what is needed: whet your knives, prepare to bite: may your seditious serpent rise up to its full height, a proud royal sceptre, imposing its tyrannical rule with silent, inscrutable violence.[9]

the call is not addressed (as is obvious, though Mr Aranguren and this or that other 'sharp' critic may have thought otherwise) to the Moroccan people who live, who barely exist, in the unacceptable conditions we all know of, but, rather, to the ghostly people of the legend. The incitement to invade and annihilate the oppressive and retrograde Spain of the Franco regime is no doubt liberating for us, but that liberation is of no interest to those whom Count Julian has summoned. The whole game is played out between Spaniards: the Moor who is the pretext is merely a spectator.

In *Juan sin tierra* and *Makbara*, the critical reading of the traditional anti-Islamic discourse is extended from the Hispanic area to the whole of the Western world. Although the clichés, prejudices and stereotypes continue to be the same – barbarousness, despotism, backwardness, cruelty, irrationalism, impermeability to the language of progress and an etc too long to bear repeating – the sexual spectres in the latter case are not centred round the terrors evoked by that intimate, determined, unassimilable enemy with which Spain had to contend for centuries; sex is seen, rather, in its seductive guise as a promise, a sensual outlet or an alternative to the puritan conformity in which the bourgeois European is being asphyxiated. When English or French writers turn to the Near East or the Maghreb in search of liberating experiences, they do so in the vanguard or in the shadow of colonial armies representing imperial powers that have turned the Afro-Asiatic countries, as Said opportunely recalls, into the brothel and the dump heap for the poor, the unemployed, the delinquents and the adventurers of the colonialist countries. The Oriental world then gives concrete form to the dream of 'free' and – in a word – 'cheap' sex, which the bourgeois artist futilely hankers after in his own milieu. Sensual revelation, whether that of a Flaubert or of a Gide, objectively implies a relation based on power – the dominator and the dominated – in which the European not only possesses or enjoys the alien body but analyses and interprets it, speaks for it in an imitation of its voice: a class relationship inasmuch as it is a race relationship – even the *petit blanc* acts like a bourgeois towards the Asiatic or African 'native' – with which, like it or not, the colonizer or ex-colonizer must contend (either consciously or by deluding himself) as long as the current iniquitous differences between industrialized states and the rest of the world continue to prevail. It is futile to point out that, except for the extensive commercialization of 'Oriental sex' – of which the proliferation of saunas and Thai massage parlours is a mere sample – this promise of happiness based on the economic and social inequality of peoples corresponds to no concrete reality: acquaintance or contact with other civilizations teaches us that the number of taboos which structure them is approximately the same everywhere, even if they are distributed differently.

The same two-faced reality of the 'promise of happiness' – in opposition to the puritanical and hypocritical bourgeois order – and colonial oppression (which confers on those presumably liberated the awkward but inevitable role of colonists) frequently determines the texture of the meandering narration of *Juan sin tierra*. The narrative discourse of Part III, for instance, is woven and unwoven like Penelope's tapestry, the victim of this insoluble dichotomy. Ambiguity becomes apparent in the highly significant choice of characters with whom the person addressed as 'tú' identifies and emulates: Friar Alselm Turmeda, Father Foucauld and T. E. Lawrence. While his definitive conversion to Islam permits the first-named to attain a full and satisfactory sensual life (Fray Turmeda defrocks himself and takes a wife at the court of the King of Tunis), the secret motivations – impulses – of Lawrence and Foucauld find their only expression within the context of the Anglo-French imperial expansion to which – despite their Islamic sympathies and affinities – both actively contribute; the 'benefits' of their politico-religious crusade do not accrue to the Bedouins or the Senusis but to the hegemonic powers that the two represent. Nor does their 'personal realization' – sexual or sublimated – as recounted in *The Seven Pillars of Wisdom* and the *Oeuvres spirituelles* contribute to the personal realization of the 'natives'. The phallus/non-phallus, dominator/ dominated dialectic does not end when the terms become inverted. The only liberation of *Juan sin tierra* – beyond that of sex and historical reality – will be achieved in the area of literary creation, or the kingdom of Utopia.

The search for sexual happiness that impels the angel of *Makbara* excluded from the bureaucratic paradise to follow after the Moorish or African phantom embodied in the pariah who sells his physical strength to the industrial world could be interpreted by hasty readers of the work (and a great number of critics and reviewers fall into that category) as a hymn to the fecundating potency of the male sex organ: in fact, what the text suggests is much more ambiguous and complex. The *muhaxir* (émigré) who, after a childhood as an orphan in colonial Morocco and his apprenticeship in slavery in the hell of the tanneries, sows horror in his wake as he makes his way along the boulevards of Paris, might be one of the innumerable Maghrebi workers whose situation Tahar Ben Jelloun has summarized so beautifully in his essay entitled 'La plus haute des solitudes'. He is none the less something more.

A simple physical examination of the person in question indicates that, on the one hand, he has no ears (rats have gnawed them away), and on the other, he possesses a male organ whose scandalous dimensions impede or hinder his sex life (this phallus, object of the desires of the vagabond angel who roams the world in the guise of a woman, is for him a curse). This *meteco* is thus not just any North African émigré. He also sums up, in condensed and caricatural form, the Occidental phantasmagoria concerning Islam and the Arabs: strange, opaque, deaf, because he has no ear(s), to the logical and 'rational' discourse of Europeans, he expresses himself in a language incomprehensible to them. Possessing an immense, aberrant sex organ makes him the target of jokes and the object of revulsion. Unlike Count Julian, the hero with a divided self, he is not simply an embodiment of Hispano-Christian fantasy, but a symbiotic character, given concrete form by the hostile and reproving gaze of those whose path he crosses: a bogeyman by antonomasia, at once invisible (the stares of self-righteous bigots pass right through him) and threatening (in so far as he accepts and thereby actualizes the negative or odious characteristics that the average Eurocrat is inclined to attribute to him). Only the fallen angel, inverting the usual scale of values, will be able to love and chase after this pure sex organ with no voice and no ears, from the colonial garrisons of the Foreign Legion to the sewers of a futuristic and dehumanized metropolis. An impossible love, not because of an arbitrary decision on the part of the narrator or the *halaiquí nesrani*, the foreign storyteller who takes up the tale in the closing pages of the work, but, once again, because of the strategic position of the author vis-à-vis the material narrated.

One last observation: the Oriental or Moorish *tableau* of *Count Julian* and *Juan the Landless* gives way in *Makbara* to a deforming mirror – though a mirror none the less – of colonial and post-colonial Morocco. The Moroccan world – viewed with the moral indignation and the human and aesthetic fascination which the intimacy and sympathy of the author in relation to that world gave rise to – appears in numerous passages of the novel. The 'reading of the space in Xemáa-el-Fna' in particular is based on that antinomy: avoiding at one and the same time the exclusively moralistic vision which rejects anachronistic pre-industrial virtues such as leisure, playfulness, festive spirit, etc, and the exclusively hedonistic perspective, indifferent to the exploitative pyramid underlying the free, plural space of the market square. Accepting only the first would be to condemn oneself to writing only a pamphlet of social criticism: limiting oneself to the second would be a grave betrayal of human solidarity and affection. Such a dilemma, already present in other works of mine such as *Señas de identidad* [*Marks of Identity*] and *Campos de Níjar*, relentlessly goaded me on in my reading of this minuscule island of freedom 'in an ocean of iniquity and poverty'. Yet this reading is not merely (as it might seem to be at first glance) an exercise in nostalgia but, rather, a gamble on the future. When I ponder the art of the tale-teller in Xemáa-el-Fna, I think of what Bakhtin says about the world of Rabelais: 'It always opens a *joyful* breach in a more distant future, which will make the *relative* progress and the *relative* truth accessible to his time and to the immediate, foreseeable future seem laughable.'

Yet even though the Moroccan presence is real, the critics are no doubt right to maintain that *Makbara* is not a work about Morocco either, and that very probably it will be of no concern to Moroccans, outside of a handful of informed readers. Like *Count Julian* and *Juan the Landless*, it is still a novel for Europeans, and its Islamic background does not represent the Arabs for whose political, social and economic liberation the author of these pages has fought for years, but, rather, presents a 'Moor' who is a grotesque freak, deformed by the 'white' imagination. A careful reading of the text by a Muslim cannot disregard this fact. For if *Makbara* points in the direction of the liberation of human beings through love, it nevertheless still operates within the time-worn dialectic of mirror-image otherness which the Christian West created in opposition to the Islamic East, and which prevents our seeing the latter and its men and women as something close and familiar, whose differences from ourselves are not greater but lesser in number than the myriad points of contact, a literary factor which must necessarily enter into the reader's calculations.

Notes

1 In Spanish the noun *Oriente* and the adjective *oriental* refer generally to Asiatic countries East of Europe, and especially to the Islamic countries of

the Near East. I have followed the author's usage, in which *Oriente* and *oriental* are most frequently used in the latter sense. The same is true of other writers represented in this volume of essays [*translator's note*].

2 Edward W. Said, *Orientalism*, New York, Pantheon Books, 1978, p. 20. For this essay I have based my translation on the edition cited in the original text of *Crónicas sarracinas*, pp. 27–8: *L'Orientalisme*, translated from the American by Catherine Malamoud, Paris: Editions du Seuil, 1980. [*translator's note*.]

3 English translations of *La reivindicación del conde don Julián sin tierra* (Serpent's Tail, London 1989) and *Makbara* (Viking Press, New York 1976) by Helen Lane.

4 A reference to the full title of the Spanish original: *La reivindicación del conde don Julián*, Mexico City: Joaquín Mortiz, 1970.

5 Ramón Menéndez Pidal, *Floresta de leyendas heroicas españolas: Rodrigo, el último godo*, Madrid, 1942.

6 *Apud* Miguel Martín, *El colonialismo español en Marruecos* Paris: Ruedo Ibérico, 1973.

7 Xavier Domingo, *Erótica hispánica*, Paris: Ruedo Ibérico, 1972.

8 The Arabic phantasmagoria and the sexual interpretation of the Saracen invasion of the Peninsula also contribute to the vision of certain European Orientalists. Thus, in the view of Raymond Charles, a stubborn defender of the French presence in Algiers:

> For almost eight centuries, Spain served as an outlet for the destructive rage, the thirst for blood and the lasciviousness of its Islamic invaders – for its *Schadenfreude*, a product of a physiological necessity based on sexual anxiety – and the spasmodic convulsions, the sensual frenzy that at times have an enervating effect, and at others stimulate the modulated laments and paroxysmal invocations of Flamenco, express, even more directly than Goya, the age-old embrace of the Moor, in which tirelessly rekindled lust excludes any and every intervention of the spirit [!].

Paris, *L'Évolution de l'Islam*, 1960.

9 From English translation by Helen Lane, in edition cited in note 3, above, p. 113.

On Literature Considered
as a Criminal Activity

In those countries in which a dictatorship rules in one form or another, whether it be military, political, social or predominantly ideological; in those States in which the people do not have in practice the right of free speech, that is to say in approximately three-quarters of the 'advanced' world in which we live, literature offers a curious particularity that has not as yet been studied with the attention it deserves: that of constituting a more or less statutory offence in the different codes of 'social and moral defence' established by the powers that impose the monopoly of their own discourse by wrongly identifying it with the voice of society. The work of literature, whether it be called a novel, story, poem, drama or essay, then assumes the characteristics of a crime, and its author, the material author of the misdeed, the characteristics of a criminal.

Spanish writers – at least certain of us Spanish writers – have enjoyed this exciting privilege for the space of nearly forty years: that of being compared with thieves, renegades, bandits, guerrilla fighters, hold-up men: that of figuring, along with gypsies, vagrants, thugs and other harmful species, within that vast and imprecise pre-delinquent category referred to as 'a danger to society'. I remember that at the beginning of the 1960s an official spokesman of the regime solemnly declared me to be a 'gangster wielding a pen': another stated with assurance that my name 'was much better known in police stations than in bookstores', and not precisely because our agents of public order were men of great learning; and a team of the aforementioned guardian angels turned up to search the warehouse of the publishing house that had brought out some of my works in order to make sure that my criminal writings were not carefully hidden away there (which for them would have constituted a crime known as a cover-up).

Finding myself as I did in a foreign country, that is to say safe, at least physically, from the penalties logically entailed by any criminal activity, this identification, rather than making me sad, made me smug. Literature was, literature could be a crime. The writer – even one as harmless as myself – could become a lawbreaker. The official propaganda which, singling me out from my worthy colleagues, situated me – as it situated Alberti, Arrabal, Sastre and so many others – in the same camp as a Quico Sabater or el Lute,[1] filled me with pride. I need not say that my condemnation to the moral ostracism of these latter was infinitely more precious to me than the company of or dealings with all the writers, intellectuals and academic scholars who meant something in the Spain that we were having to put up with at the time. That my tomes or my slim volumes earned me such a privilege gave them in my eyes a dignity that no critical praise – however lofty or flattering – could ever confer on them.

My case, as is obvious, was not unique, nor was that of Spain. Even today, the great majority of Hispanic nations live under systems in which the written word is dangerous; literature can constitute a crime and the writer can be turned into a criminal and be treated like one. In Argentina, Chile, Uruguay, Paraguay, the illegal power of literature has led to the imprisonment, kidnapping, disappearance or death of dozens of authors (what has become of Julio Castro?, of Haroldo Conti?, of Rodolfo Walsh?), authors whose writing has been made the equal not only of an act of sedition but of a common, ordinary and vulgar legal offence by the dictators at present on duty: when I presented myself at the Argentine Embassy in Paris, in the company of a number of French intellectuals, to demand information concerning a number of colleagues who had disappeared, His Excellency the Ambassador stated that the journalists and writers whose fate we were interested in were, in reality, common criminals. Writing a letter of protest or penning a nonconformist poem was equivalent in the Argentina of Videla to a robbery or a hold-up (I do not know whether these were offences aggravated by being committed at night or as premeditated acts of treason).

In the countries of the Soviet bloc – among which I include Cuba – the outlook is no brighter: though their purposes and ideologies may be poles apart, nothing resembles one dictatorship more than another as regards the future that awaits writers who refuse to write from dictation. From the enthronement of Stalinism to the end of the 1920s, Russian literature was relegated to the status it had had during the czarist era, that of a virtually criminal practice, and the writer – whether his name was Babel, Mandelstam or Pilniak

– met with the same fate as millions of political and social prisoners and common criminals: imprisonment, labour camps, extermination. Now that the most brutal aspects of Stalinism have been eliminated, the Soviet regime has refined its methods somewhat, yet the figure of the writer as a lawbreaker remains. The criminal who wields a pen is ordinarily sent to a centre of re-education through hard labour, as in the case of Guinzburg, or to a psychiatric hospital, as in that of Pliutch. As a notorious ex-criminal, the writer Andrei Siniavski declared, in his eloquent speech on dissidence at the Venice Biennale, 'If art is the same thing as robbery and crime, it is because it has a value: it is a *reality*.' This led him to pose the question as to whether art, any form of art, may not be a crime: 'a crime affecting society, affecting life itself'.

The question is most à propos: tearing ourselves away from the abstractions of art for art's sake and from writing as a game, we are forced to reflect on a series of problems that go beyond the framework of purely aesthetic considerations. Even if the gratuitous element, the ludic factor have always been essential ingredients of the literary work, the concept of literature as a crime in the greater part of today's world belies the claims of certain individuals that it is possible to create an ethereal, self-sufficient art, completely apart from social life: even the fabrication of *bibelots d'inanité sonore* may turn out to have a possible hidden criminal coloration, as is proved by the delinquent nature attributed to Mallarmé's poetry in China or in the USSR. Poetic purity, if carried to its ultimate consequences, can also assume, depending on the circumstances and the regime, the characteristics of a statutory crime.

The transformations brought about in Spain in recent years – the gradual collapse of the authoritarian institutions bequeathed to the country by the dictatorship; the restoration of political and trade-union freedoms; the liquidation of rigid state centralism; the abolition of censorship, etc – have meant the end of along nightmare in the field of culture: the appropriation and monopoly of language by Power and its servants, the piracy or kidnapping of the real meaning of words to the point of total absurdity (think, for example, of that of 'organic democracy' applied to the Francoist legislative bodies, or the euphemistic designation of censorship as 'orientation and consultation', and even making the latter dependent later on upon a mysterious Department of Popular Culture: I need scarcely point out that neither democracy, nor the people, nor culture had anything at all in common with such outrages).

The right of free speech and consequently to disagreement, the creation of a free and plural discursive space are today an undeniable reality, and after the miserable diet of the previous regime we all have reason to congratulate ourselves. Despite a few unfortunate incidents which, more than symptoms, are vestiges of the situation in the past, systematic heterodoxy as a life choice has finally disappeared from our everyday horizon: literature has lost its potentially delinquent nature and the writer his exalted or shameful status as a criminal.

It would naturally be inappropriate – and in addition quite irrelevant – if I were at this point to lament such a situation: the progressive recovery by bourgeois democracy of all the voices and discourses that have been raised against it for political, ethical, social, ideological or sexual reasons. The phenomenon, moreover, is not exclusively Spanish: it is making its appearance, to a greater or lesser degree, in all the industrialized countries of the Western world. Disagreement, rebellion, dissent may be turned into profitable merchandise and transform notorious past 'delinquents' into amiable spokesmen for a domesticated and monetarily rewarding opposition. (The same development, in an aggravated form, is taking place in those countries in which a revolution that in its beginnings was popular and spontaneous has become institutionalized. Marxism then comes to be not a dialectical method for continually transforming reality, but instead a mechanism for glorifying the existing situation, and the bard is invited to applaud. This is the lamentable case of a certain rebellious ex-poet now in exile, an author already far from producing works of talent, who has been turned for the last twenty years into a pompous official mandarin and a skilled ventriloquist.)

In the face of such a situation, those of us who continue to think of ourselves as morally delinquent – that is to say, identified with the struggles of those who for various reasons do not accept being integrated into the system of bourgeois democracy and restrict themselves to living and acting on its periphery from a position of deliberately assumed marginality – must adopt an attitude of resolute dissidence, avoiding, each and every day, in so far as possible, the temptations and the traps of an omnipresent, sterilizing respectability.

In a lecture I gave some years ago now, I defined the role of the writer in today's world as that of a provocateur, and taking into account the existence of States subjected to a dictatorship and that of societies of greater or lesser permissiveness, I made a distinction between two levels of provocation. In those countries in which a monopoly of language is established by the caste that wields power there are, as is obvious, provocative subjects (speaking of the living conditions that exist in the countries of the East or in South American dictatorships is a good example of this). In those countries that enjoy a permissive society, among which we may happily include Spain, as political, social, moral and sexual taboos disappear, there also disappear those subjects that are the object of a possible 'danger to society', and the writer determined to resist the tremendous integrative force of the system finds himself obliged to interiorize his provocation, introducing it into language itself. He is not content to be a dissident in the face of society, in the face of life; this is now more or less accepted and in no way constitutes a crime: he must also manifest his dissidence, following the admirable example of Fernando de Rojas, by deliberately violating the laws and canons observed by the cultural community within which he lives and works. The literary taboo, the linguistic taboo, today as yesterday, continue to play an important repressive role, and every creator may regard them as restrictive, oppressive phenomena when they are brought into direct confrontation with his own project. It matters little that, condemned in the beginning, tolerated next, and then finally accepted, his literarily transgressive conduct may be integrated with the passage of the years into that nebulous and sinister entity that penny-a-liners call 'the national patrimony': as is proved to us by the case of Rojas's *La Celestina*, the process of assimilation may drag on for centuries and maintain intact, where official stomachs are concerned, its extraordinary power to resist digestion, to prove upsetting. To assume, consciously and deliberately, an ethically and artistically 'criminal' behaviour – however well tolerated this may be in our present liberal societies – is always the best antidote against the frightening evaluation of the writer or the artist as a national treasure.

We here arrive at the very root of the problem. Is it possible for the writer, for the intellectual, to preserve his potential criminality from the dangers that the ever-enjoyable and desirable regime of permissiveness brings with it? Does the disappearance of the risk of punishment, whether physical (prison, banishment, internment in an asylum) or exclusively material or moral (forbidding the right to work, loss of a job, ostracism) automatically presuppose the end of ethical yet socially transgressive behaviour, of literature as an occupation made synonymous with the criminal act by a silent and morally upright majority?

I believe not, and even leaving aside the repressive violence of certain democratic societies with regard to writers and artists who are provocative in the twofold sense of the term – it would suffice to call to mind the 'social execution' of men such as Malcolm X, George Jackson or Pier Paolo Pasolini, admirable both as human beings and as literary figures – experience shows us that the writer who accepts, knowingly and deliberately, the task of extracting the common denominator of all the oppressions that afflict our advanced industrial societies today will be an individual whom the system will find it difficult to reintegrate, since his protean condition as a gypsy in the face of the peasant, a black in the face of the white, a worker in the face of the boss, a woman in the face of the man, a young person in the face of the adult, a homosexual in the face of the heterosexual, in addition to his fundamental rejection of a literary language that is a worn-out hand-me-down imposed on him, will of necessity force him out on to the edges of society, conferring on him the invincible strength of the pariah: the unconditional freedom of someone who has nothing to lose.

Once there, his twofold dissidence in the face of life and of the revered literary canon will allow him to fight in a field in which attempts to rescue him will turn out to be, if not fruitless, at best difficult. 'A tolerated delinquent', as in Spain today all traditionally disavowed and persecuted groups and minorities are tolerated, will be able to carry on a centrifugal and energetic labour, capable of offsetting, thanks to its radical virulence, the centripetal, integrative tendency of official and paraofficial culture.

In conclusion: in so far as it does not accept life as it is, art is a form of dissidence that has been subject throughout history to a repeated conceptualization as criminal. A nonconformist both with respect to society and to canonized literary expression, the creator may once again lay claim, without vanity, but at the same time without false modesty, to his shameful, and to him exalting, status as a transgressor.

Notes

1 Quico Sabater was the last of the Anarchists to continue by force of arms the struggle against Francoism. *El Lute* was a sort of gypsy George Jackson, imprisoned for common crimes.